# The Many Geographies
# of Urban Renewal

EDITED BY

Douglas R. Appler

# The Many Geographies
# of Urban Renewal

*New Perspectives on the Housing Act of 1949*

TEMPLE UNIVERSITY PRESS

*Philadelphia* • *Rome* • *Tokyo*

TEMPLE UNIVERSITY PRESS
Philadelphia, Pennsylvania 19122
*tupress.temple.edu*

Library of Congress Cataloging-in-Publication Data

Names: Appler, Douglas R., editor.
Title: The many geographies of urban renewal : new perspectives on the
Housing Act of 1949 / edited by Douglas R. Appler.
Description: Philadelphia : Temple University Press, 2023. | The chapters
included in this book were originally presented at a conference titled
Reassessing the History of the Federal Urban Renewal Program: 1949–1974
on September 27, 2019 at the University of Kentucky. | Includes
bibliographical references and index. | Summary: "Examines the impact of
urban renewal programs on small cities and other under-explored U.S.
sites"— Provided by publisher.
Identifiers: LCCN 2022053663 (print) | LCCN 2022053664 (ebook) | ISBN
9781439921708 (cloth) | ISBN 9781439921715 (paperback) | ISBN
9781439921722 (pdf)
Subjects: LCSH: Urban renewal—United States—History—20th century. |
Urban renewal—United States—Case studies.
Classification: LCC HT175 .M368 2023  (print) | LCC HT175  (ebook) | DDC
307.3/4160973—dc23/eng/20230317
LC record available at https://lccn.loc.gov/2022053663
LC ebook record available at https://lccn.loc.gov/2022053664

Printed in the United States of America

9  8  7  6  5  4  3  2  1

# Contents

    Urban Development Corporation / STACY KINLOCK SEWELL          140

7   The Dispossessed: Urban Renewal and Relocation in
    St. Louis County / COLIN GORDON                              159

8   Healthy Housing and the Health of the State / LEIF FREDRICKSON   175

9   Urban Renewal through Rehabilitation and Restoration
    / FRANCESCA RUSSELLO AMMON                                   195

    Contributors                                                 217

    Index                                                        219

# Acknowledgments

I would like to extend my thanks to the staff at Temple University Press for their continued support during the production of this volume. I would also like to thank the anonymous reviewers for encouraging the press to accept the initial book proposal, as well as for sharpening the ideas found in early drafts. Most important, I would like to thank the contributors themselves. Everyone who participated in this project has been collaborative, thoughtful, and committed throughout, from its infancy as a grant proposal through to its publication. Working with this group of scholars has been a pleasure!

*The Many Geographies of Urban Renewal* was made possible in part by a major grant from the National Endowment for the Humanities: Democracy demands wisdom. Any views, findings, conclusions, or recommendations expressed in this book do not necessarily represent those of the National Endowment for the Humanities.

# The Many Geographies
# of Urban Renewal

# Introduction

Douglas R. Appler

Shortly after the Housing Act of 1949 was signed into law by President Harry Truman, the Senate Committee on Banking and Currency published a guidebook titled *The Housing Act of 1949: What It Is and How It Works*. In this publication, the committee declared:

> From any angle, citizenship, health, appearance, taxes, or property protection, it is better to pay now for the cost of clearing slums and thereby get rid of them than to continue paying the mounting costs of slums and suffer their destructive effects upon human lives and property indefinitely.[1]

The committee described the act as enabling "a comprehensive attack upon slums and blighted areas by local communities."[2] It accomplished this primarily through Title I of the act, which provided grants and low-interest loans to local governments across the United States in order to subsidize locally planned redevelopment projects targeting "slums and blighted areas."[3] Administered first by the Housing and Home Finance Agency (HHFA) and then by its successor, the Department of Housing and Urban Development (HUD), this program was used by 1,258 communities of all sizes between 1949 and its termination in 1974.[4]

At its beginning, the program that would eventually become known as "urban renewal" was defined by the confidence that policy makers, planners, and designers had in their ability to solve complex urban problems through technocratic expertise and the power of demolition. By the final years of the program, urban renewal was widely seen as a failure, with many former neighborhoods having been replaced by parking lots rather than businesses or new housing. Even when redevelopment projects were considered successful in the sense that they were completed as planned, they were often made possible through the clearance of black, immigrant, and low-income neighborhoods whose residents were largely excluded from the planning process. As urban renewal took place during the height of the civil rights era, residents of many threatened neighborhoods vocally opposed redevelopment plans that were often discriminatory in character. For these reasons, along with many others, urban renewal became a lightning rod for public criticism. Far from solving the problems facing distressed urban communities, it frequently compounded them, disrupting the social, political, and economic networks that low-income households depended on to survive and simply pushing poor households deeper into poverty in other parts of the city.

While urban renewal has been the subject of significant scholarship since its inception, the country's experience with this program was much more varied than that research might suggest, and we do a disservice to urban and policy history if we treat this narrative as complete. Current research is diversifying our understanding of urban renewal by developing new historical, cultural, and geographical lenses that can be used to view the program and its consequences for the country at large. This book is driven by several of these increasingly significant themes. For example, nearly three-quarters (74.7 percent) of the cities that used urban renewal funds had populations of fewer than fifty thousand people, yet their experiences remain largely absent from the academic literature.[5] Urban renewal histories in the Southeast, Southwest, and West are also finally beginning to receive their due.[6] Many of these new studies examine cities such as Austin, Texas, or Los Angeles, California—cities that were growing during this period, rather than suffering industrial and population decline.[7] Another subset of studies documents the role of colleges and universities as partners in the urban renewal process, a practice that was made possible as a result of amendments to the act in 1959.[8] The idea of examining urban renewal for its role in building rehabilitation, rather than clearance, has also begun to attract attention.[9] These works have helped researchers identify variations in the use of urban renewal funds guided by local political culture, economic differences, and visions for the future. This trend is likely to continue, fueled in part by the increasing availability of data that match the nationwide scope of the program. Because this information has become more accessible, it is possible to better contextualize earlier research, contrast the experiences of diverse geographies, and identify trends or connections that cut across jurisdictional boundaries. Reflecting these shifts, this book presents the experiences of small cities, large cities, and suburbs, and it includes perspectives from state and territory levels as well. It also provides guidance for scholars seeking to expand the narrative of urban renewal in both novel and familiar places. With luck, it will encourage new research that allows us to better understand what was arguably the most significant urban policy of the twentieth century.

## The Policy Context for Urban Renewal

The Housing Act of 1949 was not the federal government's first foray into the housing market. In the early months of Franklin Roosevelt's first term, he broke with the laissez-faire tradition of his predecessors and introduced a number of programs to produce affordable housing and stabilize a market that was essentially collapsing during the bleakest years of the Great Depression.[10] Through its Housing Division, the Public Works Administration (PWA) produced approximately twenty-five thousand high-quality housing units across the country.[11] These developments are regarded by some as being among the best public housing units the government ever built.[12] Roosevelt's first year also produced the Emergency Farm Mortgage Act and the Home Owners Loan Corporation (HOLC), both of which effectively took unregulated, poorly structured loans and converted them to modern, self-amortizing mortgages with regular monthly payments.[13] If these programs looked backward to address old problems, the National Housing Act, passed in June 1934, looked forward to prevent them from occurring in the future. The Federal Housing Administration (FHA) penned into existence many of the programs that would create the modern housing market and launch America's identity as a suburban nation. Through the FHA and its mortgage insurance programs, the federal government took much of the risk of a mortgage off the local bank's shoulders and created minimum standards for new residential construction. As a result, banks were more comfortable lending money for new construction. For all the considerable good they did to stabilize the housing market and encourage construction during the Depression, however, HOLC and FHA policies also played a central role in segregating America's cities and suburbs.[14] Supported by the actions of private real estate professionals, banks, local governments, and others, these policies set the stage for decades of white flight and equity building in suburbia while minimizing access to the major wealth-building opportunity of the twentieth century for African American and minority households.[15] Instead, these marginalized groups were largely restricted to living in inner-city neighborhoods of declining value, building their own homes with limited resources, or buying their homes with less well-regulated financial instruments.[16]

The 1930s were very active years for housing policy in the United States. Just three years after the passage of the National Housing Act, a new landmark housing act was passed, the Housing Act of 1937. Though it was far from an unqualified success, the Housing Act of 1937 created the United States Housing Authority (USHA) and sought to expand the federal government's role in producing affordable housing. The USHA was hamstrung by a number of issues, including a cap on the amount of money that could be spent per unit; the political necessity of local control of the projects, which encouraged segregation; and the onset of World War II.[17] Because of its financial constraints, the housing units were neither as spacious nor as well built as their PWA predecessors, and they lacked many of the amenities that had made the earlier developments so popular.[18] During World War II, the federal government became much more involved in housing production due to the demands of the defense industry. The Lanham Public War Housing Act was the primary vehicle that facilitated the construction of the housing and community facilities needed to support war workers.[19] While most of the housing built through the Lanham Act was temporary, some was more substantial and remained in use after the war as public housing.

Following the war, President Truman sought to bring all the federal government's various housing and housing-support programs together under one administrative roof. The Housing and Home Finance Agency was the result, and while it was essentially a collection of existing programs, its structure makes it clear just how involved in the housing market the federal government had become by the dawn of the urban renewal era.

Created in 1947, the HHFA consisted of three constituent agencies. The first agency was the Home Loan Bank Board, which oversaw the Federal Home Loan Bank System, the Federal Savings and Loan Insurance Corporation, the Federal Savings and Loan Associations, and the Home Owners' Loan Corporation.[20] The second agency within the HHFA at its formation was the FHA, which had been established through the National Housing Act in 1934. The third agency within the HHFA at its creation was the Public Housing Administration (PHA). The PHA was the new name given to the USHA. In addition to the work of the old USHA, the PHA had the responsibility of liquidating the assets of several wartime emergency housing programs, including those constructed through the Lanham Act.[21]

The challenges facing the new HHFA were very different than those that had prompted the creation of its constituent parts. Instead of the crashing home values and limited credit of the Depression era, the country now faced a white-hot housing market struggling to keep up with demand. The situation in 1947 was described in the HHFA's first annual report, published in 1948:

Despite substantial housing production achievements, it was apparent throughout 1947 that the Nation's housing problems were far from being solved, and that we would be confronted for some time to come with a severe housing shortage, particularly of rental and low and moderate priced sales units. It was also apparent that the problem could not be considered in terms of volume alone; much of the housing produced during 1947 was at prices beyond the reach of a great part of the potential market. The heavy demand for housing, however, meant a ready market for the homes that were constructed during 1947, although undoubtedly many persons bought at prices that will put a severe strain on their long-range financial capacity.[22]

Faced with these challenges, as well as the increasing evidence of declining urban environments nationwide, housing advocates, the real estate industry, city officials, and various stakeholder groups prepared what would become the Housing Act of 1949.[23]

## The Housing Act of 1949

In the Declaration of National Housing Policy that begins the Housing Act of 1949, Congress called for

> housing production and related community development sufficient to remedy the serious housing shortage, the elimination of substandard and other inadequate housing through the clearance of slums and blighted areas, and the realization as soon as feasible of the goal of a decent home and a suitable living environment for every American family.[24]

On the surface, these are noble goals. It is hard to argue against the idea of "a decent home and a suitable living environment for every American family."[25] Over time, however, it became clear that achieving the dual goals of slum clearance and quality housing for every American family was beyond the administrative, planning, and financial capacity of the era, particularly given the significant limitations present in the Housing Act itself.

As has been noted elsewhere, the Housing Act of 1949 was drafted to obtain the support of competing interest groups who did not necessarily seek the same outcomes.[26] The battles between public housing advocates and the real estate industry resulted in a housing act that could easily reduce the amount of housing available to low-income households, increase overcrowding in other low-income neighborhoods, and fail to find private-sector buyers for property once cleared.[27] Yet despite its highly visible flaws, or perhaps because of them, cities saw the slum clearance program as a lifeline following decades of disinvestment during the Depression and the resource-scarce war years.

Title I of the Housing Act of 1949 allowed the federal government to provide loans to pay for two-thirds of the total cost of a slum clearance project, in addition to providing funds for initial planning.[28] The local government was responsible for providing the remaining third of the project's cost. In a typical clearance project, the local government, or its designated public agency, was obligated to prepare and obtain federal approval for a redevelopment plan for the project area and it was required to prepare a plan to rehouse the affected neighborhood residents. It could purchase the properties in the desired area or seize them through eminent domain. Once the local government had obtained ownership of all the parcels, removed the residents, bulldozed the buildings, and consolidated the properties, it then typically sold the land to a developer to actually build the project and put it into its new use. It then used the funds from the sale of the property to repay the loans it had received from the federal government.[29] Thus, for a relatively small investment, the city would be rid of its slum neighborhoods and be rewarded with gleaming new apartments, office space, or institutional facilities on a scale that would never have been possible without federal involvement. Because of the fear of falling behind the suburbs, the hubris of political and technocratic elites, and the classism and racism that were endemic to political life in the American city, the idea of "saving" the city through demolition blossomed.[30]

Not surprisingly, given the socioeconomic status of residents in neighborhoods targeted for clearance, many of the consequences of this approach were borne by the nation's most vulnerable populations. While there were exceptions to this rule, urban African American and minority populations were largely excluded from the first wave of suburban expansion through a combination of federal and local practices and often had little choice but to stay in precisely the type of area that cities were engaged in clearing. Segregation, discriminatory lending, racially restrictive covenants, and exclusionary zoning made sure that the majority of African American families who moved from rural areas to cities during the Great Migration stayed in the cities and did not have access to the same suburbs as white families.[31] And while the FHA-supported subdivisions popping up on the urban fringe were almost entirely closed to African Americans, circumstances within the urban core were hardly less restrictive. Redlining prevented significant FHA-insured real estate investment in minority or racially mixed neighborhoods, and in the racially segregated housing markets of the late 1940s and early 1950s, it was extremely difficult for growing urban African American populations to move into other neighborhoods.[32] The resulting overcrowding, lack of access to capital from legitimate lenders, and reluctance on the part of policy makers to invest in infrastructure that would support those neighborhoods accelerated their decline. Within this context, minority neighborhoods were increasingly framed as nuisances for the rest of the city to suffer, making the idea of slum clearance all the more appealing to policy makers.[33]

From the outset, the Housing Act of 1949 was a vehicle for slum clearance with a poorly defined relationship to the production of affordable housing and a deceptively hostile relationship to the residents of targeted neighborhoods. "Redevelopment" in the context of the Housing Act of 1949 could have meant almost anything as long as it was part of a plan developed and approved by the local government. If the land had previously been used for housing, once cleared, it did not have to be used for housing at all, much less public or below-market-rate housing.[34] And while the language of the Housing Act of 1949 required local public agencies to develop a suitable relocation plan before a project could be approved, those plans often consisted of little more than half-hearted efforts to move residents onto the waiting list for existing public housing.[35] There was no requirement that displaced households be guaranteed new housing anywhere, only that there be a plan for relocation. Even when nominally successful in finding new homes, relocation typically meant a radical disruption of the social and economic fabric that had previously held those communities together. And the pace of construction of new public housing units was slow. While Title III of the act authorized the production of 810,000 new dwelling units, it would take twenty years before the 810,000 units promised in the 1949 act were built.[36]

While its reputation as a slum clearance program had been firmly established by the likes of Robert Moses, Ed Logue, and others, the practice of urban renewal did change over the course of the program's existence in response to the lessons that planners and policy makers were learning. The 1954 amendments to the Housing Act, for example, allowed local governments to adopt rehabilitation as another tool for addressing blighted neighborhoods in addition to clearance. This led to the popularization of the term "urban renewal" rather than "slum clearance." The experiences of Baltimore, Philadelphia, and other cities demonstrated that rehabilitation could be a more effective way to approach neighborhood renewal than clearance.[37] By using urban renewal funds to bring marginal buildings up to code, officials were able to rehabilitate the physical fabric of these neighborhoods rather than clearing them. Rehabilitation was far from a panacea, however, as a failure to address the underlying social issues facing these neighborhoods led many such efforts to quickly return to their preintervention states.[38]

Permitting rehabilitation also, somewhat paradoxically, laid the foundation for historic preservation activities to be supported by urban renewal funds, beginning with the 1959 College Hill Plan prepared by the Providence Preservation Society in Providence, Rhode Island, and occurring elsewhere in subsequent years.[39] Though this type of urban renewal–based preservation success story was rare at the time, it helped open the public's eyes to the possibilities of neighborhood rehabilitation and reuse. Speaking broadly, the heightened levels of community activism provoked by the threat of urban renewal and other mid-twentieth-century urban "improvements," such as interstate highways, paved the way for greater appreciation of historic urban neighborhoods and landmarks. These grassroots advocacy efforts helped create an environment conducive to the passage of the National Historic Preservation Act of 1966 and to the rapid expansion of the historic preservation movement nationally. Although this perspective is most famously associated with Jane Jacobs and *The Death and Life of Great American Cities*, and with New York City's Landmarks Law following the clearance of Penn Station, it was an experience and response shared by activists in countless small and large communities across the country.[40]

The 1954 amendments also required local governments to prepare what was known as a Workable Program for community improvement and provided financial support for building local planning capacity through the Section 701 program. The requirement for a workable program was significant because it encouraged the adoption of land use planning, building codes, and other best practices for land development, more firmly entrenching the planning profession within the bureaucratic structure of local governments, both large and small, while also helping encourage the construction of safer buildings through standard codes.[41] According to the 1961 HHFA guidebook on the subject, the Workable Program consisted of seven elements: codes and ordinances, a comprehensive community plan, a neighborhood analysis, administrative organization, financing, housing for displaced families, and citizen participation.[42]

Shaped in its later years by the advances of the civil rights movement, the various successes and failures of the war on poverty (including the Model Cities program), the Civil Rights Act of 1964, the Historic Preservation Act of 1966, the Fair Housing Act of 1968, and the National Environmental Policy Act of 1969, urban renewal developed new programs and procedures that reflected the complex realities of America's cities in the mid-twentieth century. Ever so gradually, Congress also moved in the direction of trying to address the financial toll of urban renewal and other programs on those households forced to move as a result of federal initiatives. While it did nothing to address the damage done during the first twenty years of urban renewal, Congress finally took meaningful action in the form of the Uniform Relocation and Real Property Acquisition Policies Act of 1970.[43] This act significantly increased the amount of compensation households would be entitled to claim when federal projects required their displacement. The cost of urban renewal projects rapidly increased because the federal government was suddenly required to pay for something approximating the actual cost of relocation for the households and businesses it displaced.[44]

## The End of Urban Renewal and an Assessment of Its Legacy

By the early 1970s, the expansive scope of urban renewal was increasingly at odds with the goals of the Nixon administration, which sought to minimize and decentralize the role of the federal government in local decision-making processes. This stood in stark contrast to the philosophy that had prevailed during the early Kennedy and Johnson years, when the federal government was seen as providing leadership on urban issues. This, combined with the administrative inefficiencies created by the federal government operating so many different legacy urban and anti-poverty grant programs, led to a reckoning of sorts for HUD.[45] The Housing and Community Development Act of 1974 formally ended the federal urban renewal program, along with Model Cities and five other federal grant programs.[46] In their place, it channeled those funds toward the new Community Development Block Grant (CDBG) program and ushered in the "community development" era of federal urban policy. This new approach gave local governments greater authority over how federal grant funds could be spent, required less onerous measures for federal approval and oversight, minimized direct federal involvement in local decision-making, and increased the capacity of local groups, such as community development corporations (CDCs) and other nongovernmental entities, to undertake neighborhood development projects.[47]

Over the course of its existence, 3,284 projects or programs of different types were approved for funding under the auspices of Title I of the Housing Act of 1949.[48] Funds were disbursed to all fifty states, the District of Columbia, Puerto Rico, the U.S. Virgin Islands, and Guam.[49] By its conclusion, a program that began primarily as a vehicle for slum clearance had expanded to include eleven different categories of intervention, including code enforcement projects, general neighborhood renewal plans, community renewal programs, assistance for disaster areas, and traditional urban renewal projects, among other types of programs.[50]

While grants ceased to be made under Title I of the Housing Act of 1949 with the passage of the Housing and Community Development Act of 1974, the lessons learned as a result of the federal urban renewal program heavily influenced its successor programs and in many ways still guide city planning practice today. The CDBG program, for example, has been in place for almost twice as long as the urban renewal program, and it remains very popular among local government officials.[51] As would be expected given the program's origins, CDBG bears the heavy imprint of the Housing Act of 1949 and its subsequent amendments. The specified "national objectives" driving CDBG, for example, include "activities which aid in the prevention or elimination of slums or blight," and permitted activities include rehabilitation projects, historic preservation activities, disaster relief, and planning and capacity-building efforts.[52] The CDBG program is much more flexible than urban renewal ever was, though over the course of its existence, that flexibility has been both a strength and a weakness.[53]

Among other successor programs, the lessons learned from urban renewal are even more apparent, if less explicitly articulated. The Choice Neighborhoods program, for example, approaches disinvested neighborhoods with high concentrations of public housing from almost the exact opposite perspective of the viewpoint that drove urban renewal. Far from trying to erase disinvested neighborhoods from the map, as was the intent in 1949, typical Choice Neighborhoods grant recipients recognize the many complex, interlinked systems that need to function in order to make an urban neighborhood better address the needs of its residents. These projects include high levels of community engagement in the planning and project management process, varied types of housing, enhancements to educational facilities and programs, public transportation improvements, and better access to high-quality jobs, health care, and other systems.[54] The original Housing Act of 1949 targeted problem neighborhoods and sought a purely physical solution—clearance. Urban renewal was gradually transformed by policy makers to permit rehabilitation, increased levels of community involvement, and ultimately a greater recognition of the potential human cost of these projects. Its modern descendants seek to create quality neighborhoods that can be enjoyed by the residents who call the neighborhood home. Yet one is very much a product of the lessons learned through the other. New lessons can only be learned, however, if this period in urban history continues to be studied.

## Contents of the Book

The chapters included in this book were originally presented at the "Reassessing the History of the Federal Urban Renewal Program: 1949–1974" conference on September 27, 2019, at the University of Kentucky. Supported by a grant from the National Endowment for the Humanities, the conference came about because of the reasons identified earlier in the introduction—new information was becoming increasingly available, and the interpretation of that information was prompting new questions about how urban renewal had shaped the American landscape. The chapters included in this volume provide an opportunity to understand the types of questions that are being raised by this data.

In the first chapter, authors Brent Cebul and Robert K. Nelson draw attention to the work of the Digital Scholarship Lab at the University of Richmond and its newly released *Renewing Inequality* map. The map takes advantage of a range of formerly difficult-to-access federal data sources and presents, with stunning clarity, the scope of the federal urban renewal program, as well as its consequences for minority households, on a project-by-project basis for the entire United States through 1966. Just to draw attention to one of the data sources behind the map, the *Urban Renewal Directory*, published by HUD throughout the late 1960s and early 1970s, provides a running list of all projects approved, along with the project names and identification numbers, financial information, and approval dates. The June 1974 *Directory*, which covered projects through the conclusion of the program, is essentially a complete list of approved urban renewal projects and programs for the duration of the urban renewal program. This list covers all cities, states, and territories that participated in urban renewal. While not invisible in years past, this list is much more accessible today because it has been digitized and is available online. Chapter 1 introduces the scope of the data that is now widely available, as well as the capabilities of the map itself, while also examining the long-lasting fiscal consequences of urban renewal, which has traditionally been framed as requiring only a minor local investment. To further this analysis, this chapter draws attention to the experiences of cities in several southeastern states that made use of urban renewal funds.

While the increasing digital availability of relevant data is one of the most exciting aspects of current urban renewal research, new sources of data must first be found before that information can be put online. Much of it can only be encountered by doing the yeoman's work of visiting state and municipal archives or opening forgotten file cabinets in local planning offices. In his chapter, David Hochfelder provides guidance for conducting research at the state and local scale in the state of New York. Reaching far beyond the well-documented projects in New York City, Hochfelder uses local and state archival resources to bring to light the experiences of Elmira, Jamestown, and Painted Post, among other upstate communities.

The next section of the book emphasizes not the process of recovering data but the stories of the varied and diverse geographies to have used urban renewal funds. In Chapter 3, Benjamin D. Lisle introduces readers to the struggling mill town of Waterville, Maine, which had a population of 18,695 in 1960. Waterville undertook two urban renewal projects. In the face of hard times for the city's paper mills, Waterville first sought to essentially turn its downtown into a shopping mall to appeal to tourists. Its second project cleared a working-class neighborhood composed of Lebanese and French Canadian mill workers. This experience in some ways mirrored the power dynamic more often seen in larger cities, with the burden of urban renewal falling most heavily on minority and immigrant populations, but with ethnic geographies that were shaped by rural New England's industrial past.

Moving away from central Maine and into the Sun Belt, Robert B. Fairbanks's chapter highlights the experiences of the Texas cities of Grand Prairie and Lubbock. The postwar growth experienced by these two cities challenges the traditional urban renewal narrative of aging Rust Belt cities seeking to lure residents back from the suburbs. Grand Prairie, in particular, stands in contrast with that narrative in a number of ways. Its Dalworth project rehabilitated an African American neighborhood instead of clearing it. Most of the previous residents retained ownership and remained in the neighborhood after renewal, and the rehabilitation loans that supported this transition were insured by the FHA. While there was significant relocation of residents, and the project reinforced a segregated residential pattern, it was successful in ways that many better-known projects were not.

Chapter 5 introduces another geography that is rarely encountered in studies of urban renewal. Like the Sun Belt and central Maine, U.S. territories do not fit the typical view of the program as addressing the needs of major legacy cities. This is unfortunate for many reasons, not the least of which is that Puerto Rico made heavier use of urban renewal than did thirty-four states. After briefly introducing the experiences of other territories, the author offers a Commonwealth-wide view of urban renewal as used in Puerto Rico, emphasizing the progressive populism that defined much of the urban renewal era (in contrast to the conservative politics in the continental United States) and the consequences of urban renewal for the built environment. The chapter suggests three possible areas of future study, including the relationship between urban renewal and the vernacular architectural form known as the casita, the decision by Puerto Rican officials not to use urban renewal to engage with the buildings surrounding central plazas, and the connection between urban renewal and the development of the architectural style known as tropical modernism.

In Chapter 6, Stacy Kinlock Sewell approaches urban renewal from the state perspective, examining the New York State Urban Development Corporation (UDC). The story of the UDC draws attention to the failure of many local officials to effectively complete the projects they started. In the small cities and towns of upstate New York, as in many other locations, slum clearance might be framed as the "easy part," while redevelopment for many proved to be a much more difficult challenge. Sewell discusses the work of the UDC and its experience being the "developer of last resort."

The book's next chapter examines the experience of Elmwood Park in St. Louis County, Missouri. One of the primary themes of Colin Gordon's discussion is the centrality of the concept of "relocation" and the degree to which it was mismanaged in the case of this small, predominantly African American St. Louis suburb. Providing a fine-grained examination of the process by which the community was dismantled, Gordon calls out the county officials' incompetence and willful avoidance of their responsibilities to address the relocation needs of the affected residents.

While some cities almost seemed to prioritize disrupting the lives of their poorest citizens, others initiated their renewal efforts using both a public health and a rehabilitation perspective. In his chapter, Leif Fredrickson uses the experience of Baltimore, often seen as an urban renewal pioneer, to examine how urban renewal related to other existing city improvement efforts, most specifically its public health initiatives that predated the Housing Act of 1949. In the mid- to late 1940s, Baltimore was well known for its health code–based "Baltimore Plan," which prioritized strict code enforcement as a way to improve health outcomes in former slum neighborhoods. But while it attracted significant attention nationally, it was a very slow process, and its positive results were also often short lived. Following the passage of the Housing Act of 1949, the city gained new tools to use, and so began an uneasy working relationship between the city's Public Health Department and its redevelopers. Fredrickson charts the city's path from a public health–based rehabilitation effort to one that ultimately had the counterproductive consequence of pushing additional low-income households into already overcrowded neighborhoods, worsening public health outcomes.

The final chapter in this book examines one of the most significant shifts in the program: its expansion to include rehabilitation as an option for neighborhood renewal in addition to clearance. Because it provided a less expensive, and possibly less traumatizing, option for addressing the physical liabilities of a "blighted" neighborhood, rehabilitation was a popular option for many cities once it became available. Francesca Russello Ammon's chapter considers the various consequences of this approach to urban renewal practice, with a particular focus on how it began to incorporate not just rehabilitation but historic preservation as well.

## Conclusions and Future Directions for Research

These chapters draw attention to the benefit of looking outside familiar locations to paint a more complete picture of a federal program whose effects were felt across the country. Taken as a whole, they showcase the diversity, perhaps unexpected, of how different communities experienced the federal urban renewal program. Urban renewal was used to respond to both industrial decline and industrial growth. It was encouraged by both progressive populists and local chambers of commerce in wildly different political and cultural contexts. It was used in both the smallest and largest cities. It was responsible for both clearance and the rehabilitation of existing buildings.

Beyond just saying that "urban renewal happened here too," these chapters point to real differences, many of which challenge long-held assumptions about the program and its consequences.

These chapters also help draw attention to several areas that hold promise for future research, particularly those that are made possible by the greater accessibility of data that make plain the breadth and scope of the program. Probably the most significant shift in the near future, along with an expansion of the number of small and medium-sized cities being studied, will be the addition of a greater number of comparative studies that incorporate multiple sites within the same research project. Stand-alone, intensive case studies are always going to be a valued part of urban renewal scholarship for the detail and depth they provide, but the ability to quickly identify projects that share geographical, political, chronological, or social characteristics has opened new doors for future research. A regional approach, for example, would be useful not only for the Southwest, where Fairbanks has pioneered research at that scale, but also for the Midwest, the Southeast, and other geographies. One could imagine a study of urban renewal projects along any, or all, of the Great Lakes, for example, or along the Ohio River or the Merrimack River. In each of these cases, projects thus identified can be used as the entry point for understanding broader questions about the region, its economic history, its culture, and in many ways its modern prospects for success.

Continuing the idea of assembling a group of case studies based on a unifying characteristic, a project examining how urban renewal affected immigrant and ethnic neighborhoods in a variety of cities—large and small, and from all corners of the country—would be tremendously useful. Lisle's chapter, and other current work, hints at the need for this topic, but it deserves greater attention.[55] Another badly needed volume would explicitly connect post–Civil War African American communities with the urban renewal projects that cleared or threatened them. This would help raise the profile of these communities as valued and historic American settlements and would also make plain their continued targeting by various levels of public policy.[56]

Leaning on the 1974 *Urban Renewal Directory*, studies that seek to address all projects within one city are also a logical next step, drawing attention to the ways local expectations for the program changed over time as neighborhood leaders became more effective organizers and as program administrators became more receptive to other forms of "renewal." Taking a cue from Fredrickson's chapter, this approach may make it easier to understand the local policy frameworks that supported urban renewal and the diversity of challenges that local policy makers and community leaders sought to address over the life of the program. Single-city studies also present an opportunity to emphasize architectural traditions lost and gained. For better or worse, many urban renewal projects pushed out traditional building types and replaced them with something entirely different. Questions about the value of both to modern community members remain worth asking.

If nothing else, the chapters assembled in this volume make clear that we do not know urban renewal as well as we think we do. We have a better understanding of its reach than did earlier scholars, but we have only just begun to raise the questions required by that shift in perspective. From a researcher's point of view, however, recognizing that our understanding of a topic is deficient is a good thing because that means there is so much more for us to learn. Hopefully the work presented here will help move our collective questioning forward.

## NOTES

1. U.S. Senate Committee on Banking and Currency, *The Housing Act of 1949: What It Is and How It Works* (Washington, D.C.: U.S. Government Printing Office, 1949), 1.

2. U.S. Senate Committee on Banking and Currency.

3. Housing Act of 1949, July 15, 1949, chap. 338, 63 Stat. 413 § 2, "Declaration of National Housing Policy."

4. Department of Housing and Urban Development, *Urban Renewal Directory: June 30, 1974* (Washington, D.C.: U.S. Government Printing Office, 1975), 1.

5. Douglas R. Appler, "Changing the Scale of Analysis for Urban Renewal Research: Small Cities, the State of Kentucky, and the 1974 Urban Renewal Directory," *Journal of Planning History* 16, no. 3 (August 2017): 200–221.

6. See generally J. Rosie Tighe and Timothy J. Opelt, "Collective Memory and Planning: The Continuing Legacy of Urban Renewal in Asheville, NC," *Journal of Planning History* 15, no. 1 (2016): 46–67; Sarah Judson, "'I Am a Nasty Branch Kid': Women's Memories of Place in the Era of Asheville's Urban Renewal," *North Carolina Historical Review* 91, no. 3 (July 2014): 323–350; Cheryl Rodriguez and Beverly Ward, "Making Black Communities Matter: Race, Space, and Resistance in the Urban South," *Human Organization: Journal of the Society for Applied Anthropology* 77, no. 4 (2018): 312–322; Lydia Otero, *La Calle: Spatial Conflicts and Urban Renewal in a Southwest City* (Tucson: University of Arizona Press, 2010); Andrew Busch, "'Building a City of Upper Middle Class Citizens': Labor Markets, Segregation, and Growth in Austin, Texas 1950–1973," *Journal of Urban History* 39, no. 5 (2013): 975–996; Elsa Devienne, "Urban Renewal by the Sea: Reinventing the Beach for the Suburban Age in Postwar Los Angeles," *Journal of Urban History* 45, no. 1 (2019): 99–125. Christopher Silver should be recognized as a pioneer in discussing urban renewal in the Southeast, and Robert Fairbanks is one of the early advocates of examining urban renewal in the Southwest.

7. See also Fairbanks, this volume.

8. Henry Louis Taylor Jr., Gavin Luter, and Camden Miller, "The University, Neighborhood Revitalization, and Civic Engagement: Toward Civic Engagement 3.0," *Societies* 8, no. 4 (2018): 106, https://doi.org/10.3390/soc8040106; John L. Puckett and Mark Frazier Lloyd, "Penn's Great Expansion: Postwar Urban Renewal and the Alliance between Private Universities and the Public Sector," *Pennsylvania Magazine of History and Biography* 137, no. 4 (2013): 381–430; Paul R. Mullins, "Racializing the Commonplace Landscape: An Archaeology of Urban Renewal along the Color Line," *World Archaeology* 38, no. 1 (2006): 60–71. For the origins of Section 112, see Charles Fels et al., "The Private Use

of Public Power: The Private University and the Power of Eminent Domain," *Vanderbilt Law Review* 27 (1974): 681.

9. See Ammon, this volume; Stephanie R. Ryberg, "Historic Preservation's Urban Renewal Roots: Preservation and Planning in Midcentury Philadelphia," *Journal of Urban History* 29, no. 2 (2013): 193–213.

10. Though Herbert Hoover should be given credit for the Home Loan Bank Act of 1932.

11. Gail Radford, *Modern Housing for America* (Chicago: University of Chicago Press, 1997), 91.

12. Joseph Heathcott, "The Strange Career of Public Housing: Policy, Planning, and the American Metropolis in the Twentieth Century," *Journal of the American Planning Association* 78, no. 4 (2012): 360–375; Nicholas Dagen Bloom, *Public Housing That Worked: New York in the Twentieth Century* (Philadelphia: University of Pennsylvania Press, 2008), 31–35.

13. James Stewart Olson, *Saving Capitalism: The Reconstruction Finance Corporation and the New Deal 1933–1940* (Princeton, NJ: Princeton University Press, 1988), 92; Jonathan D. Rose, "The Incredible HOLC? Mortgage Relief during the Great Depression," *Journal of Money, Credit, and Banking* 43, no. 6 (September 2011): 1073–1107; Charles Courtemanche and Kenneth Snowden, "Repairing a Mortgage Crisis: HOLC Lending and Its Impact on Local Housing Markets," *Journal of Economic History* 71, no. 2 (2011): 307–337.

14. Kevin Fox Gotham, "Racialization and the State: The Housing Act of 1934 and the Creation of the Federal Housing Administration," *Sociological Perspectives* 43, no. 2 (Summer 2000): 291–317; David M. P. Freund, *Colored Property: State Policy and White Racial Politics in Suburban America* (Chicago: University of Chicago Press, 2007).

15. LaDale C. Winling and Todd M. Michney, "The Roots of Redlining: Academic, Professional, and Governmental Networks in the Making of the New Deal Lending Regime," *Journal of American History* 108, no. 1 (June 2021): 42–69.

16. Beryl Satter, *Family Properties: Race, Real Estate, and the Exploitation of Black Urban America* (New York: Metropolitan Books, 2009); Andrew Wiese, *Places of Their Own: African American Suburbanization in the Twentieth Century* (Chicago: University of Chicago Press, 2004), 67–93.

17. Heathcott, "The Strange Career of Public Housing," 364.

18. Radford, *Modern Housing for America*, 191, 192.

19. Heathcott, "The Strange Career of Public Housing," 364–365; Zenia Kotval, "Opportunity Lost: A Clash between Politics, Planning, and Design in Housing for Pittsfield, Massachusetts," *Journal of Planning History* 2, no. 1 (2003): 25–46.

20. Housing and Home Finance Agency, *First Annual Report* (Washington, D.C.: U.S. Government Printing Office, 1948), 35.

21. Housing and Home Finance Agency, IV-1.

22. Housing and Home Finance Agency, I-2.

23. Alexander von Hoffman, "A Study in Contradictions: The Origins and Legacy of the Housing Act of 1949," *Housing Policy Debate* 11, no. 2 (2000): 299–326.

24. Housing Act of 1949, § 2.

25. Housing Act of 1949.

26. Von Hoffman, "A Study in Contradictions," 299–326.

27. June Manning Thomas, *Redevelopment and Race: Planning a Finer City in Postwar Detroit* (Baltimore: Johns Hopkins University Press, 1997), 55–81; Jon Teaford, "Urban Renewal and Its Aftermath," *Housing Policy Debate* 11, no. 2 (2000): 443–465; Ann Pfau and Stacy Kinlock Sewell, "Newburgh's Last Chance: The Elusive Promise of Urban

Renewal in a Small and Divided City," *Journal of Planning History* 19, no. 3 (2020): 144–163.

28. U.S. Senate Committee on Banking and Currency, *The Housing Act of 1949*, 3–8.

29. U.S. Senate Committee on Banking and Currency.

30. Francesca Russello Ammon, *Bulldozer* (New Haven, CT: Yale University Press, 2016), 140–181.

31. Andrew H. Whittemore, "The Role of Racial Bias in Exclusionary Zoning: The Case of Durham, North Carolina, 1945–2014," *Environment and Planning A: Economy and Space* 50, no. 4 (2018): 826–847; Sonia Hirt, "The Rules of Residential Segregation: US Housing Taxonomies and Their Precedents," *Planning Perspectives* 30, no. 3 (2015): 367–395; Richard Rothstein, *The Color of Law: A Forgotten History of How Our Government Segregated America* (New York: Liveright Publishing, 2017), 59–75.

32. Douglas S. Massey and Nancy A. Denton, *American Apartheid: Segregation and the Making of the Underclass* (Cambridge, MA: Harvard University Press, 1993); Arnold R. Hirsch, *Making the Second Ghetto: Race and Housing in Chicago, 1940–1960* (New York: Cambridge University Press, 1983).

33. U.S. Senate Committee on Banking and Currency, *The Housing Act of 1949*.

34. Teaford, "Urban Renewal and Its Aftermath."

35. See Gordon, this volume; Douglas R. Appler and Julie Riesenweber, "Urban Renewal through the Lens of Unsuccessful Projects: The Pralltown Neighborhood of Lexington, Kentucky," *Journal of Planning History* 19, no. 3 (2020): 164–186.

36. Von Hoffman, "A Study in Contradictions," 315; Housing Act of 1949, § 305.

37. See Ammon, this volume; Stephanie R. Ryberg, "Historic Preservation's Urban Renewal Roots: Preservation and Planning in Midcentury Philadelphia," *Journal of Urban History* 29, no. 2 (2013): 193–213.

38. See Fredrickson, this volume; Brian D. Goldstein, "Rehabbing Housing, Rehabbing People: West 114th Street and the Failed Promise of Housing Rehabilitation," *Buildings and Landscapes: Journal of the Vernacular Architecture Forum* 26, no. 2 (Fall 2019): 43–72.

39. See Ammon, this volume; Urban Renewal Administration, *Historic Preservation through Urban Renewal* (Washington, D.C.: U.S. Government Printing Office, 1963); Michael A. Tomlan, *Historic Preservation: Caring for Our Expanding Legacy* (New York: Springer Press, 2015), 49–51; Briann Greenfield, "Marketing the Past: Historic Preservation in Providence, Rhode Island," in *Giving Preservation a History: Histories of Historic Preservation in the United States*, ed. Max Page and Randall Mason, 163–184 (New York: Routledge, 2004).

40. Jane Jacobs, *The Death and Life of Great American Cities* (New York: Random House, 1961); Lauren A. R. Poole and Douglas R. Appler, "Building a Local Preservation Ethic in the Era of Urban Renewal: How Did Neighborhood Associations Shape Historic Preservation Practice in Lexington, Kentucky?" *Journal of Urban History* 46, no. 2 (2020): 383–405.

41. Carl Feiss, "The Foundations of Federal Planning Assistance: A Personal Account of the 701 Program," *Journal of the American Planning Association* 51, no. 2 (1985): 175–184; Housing Act of 1954, August 2, 1954, chap. 649, 68 Stat. 623 § 101 (c).

42. Housing and Home Finance Agency, *The Workable Program for Community Improvement* (Washington, D.C.: U.S Government Printing Office, 1961), 4.

43. Carl Bausch II Milton M. Ferrell Jr., and Harold Johnson, "Relocation—The Uniform Relocation Assistance and Real Property Acquisition Policies Act of 1970—An Empirical Study," *Mercer Law Review* 26, no. 4 (Summer 1975): 1329–1400.

44. Christopher Silver and R. Allen Hays, "Can You Compensate for a Lost Home? An Assessment of the 1970 Uniform Relocation Act," *Journal of Urban Affairs* 2, no. 1 (1980): 33–49.

45. Charles J. Orlebeke and John C. Weicher, "How CDBG Came to Pass," *Housing Policy Debate* 24, no. 1 (2014): 14–45; Michael J. Rich, *Federal Policymaking and the Poor: National Goals, Local Choices, and Distributional Outcomes* (Princeton, NJ: Princeton University Press, 1993), 22–56.

46. Orlebeke and Weicher, "How CDBG Came to Pass," 34.

47. Kenneth K. Wong and Paul Peterson, "Urban Response to Federal Program Flexibility: Politics of the Community Development Block Grant," *Urban Affairs Review* 21, no. 3 (1986): 293–309; Tony Robinson, "Inner-City Innovator: The Non-Profit Community Development Corporation," *Urban Studies* 33, no. 9 (1996): 1647–1660; Alexander von Hoffman, "The Past, Present, and Future of Community Development in the United States," in *Investing in What Works for America's Communities: Essays on People, Place and Purpose*, ed. Nancy O. Andrews and David J. Erikson, 10–54 (San Francisco: Federal Reserve Bank of San Francisco, 2012).

48. Department of Housing and Urban Development, *Urban Renewal Directory: June 30, 1974*, 1

49. Department of Housing and Urban Development, 2–5.

50. Department of Housing and Urban Development, 152.

51. Pier Domenico Tortola, "The Microfoundations of Policy Inertia: A City-Level Analysis of the Community Development Block Grant," *State and Local Government Review* 47, no. 1 (March 2015): 6–14.

52. Code of Federal Regulations § 570.208, Criteria for national objectives; Code of Federal Regulations § 570.201, Basic eligible activities; Code of Federal Regulations § 570.202, Eligible rehabilitation and preservation activities; Code of Federal Regulations § 570.205, Eligible planning, urban environmental design and policy-planning-management-capacity building activities; Department of Housing and Urban Development, Office of Community Planning and Development, *Community Development Block Grant Program: Guide to National Objectives and Eligible Activities for Entitlement Communities*, February 2001, available at https://www.hudexchange.info/resource/89/community-development-block-grant-program-cdbg-guide-to-national-objectives-and-eligible-activities-for-entitlement-communities/; "CDBG Disaster Recovery Funds," HUD Exchange, accessed January 9, 2023, available at https://www.hudexchange.info/programs/cdbg-dr/.

53. Rich, *Federal Policymaking and the Poor*, 22–56.

54. Department of Housing and Urban Development, *Choice Neighborhoods FY 2020 Implementation Grant Awards*, Accessed January 9, 2023, available at https://www.hud.gov/sites/dfiles/PIH/images/FY20_Choice_Neighborhoods_Implementation_Project_Summaries.pdf.

55. Kathryn Wilson, *Ethnic Renewal in Philadelphia's Chinatown: Space, Place, and Struggle* (Philadelphia: Temple University Press, 2015); Mike Amezcua, "Beautiful Urbanisms: Gender, Landscape and Contestation in Latino Chicago's Age of Urban Renewal," *Journal of American History* 104, no. 1 (2017): 97–119.

56. Rodriguez and Ward, "Making Black Communities Matter"; Appler and Riesenweber, "Urban Renewal through the Lens of Unsuccessful Projects."

# I

# Finding and Using New
# Sources of Data

# 1

# Toward a More Complete Reckoning

*Renewing Inequality and New
Histories of Urban Renewal*

Brent Cebul and
Robert K. Nelson

T estifying before a subcommittee of the House of Representatives in November 1963, commissioner of the federal Urban Renewal Administration William L. Slayton repeatedly emphasized that the majority of
municipalities that received urban renewal funding were not huge metropolises but small towns and villages. "Most of the larger cities undertook urban
renewal quite early," he said, "but increasingly the small communities have
become concerned with the need for eliminating blight, sustaining their econ-
omies and preserving their desirable residential qualities." He continued by
providing some numbers: "At the end of fiscal year 1953, 45 percent of the
communities in the program had populations of 100,000 or more; by 1963
this proportion had dropped to 16 percent, and nearly half of the localities
had populations of less than 25,000."[1]

It made political sense for Slayton to highlight how the urban renewal program distributed money not just to representatives' constituencies in New
York City, Chicago, Detroit, and Los Angeles. His agency would be on the
firmest ground if he could convince representatives of thousands of small
towns and rural regions that urban renewal held out great promise for them,
too—even if they didn't especially think of themselves as representing "urban" districts. Regardless of whether he had such a political agenda in mind,
Slayton's point that most of the municipalities that executed urban renewal
projects were small was an accurate one. In at least this respect, he presented
a far more complete portrait of the program than much of the historiogra-
phy on urban renewal that has flourished in the years since.[2] While that lit-

erature is beginning to change, it remains the fact that the lion's share of urban renewal scholarship has focused far more attention on the 16 percent of funded projects in large cities than on the preponderance of projects carried out in municipalities that were comparatively smaller.[3]

Slayton's testimony also points us to one productive body of evidence that can both advance our understanding of urban renewal as well as generate new questions for future inquiry: the considerable amount of data collected by Slayton's Urban Renewal Administration. In *Renewing Inequality*, the authors and a number of colleagues and collaborators developed a map that visualized the displacement of more than three hundred thousand families by federally funded urban renewal projects covering the period of 1950 to 1966, years for which displacement data has so far been discovered.[4] Beyond conveying the massive impact of the program on more than a million displaced Americans and the fact that the majority of these were families of color, *Renewing Inequality* visually illuminates Slayton's point about the magnitude and scope of the program.

This chapter builds upon the data orientation begun with *Renewing Inequality*. These data, we argue, raise a number of significant questions about the reach, racial impact, and longer-term financial and fiscal implications of urban renewal. One question we ask is regional: why did southern cities and towns that were hesitant about or openly hostile toward the federal government during the civil rights era nevertheless apply to participate in this massive federal program in such volume and frequency? The funding data amassed by the federal government hints at one answer: the hard-to-resist attraction of federal dollars. Other data for the program—that about race and displacements—hints at a fuller explanation. Far from being a lever the federal government could use to advance a civil rights agenda, the autonomy and power granted localities to administer and execute urban renewal programs meant they could avail themselves of federal funding to execute projects that did not upend but often reinforced racial and class disparities in their communities. That is, at the high tide of the civil rights movement, urban renewal, initially advanced in an optimistic "ethic of city rebuilding" and as part of a broader housing agenda, made funding available to quite literally remove black neighborhoods from southern communities.[5]

The second question we ask digs deeper into the data on program funding: how did localities finance their project contributions of one-quarter to one-third? The tables of financial data published by the Urban Renewal Administration suggest that much of these local contributions were covered in "non-cash" contributions. But those simplified statistics, we argue, just begin to hint at a much more complicated and deeply impactful story about the varying ways renewal projects were financed. Municipal debt played a central and expansive role in underwriting these projects across essentially all municipal scales and regions. Recently, scholars have begun to sketch the ways these sorts of debt obligations, floated at the high tide of liberal state building, circa 1945–1968, may have inadvertently expanded the reach and authority of a range of new actors, particularly credit rating agencies and the purchasers of municipal bonds. The enticement of federal funding accelerated the move toward expanded municipal debt, creating essential preconditions for the transition to an era of "neoliberal" urbanism and austerity in towns and villages well beyond neoliberal bellwethers like New York City.[6]

## Urban Renewal by the Numbers

The two most detailed and comprehensive aggregated sources of data about federally funded urban renewal projects (that serve as the main sources for nonspatial data used in *Renewing Inequality*) are the *Urban Renewal Project Characteristics* and *Urban Renewal Directory* reports, both published quarterly by the Urban Renewal Administration. The *Characteristics* reports were published until June 1966; the *Urban Renewal Directory* until urban renewal ended in 1974. (In 1966, HUD created a department-wide staff to centralize administration of relocations resulting from all HUD programs, including urban renewal and highway development. The *Characteristics* reports were superseded by HUD's *Statistical Yearbook*, which regrettably reported only aggregate displacement numbers and not city- or project-specific numbers.)[7]

The *Characteristics* reports presented some basic but still substantive data about the rationale and aims of each individual urban renewal project in a lengthy table that ran for dozens of pages (see Table 1.1). In keeping with the original and abiding purpose of urban renewal as a slum clearance program, two columns recording the number of "standard" and "sub-standard" housing units in each area prior to renewal presented a statistical snapshot and justification of each area's "slum" or "blighted" status. It also recorded, broken down by race (white and non-white), the number of families that were ostensibly to be relocated to better housing. The *Characteristics* reports also presented a very simplified statistical portrait of the area's future postrenewal functions in the number of standard housing units each would have and the acreage that would be designated for residential, commercial, industrial, and public functions—in short, how the area would be transformed from blight to healthy, safe, livable neighborhoods or other productive uses of the land.

Also contained within these reports are indications of the expanding and evolving goals of urban renewal projects. Though the program was initially framed in terms of improved housing and, second, as restoring commercial or industrial land to productive use, over its nearly quarter century in operation, its uses ranged far and wide. By 1963, the "basis for assistance" designated for each project—that is, the evolving legislative rationale for sup-

**TABLE 1.1 TRANSCRIPTION OF TABULAR DATA FROM THE URBAN RENEWAL PROJECT CHARACTERISTICS: JUNE 30, 1966 REPORT FOR PROJECTS DISCUSSED IN THIS CHAPTER**

| Locality and project | Program | Project number | Current status | Basis for assistance | Dwelling units | | Families | | Proposed reuse of project land (expressed in acres) | | | | | | Estimated project costs and financing ($000) | | | | Local grants-in-aid | Non-cash | | | | |
|---|---|---|---|---|---|---|---|---|---|---|---|---|---|---|---|---|---|---|---|---|---|---|---|---|
| | | | | | Sub-standard | Standard | White | Non-white | Total | Streets, alleys, public rights-of-way | Residential | Commercial | Industrial | Public | Gross project cost | Project expenditures | Net project cost | Federal project grant | Cash | Land | Demolition and removal work | Projects or site improvements | Supporting facilities | Other |
| **Alabama** | | | | | | | | | | | | | | | | | | | | | | | | |
| **Gadsden** | | | | | | | | | | | | | | | | | | | | | | | | |
| North Fifth Street | U | 6-2 | E | PO | 30 | 4 | 22 | 11 | 63.9 | 12.5 | 37.2* | 5.0 | 6.3 | 2.9 | 956 | 551 | 719 | 295 | 19 | – | 4 | 345 | 56 | – |
| **Montgomery** | | | | | | | | | | | | | | | | | | | | | | | | |
| Houston Hill | R | R-10 | C | R | 447 | – | 51 | 322 | 64.0 | 15.0 | 14.4 | 2.9 | 15.4 | 16.3* | 2,316 | 2,060 | 1,652 | 1,101 | 295 | 12 | # | 244 | – | – |
| North Montgomery | U | 1-1 | C | R | 242 | – | 20 | 222 | 51.4 | 13.8 | – | 0.6 | 35.4* | 1.6 | 1,343 | 1,302 | 1,144 | 763 | 340 | – | – | – | 41 | – |
| **Arkansas** | | | | | | | | | | | | | | | | | | | | | | | | |
| **Junction City** | | | | | | | | | | | | | | | | | | | | | | | | |
| Project No 1 | R | R-7 | C | R | 20 | – | – | 8 | 8.0 | – | 4.3* | 0.9 | 2.8 | – | 619 | 455 | 617 | 453 | – | – | – | 35 | 129 | – |
| **Colorado** | | | | | | | | | | | | | | | | | | | | | | | | |
| **Denver** | | | | | | | | | | | | | | | | | | | | | | | | |
| Avondale Neighborhood | R | R-2 | E | R | 110 | 43 | 246 | 3 | 39.8 | 6.5 | 23.8* | 9.5 | – | – | 3,581 | 2,886 | 2,381 | 1,337 | 349 | 12 | – | – | 683 | – |
| Blake Street | R | R-5 | E | R | 186 | 9 | 181 | 8 | 45.7 | 20.3 | 0.9 | 0.9 | 23.6* | – | 2,004 | 1,794 | 1,371 | 904 | 257 | – | – | 28 | 182 | |

| | | | | | | | | | | | | | | | | | | | | | | | |
|---|---|---|---|---|---|---|---|---|---|---|---|---|---|---|---|---|---|---|---|---|---|---|---|
| **Georgia** | | | | | | | | | | | | | | | | | | | | | | | |
| Augusta | | | | | | | | | | | | | | | | | | | | | | | |
| Medical College of Ga. | R | R-45 | C | U | 176 | 38 | 27 | 123 | 40.0 | 13.9 | -- | 2.2 | -- | 23.9* | 1,869 | 1,545 | 1,240 | 827 | 89 | -- | -- | -- | -- | 324b/ |
| Rome | | | | | | | | | | | | | | | | | | | | | | | |
| East First St. | R | R-89 | E | R | 222 | 24 | 6 | 143 | 107.1 | 20.8 | 81.2* | 5.1 | -- | -- | 2,914 | 2,332 | 1,374 | -- | -- | 684 | 203 | 71a/ |
| **Kansas** | | | | | | | | | | | | | | | | | | | | | | | |
| Atchinson | | | | | | | | | | | | | | | | | | | | | | | |
| Downtown | C | R-7 | C | D | NR | NR | 14 | 1 | 53.3 | 23.5 | 0.6 | 13.8* | 11.5 | 3.9 | 3,886 | 3,400 | 2,226 | 38 | 59 | -- | 167 | 910 | -- |
| **Massachusetts** | | | | | | | | | | | | | | | | | | | | | | | |
| Boston | | | | | | | | | | | | | | | | | | | | | | | |
| West End | U | 2-3 | E | R | 2,900 | 771 | 3,001 | 41 | 46.9 | 8.3 | 32.2* | 4.2 | -- | 2.2 | 19,332 | 17,556 | 17,135 | 11,423 | 3,935 | -- | 6 | 286 | 1,485 | -- |
| **New York** | | | | | | | | | | | | | | | | | | | | | | | |
| New York | | | | | | | | | | | | | | | | | | | | | | | |
| Lincoln Square | R | R-2 | E | R | 4,491 | 174 | 4,071 | 305 | 70.3 | 24.2 | 26.7* | 1.7 | -- | 17.7 | 61,242 | 48,499 | 46,319 | 30,879 | 2,697 | -- | 56 | 162 | 12,525 | -- |
| Syracuse | | | | | | | | | | | | | | | | | | | | | | | |
| Near East Side | R | R-30 | E | R | 1,346 | 346 | 278 | 847 | 101.6 | 34.1 | 26.4 | 26.2* | -- | 14.9 | 34,464 | 24,647 | 27,879 | 17,947 | 115 | 345 | -- | 2,349 | 4,747 | 2375b/ |
| **North Carolina** | | | | | | | | | | | | | | | | | | | | | | | |
| Laurinburg | | | | | | | | | | | | | | | | | | | | | | | |
| Downtown | R | R-10 | E | OB | 27 | -- | -- | 17 | 8.8 | 3.1 | -- | 3.8* | -- | 1.9 | 1,096 | 889 | 855 | 642 | 6 | -- | 5 | 77 | 125 | -- |

*Note:* A number symbol (#) entered in any column indicates that the amount involved is less than five hundred dollars ($500). Other noncash grants-in-aid (Column 25) such as credit for low-rent public housing under Section 107 of the Housing Act of 1949, as amended (identified by the symbol "a/" in Column 25) and expenditures of educational institutions and hospitals under Section 112 of the Housing Act of 1949, as amended, for land acquisition, demolition and relocation (identified by the symbol "b/" in Column 25).

* The exclusive or predominant reuse proposed under the urban renewal plan. In this report, residential reuse is indicated as predominant in projects where the acreage proposed for residential uses comprises more than 50 percent but not all of the net acres covered by the urban renewal plans. (Net acreage is defined as total acreage minus acreage proposed for streets, alleys and public rights-of-way.) The specific nonresidential reuse involving the largest number of net acres is indicated as predominant in projects where the combined acreage for all proposed nonresidential uses comprises more than 50 percent but not all of the net acres covered by the urban renewal plan.

porting local renewal projects—expanded from "blighted residential areas" (R) and "other blighted area" (OB) to include redeveloping "predominantly open area[s]" (PO) that "arrests the sound growth of the community," "open land" (O), and "disaster area[s]" (D), added in the amended Housing Act of 1956. The amended Housing Act of 1959 authorized renewal projects "located in or near a college or university area" without requiring any link to new housing (U). The 1961 Housing Act authorized hospitals to receive renewal funds without any housing requirements and also included a title enabling the FHA to insure condominium mortgages in hopes of incentivizing private home-ownership for moderate-income families.[8] By 1964, the federal government reported that 154 urban renewal projects were supporting redevelopment initiatives at 120 colleges or universities and 75 hospitals.[9] The Housing Act of 1964, which included new regulations stipulating that any municipalities receiving renewal subsidies had to establish minimum housing code standards, allowed cities to use renewal funds to enforce those codes. It also established rules requiring that the HHFA review all proposed clearance projects to ensure that similar goals could not be achieved through rehabilitation rather than wholesale redevelopment.

By the mid-1960s, then, the program was evolving away from megablock clearance projects to include more subtle and targeted instruments for renewing the built environment. The Housing Act of 1965 extended this trend through expanded code enforcement capacities to include areas outside of specified renewal sites, offered low-income homeowners rehabilitation grants, and included new grants for urban beautification projects and "general neighborhood renewal plans." This latter initiative was intended, in the spirit of the war on poverty's community participation mandates, to include a wider range of voices in the renewal planning process, including not only residents living within urban renewal sites but also those from adjacent neighborhoods. Even as the program was amended to include an ethic of participation, however, local officials and legal analysts recognized the ways code enforcement offered more precise but no less powerful means of displacing undesirable residents while maintaining and rehabilitating older housing stock that, by the late 1960s, was gaining cultural cache among a growing set of middle-class, white gentrifiers.[10]

If families moving out of substandard slum housing and revitalized uses of the land were the intended benefits of urban renewal, the *Characteristics* reports also detailed the costs, or at least the financial costs. They recorded the total gross and net costs of projects (the latter being the gross cost minus the sale and leasing of redeveloped properties) and the ways municipalities proposed to or had met their cost-sharing obligations of one-third, one-fourth, or one-tenth net project costs. These "local grants-in-aid" were broken down into cash and noncash contributions. The latter was further broken down into the donation of land, the costs of demolition and site improvements, and the development of parks, playgrounds, and public buildings other than public housing. But, as we explore, "non-cash" is, at a minimum, something of a misnomer; arguably it hides the real financial cost of urban renewal for cities, towns, and villages as several of these contributions required significant expenditures.

The data in the *Characteristics* reports afford the best aggregate and often city- and project-specific data about key issues such as the racial disparities among families displaced (55 percent of families displaced were of color, although they were 13 percent of the U.S. population in 1960), the sheer magnitude of the program in terms of the number of families it affected (more than three hundred thousand families between 1950 and 1966), the amount of land urban renewal reshaped (more than 550 square miles), and the massive amount of federal and local government dollars devoted to the program.[11] Yet the data are limited. As the explanatory notes for each report emphasized, the data presented were estimates offered by local renewal agencies. And there are good reasons to be cautious with these estimates. To receive federal funding, cities were incentivized to deem as many houses as possible substandard instead of standard. The displacement numbers reported in the *Characteristics* reports often are smaller than those that can be found in final reports and other sources about individual projects. The *Characteristics* reports also do not include important data such as the number of individual adults—the federal government did not require or fund relocation assistance for single adults—or businesses displaced. Indeed, while the *Characteristics* reports did not publish data on dislocated businesses, a 1965 report found that, through the end of September 1963, some 39,399 businesses had been displaced. Beyond families and businesses, that report also counted 65,657 individuals displaced.[12] The program would run for another eleven years.

In its use of two categories, white and non-white, the racial data presented in the *Characteristics* report are so blunt that, taken alone, they present a warped portrait of who was displaced by urban renewal. To be sure, these data do confirm that more families of color were displaced than white families. But only using two categories for race obscures the extent to which urban renewal affected ethnic and immigrant communities. For example, the *Characteristics* report records that over three thousand white families were displaced by Boston's West End project; it doesn't say that the West End was "generally considered to be one of the foreign enclaves of Boston" whose residents were first- or second-generation Polish, Italian, and Jewish families. In many cities, Latinx families were often categorized as white. The displacements listed in the *Characteristics* report for the Blake Street and Avondale Neighborhood projects in Denver, for instance, were 95 and 99 percent white, respectively; the former was a predominately Latinx neighborhood, while the latter was predominantly Latinx and Jewish.[13] The Lincoln Square project in New York City, which created the Lincoln Center performing arts complex, listed just 7 percent of displaced families as "of color," despite the fact that estimates placed the neighborhood's Puerto Rican population at around 20 percent.[14]

Finally, and most importantly, these data may convey a sense of the scale of the human impact of urban renewal but say nothing about the human experience of being displaced. For that we have to look for accounts like that of Grady Abrams, who was displaced from the Five Points neighborhood in Augusta, Georgia, when it was cleared for the expansion of the Medical College of Georgia. "It is one thing to leave your home, your neighborhood on your own, to be forced out is a different manner," Abrams reflected years later, testifying to the trauma urban renewal visited upon his community. "It takes on a different meaning. It was, to me, the closest thing to death I can think of. In fact, my neighbors and I lost relationships forever. There is nothing of the past now in Five Points that I can show my grandchildren and great grandchildren that was part of my past. Nothing at all."[15] Fortunately, reconstructing these experiences has become a primary focus of recent studies of urban renewal.

The data published in each *Urban Renewal Directory* are more accurate if less interesting. The *Urban Renewal Directory* presented data that might be thought of as a status report about urban renewal that detailed the dates that approved projects moved from planning to execution to completion as well as the federal funding that had been awarded and dispersed for each project. The funding data in *Renewing Inequality* comes from the *Directory* reports as it recorded dispersed dollars and was published for the duration of the program. The *Urban Renewal Directory* also includes an important milestone: when a project entered the "contract" phase—that is, when it moved from the planning to execution phases. These figures, however, can elide significant dimensions of the renewal project development process. Federal financing supported the clearance of land, but it did not underwrite subsequent developments. Arranging local matching funds, assembling private investors and developers, and organizing site improvements were all complex and time-consuming undertakings that could drag on long after federally supported eminent domain, relocation, and clearance had been carried out but before a project was officially categorized as complete. In New York State, the average project took eight years to complete; in New York City, the average time to completion was thirteen years.[16] One project site in Cleveland, clearance of which was begun in the mid-1960s, was not completely redeveloped until 1987, thirteen years after federal renewal subsidies ended.[17] Our data, then, sketch the temporal scope of clearance projects, but only qualitative research can describe the experience of operating a business or living within or adjacent to a long-drawn-out clearance project, its neighborhoods reduced to rubble and vast acres of open land, while public officials courted private developers.

Though these data are imperfect, when visualized—as we have done in *Renewing Inequality*—they offer both a more comprehensive and spatially and temporally granular portrait of an unprecedented quarter century of ambitious federal action to reshape American cities. In particular, the portrait that emerges shifts away from large metropolises to smaller cities, towns, suburbs, and villages, many of them spread across the South.[18]

## Bringing the South and Smaller Cities into the History of Urban Renewal

The fact that urban renewal in its last decade was disproportionately carried out by small cities and towns—with southern cities and towns comprising a growing share—raises certain political and administrative questions that might also shed new light on some of the era's most important questions of race, rights, and citizenship.

To read the headlines of southern newspapers in 1963 or 1964 would lead one to presume that a federal program like urban renewal was the last thing southern boosters and guardians of the Jim Crow racial order would have invited into their communities. As Lyndon Johnson advanced his civil rights and voting rights agenda in the wake of *Brown v. Board*, any program associated with the national liberal administration came under fire. In Montgomery, Alabama, an epicenter of the civil rights movement, a groundswell of protest rose to meet federal initiatives that appeared poised to further unsettle local, white, elite prerogatives. Fred H. White, a Montgomery business owner, fumed at one public hearing that renewal was a "part of the left wing tendency to socialize our government." According to the *Alabama Journal*, White "drew a big round of applause."[19] A few months later, the Montgomery Citizens Forum demanded $10,000 from the city to establish a study group to counteract "the barrage of propaganda" on the necessity of urban renewal and unmask the program's real intent: "to provide a foothold for federal interference in local affairs."[20]

Meanwhile, in Selma (population 28,385 in 1960), the *Selma Times-Journal* editors described renewal in preposterous terms. It was a program, the editors told their readers, that selected "homes at random . . . in which they wish to house applicants for public housing subsidies." The homeowners, in turn, were given "a limited time in which to 'renew' the house to the government's satisfaction, at the cost of the owner of course." If the homeowners failed to meet the government's expectations, renewal authorities "then condemn the properties, seize them, alter them at your (the taxpayer's) expense, and install tax subsidized tenants."[21] These bald scare tactics had very little to do with how renewal projects actually worked. They were fictions loosely based on FHA grants for renewal-related home repair projects that did, in fact, exist. Instead, this portrait mainly represents the broader racial and political conflicts of the early to mid-1960s, when civil rights activists, increasingly with the backing of national liberals, worked to democratize southern cities like Montgomery and Selma. Though Selma's city council and leading business boosters had previously sought to develop an urban renewal program, by April 1963 the program was effectively tabled over fears, as the *Montgomery Advertiser* reported, that renewal would enable "further encroachment by the federal government on individual rights."[22]

Selma's program apparently never recovered, but dozens of southern cities pursued and received renewal dollars from the late 1950s through the 1960s—the civil rights movement's "classical" phase, as Bayard Rustin called it.[23] And, while they may have been shrouded in overheated, antigovernment rhetoric, the fact that the Montgomery Citizens Forum was up in arms about a "barrage of propaganda" in favor of renewal suggests, at the very least, that there were some proponents who worked to assuage fears about the program. Montgomery had already begun two renewal programs when controversies about federal meddling started to swirl. Yet the preponderance of Montgomery's renewal projects would begin *after* the spasm of outrage over renewal: four new projects were underway by 1966.

Montgomery, population 134,393 in 1960, was on the larger end of the spectrum of southern cities undertaking new projects in the 1960s. Over the quarter century from 1950 through 1974, nearly four hundred southern cities and towns received urban renewal funding. Three-quarters of those municipalities were small, with populations of fifty thousand or fewer. While larger southern cities generally sought and received urban renewal funding earlier than smaller cities and towns, a handful of small municipalities were among the earliest to receive funds and execute urban renewal projects. Two small cities in Tennessee—Murfreesboro (with a population of less than twenty thousand) and Union City (with fewer than ten thousand residents)—were among the first ten municipalities to begin urban renewal projects in the South, in 1953 and 1954 respectively.[24]

In 1961, mere months after the student sit-in movement exploded across the South, a significant number of southern cities entered the contract phase of urban renewal projects. This was also the year that thirty-one southern cities and towns began executing their first projects. A third of those cities were larger, with populations of fifty thousand or more. Another third were tiny, with populations of less than ten thousand. The smallest—Junction City, Arkansas—had a population of just 749 people in 1960, hardly our sense of "urban." (See Figure 1.1.) Yet its project, begun in 1961, received a grant of nearly half a million dollars from the federal government and ultimately displaced eight families, all of color. Junction City may have been the smallest southern town to receive urban renewal funding, but it was arguably more representative of the typical urban renewal grantee than larger cities like New Orleans, Memphis, and Atlanta. Between 1962 and 1974, nearly three hundred southern towns and municipalities executed their first federally funded urban renewal projects. Only one in twenty of those municipalities were cities with populations larger than one hundred thousand. Almost half were comparatively tiny, with populations less than ten thousand. (See Figure 1.2.)

In sum, urban renewal was more southern and penetrated into smaller municipalities than the historical literature on the program would suggest. Given the fears about federal intervention in the local racial order, what drove southern cities, and particularly small southern cities, to seek urban renewal funding? What follows is a brief sketch of some possible incentives. But, like the story of financing these projects discussed later, this thumbnail sketch might pose more empirical and thematic questions than it answers. It also highlights another reality of renewal: the high degree of local variabil-

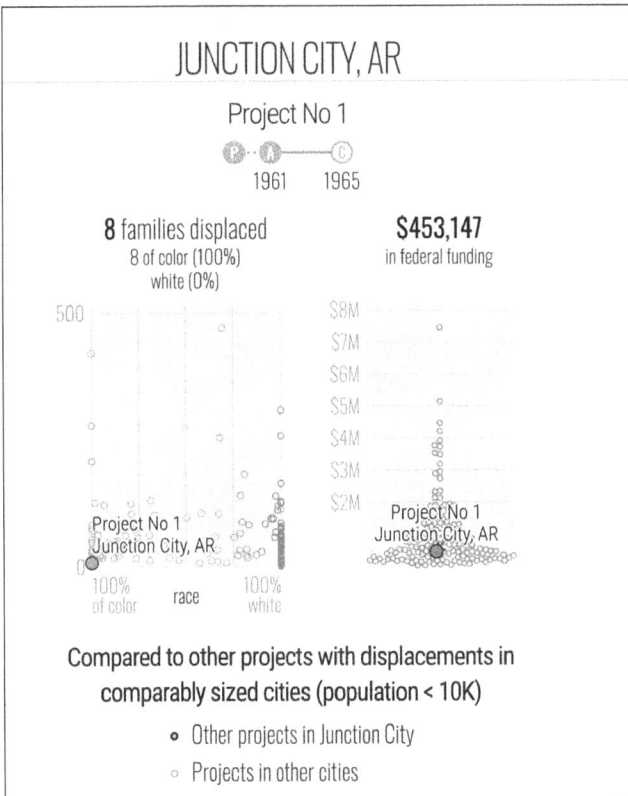

**JUNCTION CITY, AR**

Project No 1

1961    1965

**8 families displaced**
8 of color (100%)
white (0%)

**$453,147**
in federal funding

Compared to other projects with displacements in comparably sized cities (population < 10K)

- Other projects in Junction City
- Projects in other cities

**Figure 1.1**
Displacement and funding statistics for Junction City's project relative to other small municipalities.

(Sources: *Urban Renewal Project Characteristics*, 1955–1966; *Urban Renewal Directory*, 1958–1974; Digital Scholarship Lab, "Renewing Inequality.")

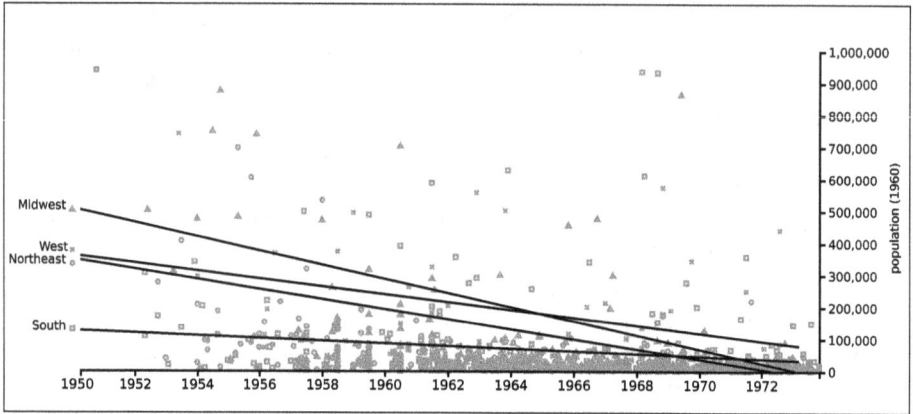

**Figure 1.2** The trend lines for every region show that urban renewal funding was increasingly awarded to smaller and smaller municipalities over the life of urban renewal.

(Sources: *Urban Renewal Project Characteristics*, 1955–1966; *Urban Renewal Directory*, 1958–1974; U.S. Census Bureau, *1960 Census of Population, General Population Characteristics*.)

ity and contingencies that this federal program allowed, variability the program in fact nurtured and depended upon for legitimacy.[25]

### The Federal Carrot?

In 1957 and 1961, Congress liberalized the local matching requirements for renewal projects. The Housing Act of 1957 allowed any local agency that underwrote its own planning costs to enjoy a three-fourths federal commitment to the program. In 1961, those three-fourths terms were extended to any community of 50,000 residents or fewer or any municipality up to 150,000 residents if that community had been designated a "depressed area" under the terms of the Area Redevelopment Administration (ARA).[26] The 701 planning program, established in the Housing Act of 1954, also offered direct subsidies to municipalities to recruit professional planners or contract with planning firms to begin the planning process for renewal projects. All of these inducements made a highly technical and seemingly large-scale project increasingly within reach for smaller, rural communities.[27]

The association of renewal with the ARA indicates the degree to which the federal government, through these and other programs, was literally invested in remaking local and regional markets. The ARA, a liberal program of the early 1960s that offered financing and grants to reindustrialize deindustrializing communities, reflected a realization on the part of federal administrators that industrial development funds alone were often insufficient

given the necessity of assembling land and, in some cases, demolishing outmoded factories or other facilities.[28] Together, the ARA and renewal offered
cities tantalizing means of returning unproductive or tax-delinquent land
to their tax rolls, offering financial and fiscal incentives—enhanced property tax yields on renewal sites was a point Slayton repeatedly drove home
in his 1963 testimony. The ARA, however, was just one way the federal government seeded development and planning efforts across the country. Regional planning bodies such as the Appalachian Regional Commission, which
took shape in the early 1960s, inculcated not only new habits of local and regional planning and economic development but did so with the backing of
federal funding and often with the goal of winning even greater levels of federal aid across a variety of program areas—from highways and renewal to
social services and job training. The ARA became the model for the Upper
Great Lakes Commission, the New England Commission, the Ozarks Commission, the Atlantic Coastal Plains Commission, and the Four Corners Commission. In 1967, those commissions established the National Association of
Regional Councils, a Washington, D.C.–based advocacy and lobbying out-
fit intended to expand federal spending for programs like renewal.[29] Throughout the 1960s, then, the federal government not only encouraged more and
more municipalities to look to Washington for all sorts of development-re-
lated subsidies but also gave them tutoring and tools to do so.

## Civil Rights Backlash? Frontlash?

But if the carrot of federal funding and economic development was one incentive, there might also have been other motivations rooted in maintaining—and bolstering—white dominance of local racial orders at the high tide
of the civil rights movement. As in many other locales, those displaced by
small southern cities were disproportionally of color. In fact, 58 percent of
the more than eight thousand families displaced by projects in southern municipalities with populations under fifty thousand were of color, the vast majority African American. Although people of color were collectively 22 percent of the population of those cities and towns, families of color were nearly
five times as likely as white families to have their homes seized and their communities decimated.[30]

Federal intervention it might be. But federal intervention with a civil rights
agenda it clearly was not, despite the program's early association with President Harry Truman's Fair Deal, housing, and civil rights agendas.[31] Quite
the opposite, municipalities large and small executed projects that decimated black neighborhoods. Years before the student sit-ins began sweeping the
South, renewal projects themselves became sites of contestation in smaller
southern cities just as they did in larger cities, no matter their region. In Gads-

den, Alabama, African Americans sought an injunction in an effort to require the city to "make housing available to Negroes in an area being redeveloped." Black residents were justifiably concerned that when their neighborhoods were cleared, they would be denied access to parcels of redeveloped land. The Gadsden injunction was blocked, and renewal of the North Fifth Street area proceeded. The presiding federal judge, Hobart Grooms, argued (and as the newspaper paraphrased him) "that it must be presumed that the City of Gadsden and its officers will act in good faith." In 1958, as white elites' massive resistance to desegregation was reaching a crescendo, the judge saw no reason to block clearance projects on suspicion of racist motives.[32]

In Junction City, the smallest municipality in the country to mount a renewal program, residents remembered long after how renewal proceeded there "in a very discriminating manner," as one (almost certainly African American) letter writer put it to the editor of the *El Dorado Times*.[33] Similarly, the first proposed urban renewal project in Richmond, Virginia—a project that would have razed relatively few houses—roused local opposition and died in the local city council. The second proposed project, which planned to seize and raze more than twelve times as many houses and displace more than five hundred families, this time in an African American neighborhood, prompted no such opposition from the city's leadership. Black resident opposition had no effect. The area was cleared and largely repurposed for a new turnpike and industrial development, worsening an already dire housing shortage for the city's African American residents.[34] In the late 1960s, a similar series of events played out in Rome, Georgia, where elites cleared out the primary black middle-class business and residential district and essentially refused to resell land to black purchasers, regardless of their ability to pay. In Rome, these clearance projects were undertaken as a wave of student sit-ins swept the downtown business district and students walked out of still-segregated and disparately resourced schools. (See Figure 1.3.) Because Rome's black residents were denied access to their former properties, not only did Rome's black businesses suffer, but the city's strongest and longest-thriving black community was devastated: 96 percent of those displaced by the East First Street renewal project were families of color.[35]

At the high tide of the civil rights movement, then, a federal program that offered local officials funding and justification for removing entire African American communities might be better understood as abetting elite efforts to preempt the civil rights movement—"frontlash"—as well as backlash to civil rights gains.[36] While not all small southern cities were as surgical in the excision of black neighborhoods as was Rome, a great many were: Fairfield, Alabama, displaced 46 families of color and none white; Marianna, Arkansas, displaced 76 families of color and none white; Newnan, Georgia, displaced 135 families of color and none white; Opelika, Alabama, displaced 138 fam-

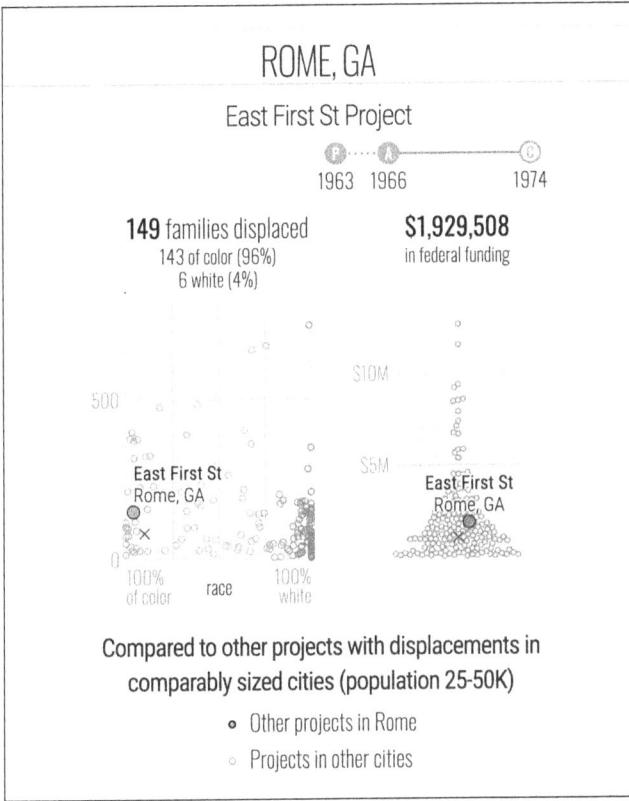

ROME, GA

East First St Project

(P)····(A)————(C)

1963  1966        1974

**149** families displaced     **$1,929,508**
143 of color (96%)             in federal funding
6 white (4%)

Compared to other projects with displacements in
comparably sized cities (population 25-50K)

○ Other projects in Rome

○ Projects in other cities

**Figure 1.3**
Displacement
and funding
statistics for the
East First St.
project in Rome,
Georgia, relative
to other small
municipalities.
(Sources: *Urban
Renewal Project
Characteristics*,
1955–1966;
*Urban Renewal
Project Directory*,
1958–1974;
Digital Scholarship
Lab, "Renewing
Inequality.")

ilies of color and only one white family.[37] Given recent scholarship on the en-twined histories of racism and the rise of mass incarceration, which fostered a far less direct form of "removal" than did renewal, scholars of urban renewal would be wise to incorporate the findings, analytical frames, and theories of the emerging carceral state literature to explore the many ways white racists made an ally of the mid-century liberal state.[38] Writing to Juanita Jelks, who faced losing her home in Gadsden, Alabama, the Reverend Martin Luther King Jr. made precisely that point: federally financed, locally prosecuted clearance projects amounted to "efforts of the segregationists to uproot your home and preserve a system that is destined to die."[39]

## Financing Renewal

If renewal endowed smaller communities with considerable new administrative capacities, the federal government's fiscal contributions, it turns out, only explain part of renewal's proliferation. Fundamental questions remain concerning smaller and southern cities' abilities to generate the matching contributions required to secure federal funds. Given the relative underdevelopment of smaller municipal governments and their limited tax bases, one wonders not only how local officials met the technical requirements of securing federal aid (e.g., preparing detailed surveys of local housing stock, generating statistical data, or preparing professional "Workable Program" reports) but also how they managed to meet their one-third or one-fourth financial matching obligations.

We know part of the answer. In terms of planning and preparing reports, the Housing Act of 1954 included generous funding for modernizing local planning capacities and hiring consultants or professional planners—and it did so regardless of whether the goal was applying for renewal funds or not. The 701 planning grant program, as Douglas Appler and others have argued, played an important role in incentivizing and teaching local governments how to undertake more recognizably modern processes and practices.[40]

But the funding question is much murkier and suggests, perhaps, deeper and wider roots to the period of financialization we most often associate with bigger cities and the post-1960s era. Take the example of Atchison, Kansas, population 12,529 in 1960. Atchison received a $2.3 million federal subsidy ($20.5 million in 2021 dollars) to completely redevelop its downtown after it sustained devastating damage in a series of summer storms in 1958.[41] (See Figure 1.4.) For a tiny city like Atchison, the matching costs associated with such a substantial grant (even under the more generous terms of renewal's disaster provision, which set the matching commitment at just 10 percent) would have been difficult if not impossible to meet out of general operating revenues. And so renewal's legislation authorized communities to meet their matching obligations in other ways: by using city manpower or resources to contribute to or offset the costs of demolition, by applying the costs of certain site improvements once the land was assembled and cleared, by including university or hospital expenditures related to renewal, or by investing in "supporting facilities," which might include building or improving parks on site or nearby that might increase the value of renewed property.[42] By December 1963, the preponderance of local matching obligations was met not through direct cash contributions but through these sorts of secondary improvements, new facilities, or land donations.[43]

Atchison made relatively little of its matching commitments in cash (only $146,000). Instead, the city met the vast majority of its obligations through site improvements ($286,000) and "supporting facilities" ($710,000), which included local expenditures on improvements, for instance, to related streets, parks, and other infrastructure.[44] Even so, these sorts of contributions often required ready capital to make improvements to a site or invest in a park or library. Despite only a small part of Atchison's contributions, according to the *Characteristics* reports, being made in cash, Atchison raised most of the

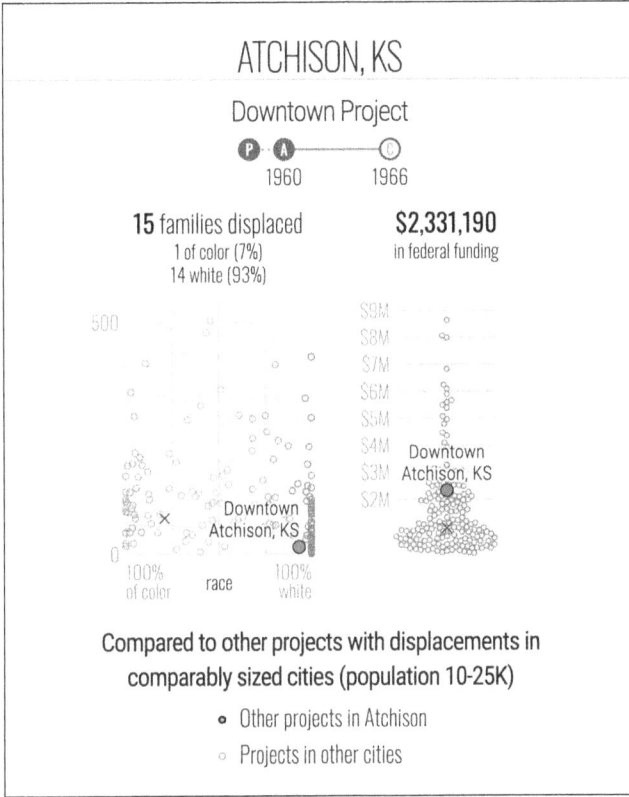

## ATCHISON, KS

### Downtown Project

**P** · **A** ————— **C**
1960        1966

**15** families displaced          **$2,331,190**
1 of color (7%)                    in federal funding
14 white (93%)

Downtown
Atchison, KS

Downtown
Atchison, KS

100%        race        100%
of color                white

Compared to other projects with displacements in
comparably sized cities (population 10-25K)

- Other projects in Atchison
- Projects in other cities

**Figure 1.4**
Displacement
and funding
statistics for the
Downtown project
of Atchison,
Kansas, relative
to other small
municipalities.
(Sources: *Urban
Renewal Project
Characteristics*,
1955–1966; *Urban
Renewal Directory*,
1958–1974;
Digital Scholarship
Lab, "Renewing
Inequality.")

capital to cover its ostensibly "non-cash" contributions by turning to the bond
market—that is, by borrowing cash. In April of 1960, Atchison voters overwhelmingly approved an $800,000 ($7.1 million in 2021 dollars) "urban renewal bond issue" to cover "the city's share" of the "plan to renovate the entire
downtown," as the *Manhattan (KS) Mercury* reported.[45]

Atchison's $800,000 bond issuance was almost certainly not the only
foray into municipal securities undertaken by the small Kansas municipality to support its renewal program. This was because the vast majority of the
federal government's share of renewal programs—the $2.3 million grant in
Atchison's case—were delivered through private lending institutions. Indeed,
private financing of public renewal programs was the standard practice. Rather than deliver direct grants to local governments, the federal government
encouraged local renewal authorities to float "urban renewal notes" in municipal securities markets. As opposed to the usual municipal bonds (like
Atchison's $800,000 note), which were paid off with general operating funds,
other sources of local revenue, and over a longer period of time (perhaps as
long as thirty years), the federal government's renewal grants both backed

and retired local urban renewal notes, which were uniquely short in duration—just six or twelve months. By turning to securities markets when interest rates were relatively low, the federal government aimed to save local governments (and itself) some interest costs around the margins of the program and route public revenues through private markets, offering subsidies and liquidity to private financial institutions as well.[46]

During the 1960s and into the 1970s, the federal government increasingly encouraged local governments to pursue debt financing.[47] While municipal debt has long been a bedrock of municipal finance, its use took off in the post–World War II suburban boom to finance school construction, especially.[48] For decades, interest rates on municipal securities were relatively low and predictable, while the relatively humdrum return for purchasers of that debt, which was tax free, became a handy place for high-tax-bracket individuals to stash their wealth and still realize a steady return. For local governments, then, the municipal bond market was a convenient and often essential pressure valve for municipal finances, enabling local governments to sell debt instruments rather than ask voters to approve higher property tax rates. As a result of this confluence of high tax rates, expanding municipal capacities, and a national system of debt financing, in the 1950s and 1960s—years we often associate with the explosion of big, national government—the fastest-growing employers, spenders, and revenue generators were subnational governments, which "outsripp[ed] the growth rate of all other parts of the economy, public or private."[49] This meant that a small, isolated city like Atchison could transcend local limitations by tapping into national networks of capital brokered by investment banks in New York City or Chicago. And, while municipal debt could require increased taxes to pay off the obligations, most analysts were optimistic: as one student of municipal finance put it in 1967, "increases in tax bases, such as property values, incomes, and sales, will probably serve as built-in growth factors for future state and local revenues."[50] In other words, as long as the debt financing stimulated or at least occurred in the context of rising property values—as officials were sure new schools or urban redevelopment schemes would deliver—there would be no need to raise tax rates. The higher yields derived from higher property values would suffice.

Consulting newspapers, legal notices, local records, and trade publications like the *Bond Buyer* yields some evidence about the types of financing that cities (and counties) pursued. In Syracuse, New York, for instance, the city sold an "urban renewal revenue note" for its Near East Side project. The $2.5 million instrument was intended to "cover anticipated first-year cash requirements" that the city planned to repay from revenues generated by "the resale of land within the project area."[51] In this case, Syracuse used debt financing to cover some portion of its matching requirements for the project based on bonds anticipating proceeds from the ultimate sale of redeveloped land.

One of the most confounding forms of local subsidy for renewal—in that it seems to be the hardest to parse—was the general obligation bond (GOB). Often floated to support a multitude of projects, these omnibus debt instruments could be used to make improvements to renewal sites or generate cash matching grants. But the same security could be used to fund a range of other priorities unrelated to renewal. In Laurinburg, North Carolina, for instance, voters approved such a debt instrument to build a new courthouse and jail on the city's Downtown renewal project, the costs for which might have been used to make a "site improvement" matching contribution.[52] More common, it seems, was that cities advertised GOBs in much more general terms, as in the example from High Point, North Carolina (see Figure 1.5), where the city floated $4.3 million to cover "Water, Municipal Building, and Street Improve-

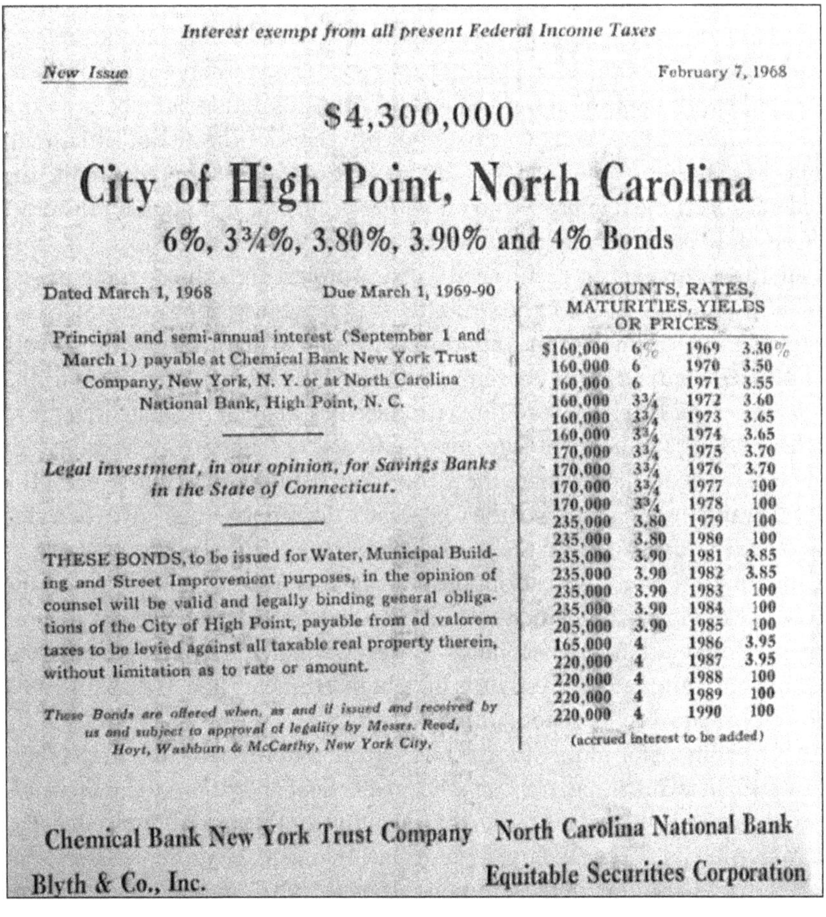

*Interest exempt from all present Federal Income Taxes*

*New Issue* February 7, 1968

**$4,300,000**

**City of High Point, North Carolina**

**6%, 3¾%, 3.80%, 3.90% and 4% Bonds**

Dated March 1, 1968 Due March 1, 1969-90

Principal and semi-annual interest (September 1 and March 1) payable at Chemical Bank New York Trust Company, New York, N. Y. or at North Carolina National Bank, High Point, N. C.

*Legal investment, in our opinion, for Savings Banks in the State of Connecticut.*

THESE BONDS, to be issued for Water, Municipal Building and Street Improvement purposes, in the opinion of counsel will be valid and legally binding general obligations of the City of High Point, payable from ad valorem taxes to be levied against all taxable real property therein, without limitation as to rate or amount.

*These Bonds are offered when, as and if issued and received by us and subject to approval of legality by Messrs. Reed, Hoyt, Washburn & McCarthy, New York City.*

AMOUNTS, RATES, MATURITIES, YIELDS OR PRICES

| | | | |
|---|---|---|---|
| $160,000 | 6% | 1969 | 3.30% |
| 160,000 | 6 | 1970 | 3.50 |
| 160,000 | 6 | 1971 | 3.55 |
| 160,000 | 3¾ | 1972 | 3.60 |
| 160,000 | 3¾ | 1973 | 3.65 |
| 160,000 | 3¾ | 1974 | 3.65 |
| 170,000 | 3¾ | 1975 | 3.70 |
| 170,000 | 3¾ | 1976 | 3.70 |
| 170,000 | 3¾ | 1977 | 100 |
| 170,000 | 3¾ | 1978 | 100 |
| 235,000 | 3.80 | 1979 | 100 |
| 235,000 | 3.80 | 1980 | 100 |
| 235,000 | 3.90 | 1981 | 3.85 |
| 235,000 | 3.90 | 1982 | 3.85 |
| 235,000 | 3.90 | 1983 | 100 |
| 235,000 | 3.90 | 1984 | 100 |
| 205,000 | 3.90 | 1985 | 100 |
| 165,000 | 4 | 1986 | 3.95 |
| 220,000 | 4 | 1987 | 3.95 |
| 220,000 | 4 | 1988 | 100 |
| 220,000 | 4 | 1989 | 100 |
| 220,000 | 4 | 1990 | 100 |

(accrued interest to be added)

Chemical Bank New York Trust Company North Carolina National Bank

Blyth & Co., Inc. Equitable Securities Corporation

**Figure 1.5** Announcement of High Point, North Carolina bond offering.
(Source: *Weekly Bond Buyer*, February 3, 1968.)

ment purposes" but did not indicate the sites or projects with any more specificity. In High Point, the timing suggests the possibility that some of these funds would support the Harrison Center Project, which had only just received HUD's approval the year before.[53] Similarly, in Alabama, where twenty municipalities operated renewal projects in 1962, most local matching requirements were made through "cash" or "project or site improvements." Montgomery, for instance, made most of its contributions in cash, and at least one bond issuance, announced in June 1957, was almost certainly tied toward improvements related to the Houston Hill and North Montgomery renewal projects.[54] In such a resource-poor and tax-averse state as Alabama, it is likely that most municipalities used debt financing to generate cash or make site improvement–based contributions.

In many cases, however, it seems that cities went far beyond the baseline matching requirements to secure federal subsidies. Federal guidelines made this an attractive approach by enabling cities to bank overage on one project's matching contribution and apply it to the local share of subsequent projects. As the head of the federal Urban Renewal Administration put it before Congress in 1963, officials called this "pooling credit."[55] The city of Cincinnati may have been one municipality that took advantage of pooling credit. The federal government approved an outlay of roughly $12.5 million for the city's "Central Riverfront" renewal project, but the city secured considerably more than that figure for costs associated with the project and subsequent improvements to the site. In 1963, the year after the project was approved, voters approved a $16.6 million capital improvement bond to make various infrastructural (see Figure 1.6) improvements to the site—which, according to the *Characteristics* reports, accounted for the city's share of the matching grant through local financing of "site improvements" or "supporting facilities" (in this case, $3.6 million went to the former and $1.1 million to the latter).[56] The local grants-in-aid section of the *Characteristics* reports, then, gives us a clue as to where to look to find the local share of renewal project costs, which, as Cincinnati's Central Riverfront project suggests, might go well beyond the baseline requirements, which was all that was reported to the federal government. Unlike urban renewal notes, however, which the federal government would back and retire, these sorts of debt instruments had to be paid off by the city itself from its general fund.[57]

The climate for municipal debt was so good in the early and mid-1960s, however, that Cincinnati took on even greater debt obligations to further subsidize renewal with local funds. As acquisition and clearance proceeded, the city secured an NFL franchise in large part thanks to Hamilton County's issuance of $44 million in revenue bonds to build the Cincinnati Bengals football team a stadium on the renewal site. The city, in this case, did not have the authority to issue the revenue bonds and instead paid down the county's

## CINCINNATI, OH

Central Riverfront Project

1962    1966        1974

**$12,472,915**
in federal funding

$40M

$30M

$20M    **Central Riverfront**
Cincinnati, OH

$10M

Compared to other projects without displacements in
comparably sized cities (population > 500K)

○ Other projects in Cincinnati

○ Projects in other cities

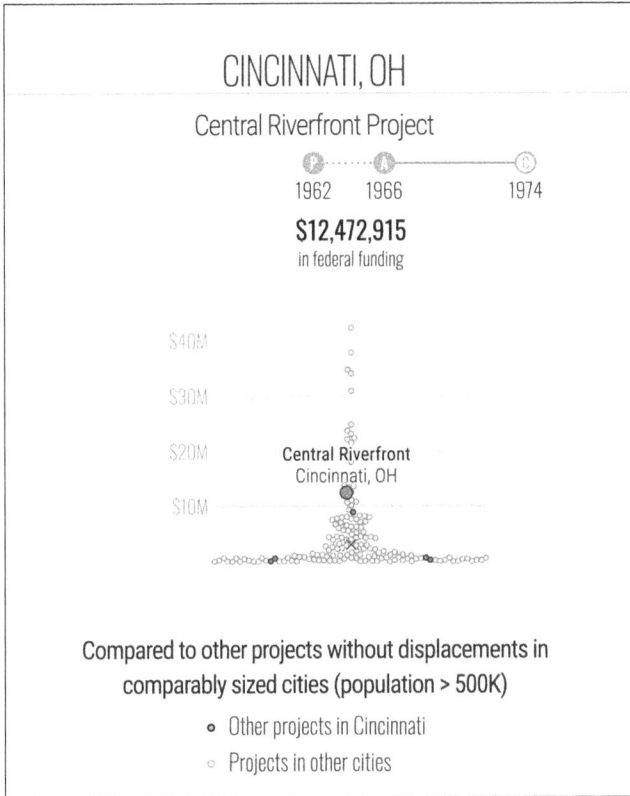

**Figure 1.6**
Funding statistics
for the Central
Riverfront project
of Cincinnati,
Ohio, relative
to cities with
populations of five
hundred thousand
or more.

(Sources: *Urban
Renewal Project
Characteristics*,
1955–1966; *Urban
Renewal Directory*,
1958–1974;
Digital Scholarship
Lab, "Renewing
Inequality.")

debt on the stadium in the form of a lease the city paid with revenue earned from the stadium itself—primarily subleases to the Bengals and Reds sports teams and game-day and other event revenues. When Riverfront Stadium was completed in 1970, the city began collecting surcharges on revenue from game tickets, parking, and concessions to retire the debt.[58] Pittsburgh used similar revenue bond instruments to build Three Rivers Stadium on its "Stadium" renewal site, which received just over $16 million in federal subsidies but cost the city at least an additional $35 million in revenue bonds.[59] Initially, however, Cincinnati's stadium did not generate enough revenue to cover the city's debt to the county. By late 1970, when inflation was taking off, one city official betrayed his concerns disguised as fatalistic optimism: "We're not paying for the stadium now," he said. "But"—as inflation continued its creep upward and made older debts decline in relative terms—"in 10 years inflation dollars will put us in the black."[60] By 1978, however, and as interest rates and inflation skyrocketed, the city was forced to dip into its general tax revenues to meet a $1 million gap between stadium income and its bond payments.[61] The initial optimism of the 1950s that the tax base or revenues inevitably would expand alongside property values and economic growth was not playing out as imagined. As the urban fiscal crises of the 1970s and 1980s set in, Cincinnati was far from exceptional in this regard.

Though we have much more to learn about specific cases and the broader story of municipal debt in the aggregate, urban renewal sheds light on how it was that, for much of the second half of the twentieth century, American municipalities outborrowed American consumers, who have received a great deal of scholars' attention.[62] In 1945, the total municipal debt market, in constant dollars, had not yet reached $20 billion. By 1960, the figure had grown to $66 billion. By 1981, however, and in the wake of the disastrous 1970s, municipal debt markets exploded, reaching at least $361 billion.[63] One result was that municipal debt became a key point of leverage for bankers and creditors in the 1970s in the high-profile restructurings of New York City and Cleveland as those cities teetered on the brink of insolvency. (Cleveland did default on its bonds.)[64] While urban renewal was certainly not the predominant source of those cities' debt, data from the *Bond Buyer* trade publication suggest that municipal governments floated at least $50.4 billion in urban renewal notes between 1954 and 1979.[65] This number makes the federal outlay of $8.6 billion between 1949 and 1974 appear comparatively paltry.

It might also prompt scholars to question whether we should view urban renewal less as a centralized federal program than a distributed local one, catalyzed but not fundamentally driven by federal aid. This further underscores just how profoundly local urban renewal was in the end. While federal legislation and funds called the program into existence, its administration and, it turns out, much of its financing came from the local level. Beyond federally subsidized urban renewal notes, general obligation bonds and revenue notes stayed on cities' books long past the completion of renewal projects: the aforementioned High Point general obligation bond was not scheduled to be retired until 1990. As interest rates and inflation soared in the 1970s and early 1980s, the cost to cities of borrowing, refinancing, or converting short-term notes to long-term debt skyrocketed. As William Tabb put it in his account of New York City's fiscal crises, that city's plight "illustrates the process by which, across the nation, the liberal 1960s turned into the neoconservative 1970s."[66] Today we might rename the transition as from liberal to neoliberal.

While the debts were carried locally, the data on the financing of renewal sheds light on the process by which local governments simultaneously grew evermore enmeshed in national and international financial systems over the course of the twentith century—that is, cities did not suddenly *become* financialized in the disastrous 1970s but rather underwent a process of acceleration and expansion. In fact, the distastrous 1970s were such a disaster largely thanks to preceding decades of borrowing. Faced with persistent and growing demands for services and economic development schemes but saddled with inferior revenue sources (relative to the federal government), cities of all sizes continued borrowing, especially as the Reagan administration waged war on intergovernmental fiscal transfers. And while that fiscal localism offered a degree of autonomy, it also invited in new nonlocal actors: credit rating agencies, bankers, and institutional investors, all of whom began imposing their preorgatives on local practices of governance and development. While scholars have noted the disproportionate power exerted by credit rating agencies and banks at moments of fiscal crises, this process of financialization suggests that those actors' interests and prerogatives were likely far broader and deeper than we may have presumed, extending into small cities as much as large. And that influence could also often come with inequities as well: as some new scholarship is revealing, a higher proportion of African American residents in a given municipality correlated with *lower* credit ratings by agencies—meaning the cost to borrow or refinance older debts for municipalities with higher minority populations was higher than for disproportionately white municipalities or suburbs. All of this made it more difficult to borrow in the first place and more costly to refinance or retire debts on the back end.[67]

The financial forces that structure urban inequality today may be somewhat subtler than renewal-era megablock clearance, but in their shared emphasis on maximizing profits and tax yields derived from property, they are a difference of degree rather than kind. The *Urban Renewal Project Characteristics* reports give us a tantalizing glimpse of the ways cities large and small raised their share of the costs of the program and points us toward much deeper continuities with and causes of a later era of urbanism in which the interests and prerogatives of capital gained an even stronger hand over local institutions. Fully grasping the ways the neoliberal urban regimes of today emerged from the high tide of highly indebted *liberal* city building might better empower us to transcend an era of neoliberal development, crafting an entirely new urban policy that emphasizes people over places and values homes ahead of short-term profits or future tax yields.

*Renewing Inequality*, its maps, and the data upon which it is based constitute merely a first step to reconceptualizing and recapturing the full history of urban renewal as well as its contemporary legacies. New histories of resistance and reaction in the South, in small cities, and in the North and West may well point to an even more literal interpretation of "Negro removal." Framed in terms of urban democracy, the disproportionate costs of the program borne by African Americans and other minorities might be understood less as an unhappy by-product of minority electoral status or the result of segregationist impulses but perhaps, in the context of civil rights demands, more as a proactive project of disfranchisement and literal banishment from the community. Similarly, qualitative archival work is essential to transcending the white/non-white binary imposed on *Renewing Inequality* by the limitations and biases of demographic data collection and construction in the past— there are a great many social histories to be written. Indeed, qualitative archival work will also be essential to fleshing out the woefully underdeveloped record of those displaced from urban renewal sites—as a basic matter of filling in the historical record but also, ideally, as a step toward justice and repair.

## NOTES

1. United States, Urban Renewal Administration, *Report on Urban Renewal: Statement of William L. Slayton, Commissioner, Urban Renewal Administration, Housing and Home Finance Agency, before the Subcommittee on Housing, Committee on Banking and Currency, United States House of Representatives, November 21, 1963* (Washington, D.C.: U.S. Government Printing Office, 1964), 402.

2. For an overview of the literature on urban renewal, see Samuel Zipp, "The Roots and Routes of Urban Renewal," *Journal of Urban History* 39, no. 3 (2013): 366–391.

3. This trend accords with the historical study of cities more broadly, in which larger cities dominate the scholarly agenda. For a survey suggesting these trends, see Richard Harris, "A Portrait of North American Urban Historians," *Journal of Urban History* 45, no. 6 (2019): 1237–1245.

4. Digital Scholarship Lab, *Renewing Inequality*, in *American Panorama*, ed. Robert K. Nelson and Edward L. Ayers, accessed January 4, 2023, https://dsl.richmond.edu/panorama/renewal/#view=0/0/1&viz=cartogram&text=sources.

5. On this "ethic of city rebuilding," see Zipp, "The Roots and Routes of Urban Renewal," and Samuel Zipp, *Manhattan Projects: The Rise and Fall of Urban Renewal in Cold War New York* (New York: Oxford University Press, 2012).

6. On the relationship between credit rating agencies and neoliberalism, see Roger Biles, "Public Policy Made by Private Enterprise: Bond Rating Agencies and Urban America," *Journal of Urban History* 44, no. 6 (2018): 1098–1112; Jason Hackworth, *The Neoliberal City: Governance, Ideology, and Development in American Urbanism* (Ithaca, NY: Cornell University Press, 2007), 15–39. For historical accounts of the proliferation of municipal debt in the twentieth century, see Alberta Sbragia, *Debt Wish: Entrepreneurial Cities, U.S. Federalism, and Economic Development* (Pittsburgh, PA: University of Pittsburgh Press, 1996); Destin Jenkins, *The Bonds of Inequality: Debt and the Making of the American City* (Chicago: University of Chicago Press, 2021); Colin McGrath, "A City Built on Debt: Federal Retrenchment, Municipal Finance, and Inequality in Dallas since the 1960s" (PhD diss., University of Pennsylvania, 2019); Michael Glass and Sean Vanatta, "The Frail Bonds of Liberalism: Pensions, Schools, and the Unraveling of Fiscal Mutualism in Postwar New York," *Capitalism: A Journal of History and Economics* 2, no. 2 (2021): 427–472.

7. Department of Housing and Urban Development, *Second Annual Report* (Washington, D.C.: U.S. Government Printing Office, 1966), 37. In addition to the data-oriented sources noted prior, HUD also published a series of pamphlets, *Urban Renewal Notes*, that offered qualitative dispatches from a wide range of projects across the country. Clearly intended as promotional materials, these sources accentuate boosterish accounts of urban renewal. Many of these resources are available digitally through HathiTrust.

8. On the 1961 Housing Act and the FHA's mortgage insurance for condos, see Alexander von Hoffman, "The Quest for a New Frontier in Housing," (JCHS Working Paper

W1-05, Joint Center for Housing Studies, Harvard University, Boston: 2010), available at https://www.jchs.harvard.edu/sites/jchs.harvard.edu/files/w10-5_von_hoffman.pdf.

9. Guian A. McKee, "The Hospital City in an Ethnic Enclave: Tufts-New England Medical Center, Boston's Chinatown, and the Urban Political Economy of Health Care," *Journal of Urban History* 42, no. 2 (2016): 259–283, figures at 263.

10. On gentrification and urban renewal in the 1960s, see Suleiman Osman, *The Invention of Brownstone Brooklyn: Gentrification and the Search for Authenticity in Postwar New York* (New York: Oxford University Press, 2011). For a contemporary appreciation of urban renewal and the powers of code enforcement in reshaping urban neighborhoods, see Judah Gribetz and Frank P. Grad, "Housing Code Enforcement: Sanctions and Remedies," *Columbia Law Review* 66, no. 7 (November 1966): 1254–1290.

11. The *Urban Renewal Project Characteristics* reports and a collection of *Urban Renewal Directory* reports whose data formed the basis of *Renewing Inequality* are available online at https://dsl.richmond.edu/panorama/renewal/#view=0/0/1&viz=cartogram&text=sources. Accessed January 4, 2023.

12. Advisory Commission on Intergovernmental Relations, "Relocation: Unequal Treatment of People and Businesses Displaced by Governments" (United States Advisory Commission on Intergovernmental Relations, January 1965), 11.

13. Marc Fried, *The World of the Urban Working Class* (Boston: Harvard University Press, 1973), 53; Kenneth E. Gray, *A Report on Politics in Denver, Colorado* (Cambridge, MA: Joint Center for Urban Studies of the Massachusetts Institute of Technology and Harvard University, 1959), VI-12.

14. Samuel Zipp, "The Battle of Lincoln Square: Neighborhood Culture and the Rise of Resistance to Urban Renewal," *Planning Perspectives* 24, no. 4 (2009): 409–433, discussion of Puerto Rican and other minority residents at 417–419.

15. Grady Abrams, "Mixed Emotions about Urban Renewal," in *The Evolution of a Negro into an Integrated Society: Opinion Editorials, Columns, Letters to the Editor, Business and Personal Letters, Poems* (n.p.: Xlibris, 2011), 283–285. On the long-term traumatic psychological impact of urban renewal, see Mindy Thomson Fullilove, *Root Shock: How Tearing Up City Neighborhoods Hurts America, and What We Can Do About It* (New York: Ballantine Books, 2004).

16. Nicholas Dagen Bloom, *How States Shaped Postwar America* (Chicago: University of Chicago Press, 2019), 42.

17. "Erieview," Encyclopedia of Cleveland History, accessed July 20, 2020, available at https://case.edu/ech/articles/e/erieview.

18. On renewal in suburban communities, see Colin Gordon, *Citizen Brown: Race, Democracy, and Inequality in the St. Louis Suburbs* (Chicago: University of Chicago Press, 2019).

19. Gene Kovarik, "Urban Renewal Stirs Words," *Alabama Journal*, December 2, 1964, 11. Such rhetoric was not entirely new but was amplified by white southerners increasingly wary of the federal government's civil rights enforcement. For instance, in 1952 the Richmond *News Leader* condemned a proposed urban renewal project as "The Shadow of Marx on Gamble's Hill." Christopher Silver, *Twentieth-Century Richmond: Planning, Politics, and Race* (Knoxville: University of Tennessee Press, 1984), 216.

20. Tom Mackin, "Urban Renewal Study Board Sought by Citizens Forum," *Montgomery Advertiser*, April 13, 1965, 2.

21. "A Free Country?" *Selma Times-Journal*, January 27, 1963, 4.

22. Frank Pace, "Citizens Halt Code Change for Housing," *Montgomery Advertiser*, April 23, 1963, 2.

23. Rustin quoted in Jacquelyn Dowd Hall, "The Long Civil Rights Movement and the Political Uses of the Past," *Journal of American History* 91, no. 4 (March 2005): 1233–1263, quote at 1234.

24. These and all other city population data are taken from the various "Summary of Population Characteristics, For the State, By Size of Place, and For Standard Metropolitan Statistical Areas, Urban Places, and Counties" tables in the respective United States Census Bureau reports (*Census of Population: 1950*, vol. 2, *Characteristics of the Population*, 1953, available at https://www.census.gov/library/publications/1953/dec/population-vol-02.html, and *1960 Census of Population, General Population Characteristics, March 31, 1961*, available at https://www.census.gov/library/publications/1961/dec/population-pc-a2.html).

25. On the place of subnational governments and localism in New Deal and midcentury liberal programs, see Brent Cebul and Mason B. Williams, "'Really and Truly a Partnership': The New Deal's Associational State and the Making of Postwar American Politics," in *Shaped by the State: Toward a New Political History of the Twentieth Century*, ed. Brent Cebul, Lily Geismer, and Mason B. Williams, 96–122 (Chicago: University of Chicago Press, 2019); Brent Cebul, Karen Tani, and Mason B. Williams, "Clio and the Compound Republic," *Publius: The Journal of Federalism* 47, no. 2 (Spring 2017): 235–259.

26. Housing and Home Finance Agency, Urban Renewal Administration, *Urban Renewal Project Characteristics, June 30, 1962* (Washington, D.C.: U.S. Department of Housing and Urban Development, 1962), 2–3.

27. Douglas Appler, "Changing the Scale of Analysis for Urban Renewal Research: Small Cities, the State of Kentucky, and the 1974 Urban Renewal Directory," *Journal of Planning History* 16, no. 3 (August 2017): 200–221; Brent Cebul, "'They Were the Moving Spirits': Supply Side Liberalism in the Postwar South," in *Capital Gains: Business and Politics in Twentieth Century America*, ed. Richard John and Kim Phillips-Fein, 139–156 (Philadelphia: University of Pennsylvania Press, 2016).

28. On the ARA, see Gregory Wilson, *Communities Left Behind: The Area Redevelopment Administration, 1945–1965* (Knoxville: University of Tennessee Press, 2009).

29. See, for example, Richard Harwood, "Regional Planning Revamped by Johnson," *Washington Post*, December 30, 1967, A3.

30. United States Census Bureau, *1960 Census of Population, General Population Characteristics*; Digital Scholarship Lab, *Renewing Inequality*.

31. The initial framing of urban redevelopment as a housing initiative associated with civil rights garnered a great deal of support from black community leaders, clergy, and civil rights activists. See, for instance, Nathan D. B. Connolly, *A World More Concrete: Real Estate and the Remaking of Jim Crow South Florida* (Chicago: University of Chicago Press, 2014).

32. "Negroes Lose Housing Suit in Gadsden," *Birmingham News*, August 19, 1958, 1.

33. A Concerned Citizen, "Revenue Sharing the Problem Solver," *El Dorado Times*, December 20, 1972, 4.

34. Silver, *Twentieth-Century Richmond*, 210–222.

35. On urban renewal in Rome, see Michelle Brattain, *The Politics of Whiteness: Race, Workers, and Culture in the Modern South* (Athens: University of Georgia Press, 2001), 275–276; Digital Scholarship Lab, *Renewing Inequality*.

36. On the concept of "frontlash" and mass incarceration, see Vesla Weaver, "Frontlash: Race and the Development of Punitive Crime Policy," *Studies in American Political Development* 21, no. 2 (2007): 230–265.

37. Digital Scholarship Lab, *Renewing Inequality*.

38. On the early literature on and significance of the twentieth-century carceral state, see Heather Ann Thompson, "Why Mass Incarceration Matters: Rethinking, Crisis, Decline, and Transformation in Postwar American History," *Journal of American History* 97, no. 3 (December 2010): 703–734.

39. Martin L. King Jr. to Juanita Jelks, 8 August 1959, in *The Papers of Martin Luther King, Jr., Volume V: Threshold of a New Decade, January 1959 December 1960,* ed. Clayborne Carson et al. (Berkeley: University of California Press, 2005), 261, available at https://kinginstitute.stanford.edu/king-papers/documents/juanita-jelks#ftnref1.

40. Appler, "Changing the Scale of Analysis"; Cebul, "'They Were the Moving Spirits'"; Carl Feiss, "The Foundations of Federal Planning Assistance: A Personal Account of the 701 Program," *Journal of the American Planning Association* 51, no. 2 (1985): 175–184.

41. "Hit Faster Pace in City's Urban Renewal Program," *Atchison Daily Globe,* June 30, 1960, 1; Digital Scholarship Lab, *Renewing Inequality.*

42. On hospitals, urban renewal, and local contributions, see McKee, "The Hospital City in an Ethnic Enclave," 262. For a comprehensive examination of universities and urban renewal, see LaDale C. Winling, *Building the Ivory Tower: Universities and Metropolitan Development in the Twentieth Century* (Philadelphia: University of Pennsylvania Press, 2018).

43. Housing and Home Finance Agency, Urban Renewal Administration, *Urban Renewal Project Characteristics, December 31, 1963,* 12–18.

44. Housing and Home Finance Agency, Urban Renewal Administration, *Urban Renewal Project Characteristics, June 30, 1964,* 30.

45. "Renewal Bond Wins," *Manhattan Mercury,* April 20, 1960, 1.

46. Urban Renewal Administration, *Report on Urban Renewal: Statement of William L. Slayton, Commissioner,* 398. It was cheaper for local governments to issue the financing because their notes were exempt from federal taxation. Had the federal government offered financing in the form of federal bonds, interest rates would have been higher to compensate for the fact that buyers would owe taxes on interest-based income. The leading New Deal and midcentury liberal economist Alvin Hansen, who played a role in conceptualizing urban renewal, explained the role federal debt played in "strengthen[ing] the financial position and liquidity of business units. . . . This vast reserve of liquid assets, constitutes a powerful line of defense against any serious recession." As a result, "our society has become a mixed public-private economy in which the powerful fiscal and monetary operations of an alert and informed government are playing a stabilizing and sustaining role." Alvin H. Hansen, *The American Economy* (New York: McGraw Hill, 1957), 33–34.

47. McGrath, "A City Built on Debt," chaps. 2–3.

48. The debt associated with school construction was especially pronounced in new suburbs, where the federal government had often offered subsidies for mortgages and highways, as well as support in some cases for sewage and other infrastructure. But public school construction, an essential aspect of suburban expansion, often operated as a sort of unfunded mandate for new suburban municipalities, and suburbs overwhelmingly financed these projects through municipal bond offerings. See Glass and Vanatta, "The Frail Bonds of Liberalism."

49. Alan K. Campbell and Seymour Sacks, *Metropolitan America: Fiscal Patterns and Governmental Systems* (New York: Free Press, 1967), 6. On the federal government's role in encouraging this expansion in variety of legal, constitutional, and programmatic domains, see Martha Derthick, *Keeping the Compound Republic: Essays on American Federalism* (Washington, D.C.: Brookings Institution Press, 2001), esp. chap. 10.

50. George H. Hempel, *Measures of Municipal Bond Quality* (Ann Arbor: University of Michigan, 1967), 7.

51. "Council OKs Urban Renewal Notes," *Post-Standard*, September 1, 1960, 6.

52. "Voters Split on Urban Renewal; More Say Yes Than No," *Cedar Rapids (IA) Gazette*, January 6, 1963, 6. Albany, New York, which constructed a massive and principally state- and locally subsidized renewal project, planned to float some $480 million in general obligation bonds in a series of smaller increments to complete its South Mall renewal project, composed principally of new downtown office buildings. "Dramatic Price Improvement Is Best in Exactly a Year," *Bond Buyer*, January 15, 1968, 53.

53. "City of High Point, North Carolina," advertisement, *Bond Buyer*, February 3, 1968.

54. "Items in New Bond Issue," *Montgomery Advertiser*, June 5, 1957, 7. See also "Montgomery's New Bond Issue," *Alabama Journal*, May 12, 1956, 4A.

55. These "credits" for local expenditures that exceeded the local matching requirements were also applied to hospital or university expenditures. As Guian McKee argues, these credits incentivized cities to invest in these sorts institutional renewal projects because they at once reduced municipal costs and created new subsidies for the broader renewal program. See McKee, "The Hospital City in an Ethnic Enclave," 262.

56. Housing and Home Finance Agency, Urban Renewal Administration, *Urban Renewal Project Characteristics, December 31, 1965*, 48.

57. "Voters Split on Urban Renewal," *Cedar Rapids (IA) Gazette*.

58. Aaron Cowan, "A Whole New Ballgame: Sports Stadiums and Urban Renewal in Cincinnati, Pittsburgh, and St. Louis, 1950–1970," *Ohio Valley History* 5, no. 3 (2005): 69.

59. Sheila Wolfe, "2 Riverfront Stadiums Boost Renewal," *Chicago Tribune*, March 23, 1971, 4.

60. Jerry Shnay, "Cincinnati Lawyer Talks Stadium Sense," *Chicago Tribune*, November 17, 1970, C1.

61. Jerry Shnay, "Many New Stadiums Facing Financial Problems," *Chicago Tribune*, January 22, 1978, B2.

62. On the politics and political economy of consumer debt, see especially Lizabeth Cohen, *Consumer's Republic: The Politics of Mass Consumption in Postwar America* (New York: Vintage Books, 2003); Louis Hyman, *Debtor Nation: The History of America in Red Ink* (Princeton, NJ: Princeton University Press, 2012).

63. "The State of the Municipal Securities Market," Securities and Exchange Commission, accessed August 13, 2019, available at https://www.sec.gov/spotlight/municipalsecurities.shtml.

64. William K. Tabb, *The Long Default: New York City and the Urban Fiscal Crisis* (New York: Monthly Review Press, 1982).

65. "$50 Bil. Notes in Urban Renewal Notes in 1954–79," *Bond Buyer*, February 9, 1981, 14. This figure raises a number of questions about potential changes in or multiple versions of urban renewal notes. As the *Bond Buyer* put it, these notes, "issued to finance urban renewal projects," were "secured by the full faith and credit of the U.S. Government." Earlier, the federal renewal administration retired urban renewal notes within six or twelve months. That hundreds of millions of dollars' worth of these obligations, ostensibly backed by the federal government, were still unretired as of 1980 suggests there may have been other categories of notes or that the federal governments mechanisms' for their retirement changed, perhaps becoming longer term or shifting from federal retirement to insuring the notes should local governments default on the debts. More research is needed.

66. Tabb, *The Long Default*, 11.

67. On discrimination in credit rating agencies, see Yaw A. Badu, Kwadwo Bawuah, and Kenneth Daniels, "Race and Municipal Bond Ratings in the Commonwealth of Virginia," *Review of Black Political Economy* 24, no. 4 (1996): 111–121. Recent studies have also suggested that credit rating agencies systematically underrated public debt versus private alternatives, against the actual historical evidence of relative default rates. See Marc Joffe, *Doubly Bound: The Cost of Credit Ratings* (Berkeley, VA: Haas Institute, 2011), available at http://haasinstitute.berkeley.edu/sites/default/files/haasinstitute_doublybound _creditratings_april11_publish.pdf. See also Jenkins, *The Bonds of Inequality*; Gordon, *Citizen Brown*.

# 2

# Toward a Social History of Urban Renewal

David Hochfelder

At the end of 1968, the National Commission on Urban Problems published its report on the state of urban America. Congress and President Lyndon Johnson had charged the commission to investigate the current condition of America's cities and recommend solutions. Their work began at the start of 1967 and grew more urgent as poverty and racial discrimination fueled protests and uprisings in cities across the country. In its introduction, the report noted that the sixteen commission members—drawn from elected officials, scholars, and planners—had traveled to two dozen cities to hold hearings, walk the streets, and meet with a broad range of residents. In their words, "We could have stayed in Washington and gathered statistics, but statistics do not tell enough about a slum." They described their visits to these cities as "vivid and moving."[1]

The members of the commission realized that the best way to understand the American city was to pay attention to local conditions and concerns while connecting these to national policy decisions and consequences. Today, historians of urban renewal have the same opportunity—to use state, local, and community resources to gain a better understanding of one of the most controversial federal policies in the nation's history. This research strategy facilitates comparison across size scales and leads us to understand how local concerns shaped, and were in turn shaped by, federal policy. Just as important, this strategy requires historians to incorporate the perspectives not just of politicians and planners but of residents and business owners, architects and construction workers—the people whose lives were most directly affected by redevelopment.[2]

It is, of course, impossible to research the history of the 1,250 towns and cities that received federal funds for urban renewal projects. One must choose locations strategically. To that end, this chapter provides guidance for researchers who want to understand the social history of urban renewal at state, local, and community scales.[3] This chapter relies heavily on the author's research in New York State. Not only did New York receive more federal spending than any other state (about one-eighth of total federal spending), but it also ranked second in the number of municipalities affected. New York was also one of only four states that helped localities pay their share of urban renewal costs. There were 251 federally funded urban renewal projects in ninety-one New York municipalities, ranging in size from villages of a few thousand residents to New York City.[4]

## Using State Records to Create a Composite Picture of Urban Renewal

In the United States, local governments and government agencies are creatures of the state. The state government delegates authority to local governments, even for mundane functions like sewer and water districts and fire departments. Thus, local governments and agencies are subject to state oversight, especially annual reporting requirements. In New York, these annual reports are filed with the state comptroller's office. In 1963, the state government passed legislation enabling local governments to set up independent urban renewal agencies. Thereafter, any local jurisdiction that wanted to apply for federal urban renewal grants and loans had to set up such an agency.

The annual reports of urban renewal agencies usually took the form of a standard four-page document: a balance sheet, an income statement, a statement of indebtedness, and a blank page labeled "Operations and Accomplishments." While many urban renewal agencies left this last page blank, others filled it in with basic information—public meetings held, buildings demolished, parcels sold to developers, and so forth. Sometimes an urban renewal agency appended a typed annual report similar to what it filed with its municipal government. In a few cases, agencies included a glossy public relations booklet. These annual reports can help build a statewide picture of urban renewal that remains sensitive to local needs and conditions.

Right away, for instance, these annual reports helped explain a puzzle. Per capita federal urban renewal spending across all New York State jurisdictions was about $100.[5] However, some outliers jumped out. Painted Post received a federal urban renewal grant of $4.4 million. For this village of 2,500 residents, this amounted to $1,760 per capita. The neighboring city of Corning topped this—it received $1,800 per capita. Elmira, about twenty-five miles to the east, received $1,300 per capita. The projects themselves had unusual names not typically given to urban renewal projects. Most project names are mundane, like "Downtown Project #2," and not names like "Comeback '72," "Agnes," and "New Elmira." Adding to the puzzle was the fact that this federal largesse came in late 1972 and 1973, as the federal urban renewal program was winding down.[6]

Their annual reports explained why these places received such large amounts of late funding for their unusually named projects. The 1972 Elmira Urban Renewal Agency report revealed that on June 23, the remnants of Hurricane Agnes hit the region hard.[7] The resultant flooding displaced over half of the city's population and damaged over 6,400 buildings. Corning sustained major damage covering nearly a square mile of the city, and Painted Post's small business district was totally destroyed. The flood killed twenty-three people in the region and caused nearly $500 million in property damage.[8]

Shortly after the flooding, the New York State Urban Development Corporation stepped in and acted as a disaster relief agency. It built emergency temporary housing for tens of thousands of displaced families. In the longer term, UDC coordinated the efforts of six communities to rebuild after the flood and filed applications for federal urban renewal money on their behalf. This was an unusual—if not unique—use of urban renewal funds made possible due to UDC's broad powers and an energetic director willing to use them.[9]

Other narrative accounts in these annual reports reveal the range of urban renewal projects across the state. Cities like Buffalo, Syracuse, and Poughkeepsie undertook massive clearance projects to build public housing and downtown civic centers, the types of projects typically associated with urban renewal. Rochester also undertook a large downtown renewal project featuring an indoor mall (since abandoned and demolished), but the city was unusual in that it built low- and moderate-income housing in collaboration with African American and Hispanic community organizations.[10]

The annual reports indicate that other places had more modest goals for their urban renewal projects. Many chose to avoid demolition and clearance projects entirely and used federal and state money to finance code enforcement, planning, and rehabilitation efforts. Hudson, for example, set up a historic district and rehabilitated buildings within it. Guilderland, a truck farming and bedroom suburb of Albany, converted an old army depot into an industrial park employing about six hundred workers. Rome's centerpiece was the reconstruction of Fort Stanwix, a National Park Service historic site. Hornell and Norwich cleared small sites for the construction of motels. Potsdam's major accomplishment was the construction of a new sewage treatment plant.

These annual reports also offer windows into the life cycle of urban renewal projects of all types. To begin with, they reveal the hopes and expectations expressed by local officials and show how eager they were to bring federal and state dollars to their towns. Batavia's 1965 report told state officials that in 1966, "Batavia's Main Street will start to take on THE LOOK OF THE FUTURE, through the cooperation of Batavia's businessmen and City Government."[11] That same year, Ellenville boasted that it could "finance its share of the U.R. program at no out-of-pocket costs" through construction of sanitary and storm sewers and a new bridge. Urban renewal was a "great opportunity for Ellenville. No other program, private or public, can match the scope of Urban Renewal" to "truly re-vitalize Ellenville's Central Business District."[12] Similarly, Binghamton's slick 1968 brochure reassured readers that construction of the first new buildings in its downtown renewal area "tell us we have passed the time of skepticism and moved into a welcome era of public acceptance that urban renewal offers the best hope for the rebirth of the city."[13] In 1973, the report from Ilion included a clipping from the local newspaper that told readers, "A project of such magnitude can only be successful if you have cooperation from the citizens. . . . The residents are strongly behind this Project."[14]

Other urban renewal agencies reported that their projects had met resistance from local residents. In Elmira (before the Agnes flooding), the Hall and Rawlings families refused to move from their homes to make way for a new Holiday Inn and car dealership. In February 1972, the county sheriff attempted to evict them but was "met with physical resistance." A local judge stayed the eviction for about a month, but ultimately the families were forced out.[15]

More sustained resistance occurred in North Hempstead. Town officials initially planned to build about one hundred units of low- and moderate-income housing in the Spinney Hill neighborhood. At first glance, this might seem like the typical story of white suburbanites opposing the entry of poor people of color, as had occurred with the blocked UDC's Nine Towns project in Westchester County.[16] But Spinney Hill was already largely African American, and its community was divided over the project. Some residents thought it was sorely needed to alleviate a shortage of affordable housing. Others opposed the plan because they did not want to change the middle-class nature of the area. Virginia Hampton exclaimed to a *New York Times* reporter, "Can't we just enjoy our home without young people on welfare coming in? I'm tired of welfare. Let them go somewhere else." Some residents opposed the project for fear it would further concentrate and segregate black people. Joseph Vaultz caustically asked, "Why don't you get Mr. Charley [the white establishment] to put some housing over in Kings Point or Sands Point? Man, you should fight to spread this housing all over. Don't dump it all here on us."[17] In 1973, the area's neighborhood association filed suit in federal court to halt the project. They lost on appeal in 1975, and the project went forward, albeit in heavily modified form. When the project was finally completed in the early 1980s, the planned multifamily housing had been replaced with twenty-five townhouses and fifty units of senior citizen housing. A "buffer strip" separated this development and the rest of Spinney Hill.[18]

Many annual reports detail the difficulty urban renewal agencies had in disposing of cleared parcels, particularly during the recession years of the early 1970s. Plattsburgh, for example, failed to find developers despite an aggressive advertising campaign. The response to that campaign was "disappointing," and the city ended it because of "the uncertainty of changing politics."[19] When the city did finally manage to interest a developer for the largest parcel, located on Lake Champlain, the developer discovered that the federal government had recently designated it as a flood plain. Because of higher insurance costs, the developer backed out. By 1980, when the city closed out its urban renewal projects, it had yet to complete property disposition in that area.[20] Peekskill launched a similar promotional campaign to no avail. City officials blamed the poor economy and the 1973–1974 oil crisis for its failure to attract a developer.[21] Port Jervis successfully sold eight parcels to developers but had trouble with the remaining eleven. John F. Hawkins, the director of its urban renewal agency, reported that "the redevelopment and revitalization of the Central Business District . . . requires an open mind and a willingness to carefully review any reasonable proposal." He called for a reconfiguration of the plan to permit senior citizen housing in the downtown area.[22] Similarly, the city of Dunkirk sought developers to build a three-hundred-thousand-square-foot indoor shopping mall on cleared land. After several developers pulled out of that project, the city scaled back its plans and contented itself with a shopping plaza anchored by a grocery store and a drugstore.[23]

Even when urban renewal projects were successfully completed, they often failed to provide the long-term revitalization promised by city officials. Many of these failures involved indoor shopping malls intended to draw shoppers from a regional catchment. Niagara Falls built Rainbow Centre, a complex that included an indoor shopping mall, hotel, and convention center. Designed to attract shoppers and vacationers from Canada, it was successful for a few years after its 1982 opening. But by 2000, the only business remaining was an off-track betting parlor.[24] Similarly, in Amsterdam, a new eighty-thousand-square-foot downtown mall opened with great fanfare in 1977. In 1980, the project added another forty retail stores and 1,200 parking spots at an additional cost of $14 million. When the project closed out in 1981, the

Amsterdam Urban Renewal Agency regarded the mall as a huge success for the city. Yet, twenty years later, retail activity had stopped. Part of the mall has been repurposed for office space.[25]

Finally, these annual reports show how some communities responded to changing federal and state priorities. By the early 1970s, public and legislative support for urban renewal had eroded. In January 1973, the Nixon administration declared a moratorium on urban renewal assistance and announced that the program would end in 1974. Afterward, urban renewal funds would be replaced with Community Development Block Grants. At the same time, the state's UDC had lost the public's confidence because of worsening state finances and suburban backlash against the introduction of public housing. Taken together, cities and towns across the state shifted their priorities from neighborhood rehabilitation to economic development. After the mid-1970s, for example, Syracuse focused its efforts on building a new football stadium for Syracuse University and a nearby luxury hotel.[26] By 1982, Jamestown had transformed its urban renewal agency into a local development corporation that offered loans to local businesses, along with some residential rehabilitation assistance.[27]

## Using Local Records to Understand Urban Renewal's Causes and Consequences

While annual reports provide insights into the range, scale, and varied outcomes of urban renewal projects across the state, locally held records permit a fine-grained analysis of the origins and effects of urban renewal on specific places. They open up several lines of inquiry. The files of local urban renewal agencies are central to understanding why urban renewal succeeded or failed in a particular place. The papers of elected officials help us understand how local needs and concerns shaped this national policy. In order to make the case for wholesale clearance, local officials typically showed the public selected photographs that depicted buildings or streetscapes in states of disrepair. However, other images, taken for appraisal purposes or by amateurs documenting urban renewal areas before clearance, often contradicted the official position that an area was "blighted" or a "slum." These photographs also revealed the built environment and material conditions experienced by area residents.

Regarding success or failure, consider the small city of Newburgh, New York. Its urban renewal program was a case study in failure, although its promotional brochures touted it as a great success. As Newburgh wrapped up its urban renewal efforts, the city's leadership looked back with satisfaction on their work. The Newburgh Urban Renewal Agency's (NURA) 1972 annual report profiled several residents whose lives had been improved by these projects. An elderly white widow who moved into senior citizen housing said, "Urban Renewal took my house, and they moved me up here. It's very nice here. I'm very happy." A white couple with two young children remarked that "urban renewal took our place; knocked it down. They just moved us out of that one and into this one. . . . The kids like the playground. . . . The kids are safe out here." A young black couple "had a rough time finding a decent apartment. . . . Often we would go look and they would say 'rented already.' . . . To be able to move into this apartment is like a whole new life for us. We love the apartment. It's just nice, really nice living here." The chairman of the agency concluded the report by asking readers to imagine "the great residential, industrial, educational complex that will arise on the banks of the beautiful Hudson River. . . . We are at the threshold of a great future."[28]

That future never arrived. Today, most Newburghers regard urban renewal as a failure. From initial planning in 1956 to finished execution in 1977, urban renewal took over twenty years. Altogether, about 120 acres of downtown land were cleared. As early as 1959, federal urban renewal administrator Charles H. Horan expressed "serious questions as to the marketability and disposition" of this area after clearance.[29] Planning consultant David M. Rosen warned in 1966 that 40 percent of the cleared land could not be redeveloped because of the steep grade.[30] Much of it remains vacant today.

Urban renewal failed in Newburgh for two reasons. Like many other cities along the Hudson and Mohawk Rivers, Newburgh experienced the same kind of urban crisis endured by larger northeastern and midwestern cities. Newburgh was fighting long-term and insurmountable demographic and economic trends. At the same time that major employers like DuPont and Stewart Air Force Base closed, the city lost its role as a regional transportation hub because of the closure of a cross-river ferry and the opening of the New York State Thruway several miles west of downtown. These trends were outside the control of city officials and planners. But a more telling reason for urban renewal's failure was political and racial conflict. This marred the project from the very beginning.[31] In 1962, Newburgh made national headlines because of a bitter conflict over welfare policy. City manager Joseph McDowell Mitchell (who would work for the John Birch Society and the White Citizens' Council after leaving Newburgh in disgrace) blamed the city's generous welfare benefits for "attract[ing] the poor rather than repelling them." The resulting controversy was the subject of a television documentary, the *Battle of Newburgh*, that painted the city in an unfavorable light.[32] In 1970, Newburgh's urban renewal plans received more bad publicity because they called for the demolition of a historic church while leaving a nearby brothel untouched. (See Figure 2.1.) NURA executive director Jack Present complained about the "screaming headlines of 'Raze the Church and Save the Brothel.'"[33] These

HOUSING CONDITION AND OCCUPANCY

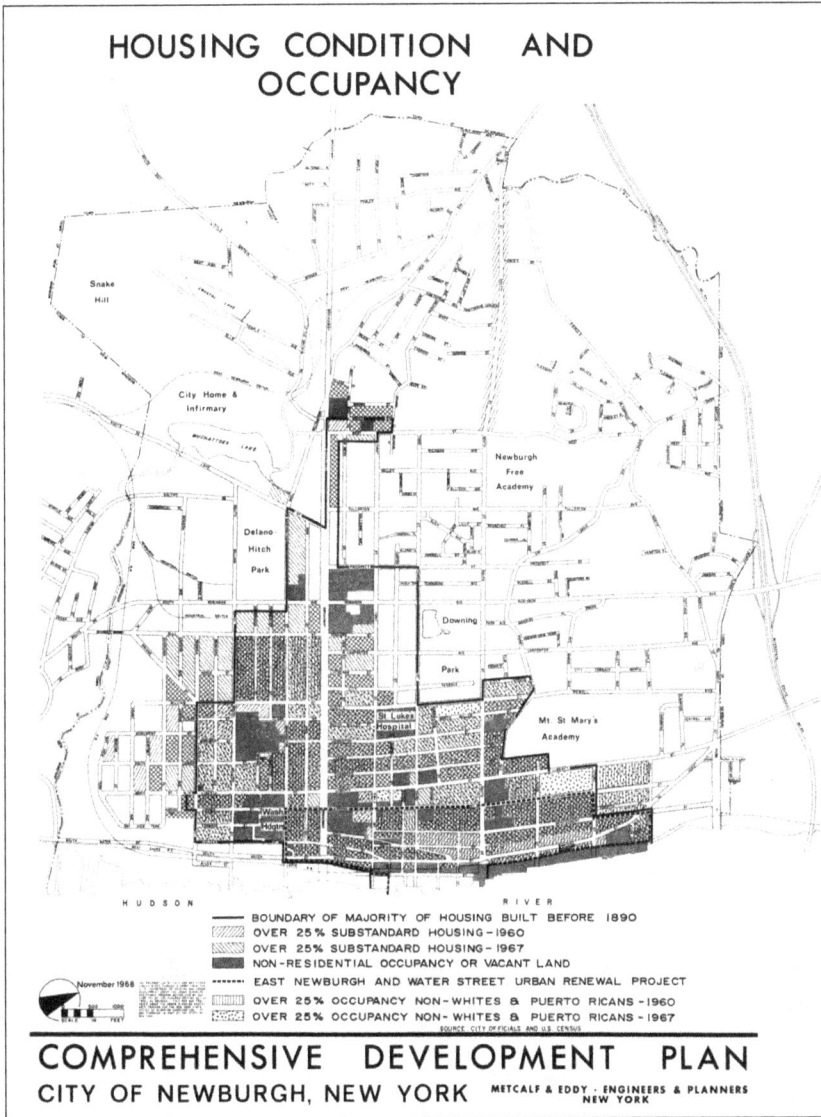

Figure 2.1 One of several maps of Newburgh, New York, included in Metcalf and Eddy's comprehensive development plan for that city, January 30, 1969. (Source: New York State Library.)

controversies, alongside the slow pace of rehousing displaced residents, convinced most observers that urban renewal had failed in Newburgh.[34]

Officials in nearby Kingston certainly reached that conclusion. In their desire to avoid the delays and conflicts they saw in Newburgh, urban renewal officials in Kingston moved quickly to demolish buildings and move out residents—even before adequate relocation housing was available. (See Figure 2.2.) When city officials began planning for a downtown riverfront renewal project in the mid-1950s, the public's response was generally enthusiastic.

But many city residents soured on urban renewal after the city began executing its plan. To do so, Kingston hired Eric Hemphill away from the Philadelphia Redevelopment Authority to direct its urban renewal agency (KURA). Although he was a well-trained and experienced urban planner, he quickly ran afoul of the local politics and culture. To many Kingstonians, he behaved as an out-of-touch technocrat who lost sight of the human dimension of renewal, especially with respect to inadequate housing for displaced families. The demolition contractor he hired left streets and sidewalks in dirty and dangerous condition. And he insisted on KURA's independence and refused to provide financial data—staff salaries and lawyers' fees for closings—to the Common Council.[35]

In 1967, residents began lodging complaints with Congressman Joseph Y. Resnick. In May, Resnick alerted HUD to these major problems. HUD responded by suspending Kingston's urban renewal funds. Resnick warned that unless KURA corrected its relocation procedures, "Urban Renewal in Kingston is dead for a long time to come."[36] At the end of June, Resnick held a one-day hearing in Kingston. After touring the renewal area and hearing complaints from local residents, he concluded that "while the basic plan to renew downtown Kingston was sound, its execution was extremely bad"—particularly its ineffective relocation assistance. Resnick characterized downtown Kingston as "virtually destroyed as a community."[37] By late July, Resnick called for the wholesale dismissal of Hemphill and the entire KURA board.[38] By the end of August, their resignations were inevitable, as HUD had made it a requirement for restoring Kingston's funding. Hemphill admitted that urban renewal was "not a painless process" but blasted his critics for lacking a basic understanding of "how the program operates." Hemphill and KURA also defended their aggressive schedule of property acquisition and demolition by pointing to the slow pace of renewal in Newburgh.[39]

In 1973, HUD hired the Real Estate Research Corporation to study urban renewal failures. It chose Kingston as one of six sites, by far the smallest. This study identified many reasons for Kingston's botched relocation efforts, including three major "National Program Related Factors." One important factor was inadequate federal oversight of Kingston's relocation procedures up to 1967. The report acknowledged that its policy recommendations came too late for meaningful reform, since the federal urban renewal program was winding down. However, the experiences of Newburgh and Kingston indicate that local failures contributed to the erosion of support for urban renewal nationally after the mid-1960s and were a major reason for the program's end in 1974.[40]

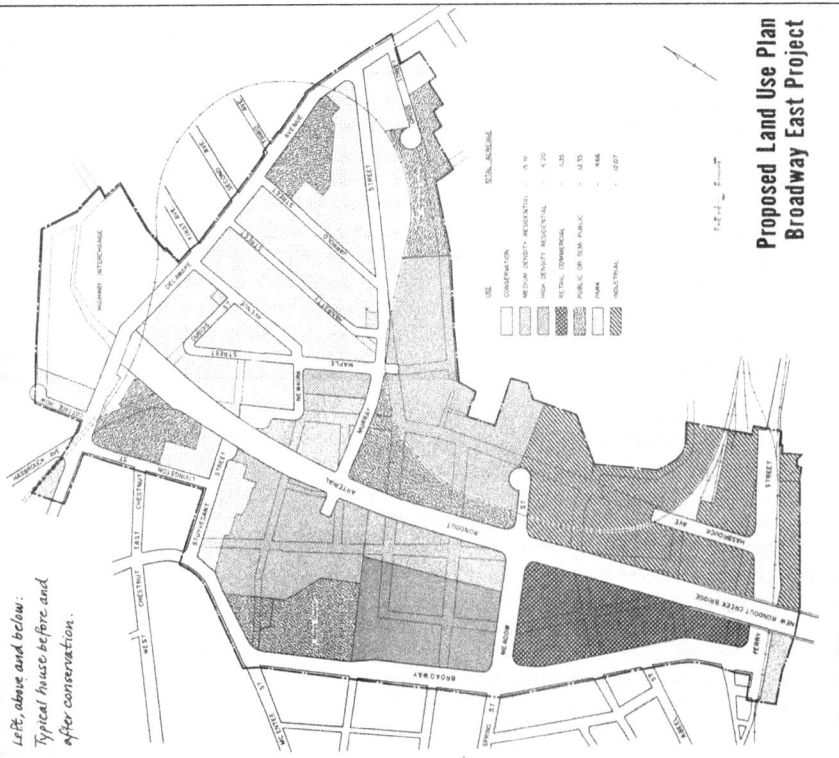

Left, above and below: Typical house before and after conservation.

## BROADWAY EAST PROJECT

116 acres of run-down, outmoded buildings and incompatible uses will be transformed into an attractive, convenient neighborhood with a new shopping center, modern industries, homes for sale and rent; parks, playgrounds, and a new Rondout Bridge and arterial highway. Conservation, or improvement of existing homes, will be stressed in the 28-acre northeast part.

**Figure 2.2** Reverse side of brochure issued by the Kingston (New York) Urban Renewal Office, created by planning firm Raymond and May Associates, April 1963.

(Source: Joseph Y. Resnick Papers, M. E. Grenander Department of Special Collections and University Archives, University at Albany, State University of New York.)

The papers of local elected officials are excellent resources as well. After New York State announced in March 1962 that it was seizing forty blocks and 1,200 buildings in downtown Albany for a modernist capitol complex, Mayor Erastus Corning 2nd stated his strong opposition. Corning criticized the seizure as unjust to the residents of the city and decried it as a vanity project of liberal Republican governor—with presidential aspirations—Nelson A. Rockefeller. Corning served as mayor from 1942 to his death in 1983 (winning eleven consecutive terms) and was the figurehead for an insular and corrupt Democratic machine. Corning's papers reveal the conflict between these two powerful politicians over the future of New York's capital city, as well as the negotiations for its byzantine financing agreement. Under this agreement, the state sidestepped a vote in the legislature or a bond referendum to fund this massive project. Instead, Albany County issued bonds to finance construction and the state paid back the county as a payment in lieu of property taxes. During the negotiations for the financing agreement, Corning and the Democratic organization reversed their opposition and avidly supported the project.[41]

One issue at stake in the weeks after the state announced its plans in 1962 was whether area residents favored or opposed the project. Corning sent out Democratic Party operatives to collect statements from residents who opposed it. A Mrs. Martin of 10 Jefferson Street told a canvasser that she wanted to stay in her apartment because it was close to "all the facilities that poor people want," including churches, schools, and downtown shopping, all "within walking distance." Her landlord, Joseph Tropp, said that he had bought the building "to get away from landlords who would not do any repairs." And he noted that at the age of sixty-six, he felt "too old to start all over again." Albert Drake of 236 Madison Street also wanted to remain: "It is hard enough for a colored person to find a decent place to live and now that I have bought this place, the State wants to take it away. It is not fair."[42]

These statements confirm several general observations about the problems of relocating residents from urban renewal areas. First, a 1961 survey showed that inner-city Albanians were dissatisfied with their cramped quarters and potholed streets but valued living near friends, shopping, jobs, churches, and social organizations.[43] Second, the groups whose lives were disrupted the most by relocation were the elderly and African Americans. The elderly were often the hardest hit psychologically and found it difficult to start over in new quarters. Black people were confined to particular areas of the city due to informal but rigidly enforced housing discrimination, and they often paid more in rent for comparable—or worse—housing than white households. And families with children had trouble finding apartments.

A final set of sources are photographs documenting the life cycle of urban renewal projects. Photographs of urban renewal sites exist for several reasons.

Most urban renewal projects created photographs for appraisal purposes as part of the process of reimbursing owners for taking their properties. Researchers can usually find them in property appraisal files. Similarly, photographers for New York State took more detailed photographs of building exteriors and interiors when owners challenged the state's appraisal and sued in the state court of appeals. Many of these captured people in their homes and places of business. In many cases, amateur photographers documented buildings and streetscapes before and during demolition. Local historical societies or public libraries often house these photos. Finally, local newspapers may retain their photo libraries from this period and may be willing to make these available to researchers.[44]

Many of these images convey the human side of urban renewal and can evoke empathy and strong emotion in the viewer. They also document the material conditions in which urban working-class families lived. Figure 2.3 is a photograph of a soon-to-be-displaced couple in their Albany apartment. Although we will likely never be able to reconstruct this couple's experiences fully, this photo strongly suggests that their impending relocation was emotionally difficult.

Interior photographs such as this one are rare. Exterior photographs are far more common. Besides those taken for appraisal purposes or by amateurs wanting to document buildings before they were demolished, proponents of urban renewal projects often photographed streetscapes to make the case that these areas were "blighted" and required wholesale clearance. In the case of Stuyvesant Town, for example, the Metropolitan Life Insurance Company used photographs of dilapidated buildings, laundry hanging on clotheslines, and a homeless man sleeping in a doorway to make the case for redevelopment. Yet many of their photos make the opposite case and depict sound structures and vital communities.[45]

## Community Records and Social Histories of Urban Renewal

Research at the community scale is essential for capturing the texture of the urban fabric shown in these photographs. Such social history research also fosters public conversations about urban renewal's legacy. Attention to the community scale can open several lines of investigation difficult to access at larger scales. These lines of investigation, however, may pose significant research challenges.

Consider Vincent and Angeline Carputo (aged seventy and sixty-two), who were displaced twice for Kingston's urban renewal program. In the mid-1960s, they lost their three-story building and family store, along with grape-

**Figure 2.3** Robert and Ethel Mather in their apartment, February 28, 1963, before their building (one of about 1,200) was razed for the Empire State Plaza. The state sent photographers into the area to document it for appraisal purposes, often capturing residents and merchants in their homes and businesses. We are grateful to photographer Mike Wren for scanning this photo and several hundred others.
(Source: Office of General Services Empire State Plaza Construction Progress Photographs, New York State Archives, Albany, NY.)

vines and fruit trees, for a downtown clearance project. Angeline Carputo told a local reporter, "It was hell when we moved. We had to move in the winter, just before Christmas. Half our furniture in the old place was stolen." Ten years later, they were forced to move again to make way for a new arterial highway. This time, however, organized (but ultimately futile) citizen opposition arose to block the arterial. She continued, "I boil. Where were they 10 years ago when we really needed them?"[46] According to an editorial in the *Kingston Daily Freeman*, "the chief argument" for the arterial, which displaced about sixty families and today divides downtown Kingston from a residential neighborhood, was to obtain state highway funds to defray $1.5 million of Kingston's local urban renewal financial obligation. The same was true in Newburgh—a major reason for a new arterial being part of its urban renewal plans was to obtain state Department of Transportation funding to defray part of the city's local obligation.[47]

The Carputo family's experience invites several avenues of research. At the policy level, this arterial appears to owe its existence to a system of perverse incentives. Perhaps much of the damage wrought by urban renewal was unnecessary to accomplish its stated goals of slum clearance and neighborhood revitalization. At the very least, this incident shows that federal funding requirements shaped Kingston's and Newburgh's urban renewal plans and that this decision in turn eroded local support for urban renewal. Incidents like these, multiplied on a national scale, help explain why urban renewal fell out of favor by the late 1960s and early 1970s. Angeline Carputo's remarks about losing their first home are consistent with what we know about the psychological trauma of displacement, characterized by sociologist Marc Fried as "grief" for a lost home and neighborhood and by urban psychologist Mindy Fullilove as "root shock." Age and socioeconomic status matter as well. The elderly, especially the elderly poor, experienced this psychological loss much more acutely than younger or more affluent residents.[48]

The issue of the elderly poor stood out in the area demolished for Albany's Empire State Plaza. Over one thousand of the seven thousand people displaced for this complex were residents of the area's one hundred rooming houses. Most were converted single-family rowhouses. Women owned and managed nearly all of them and depended on them for their livelihoods. The quality of lodgings varied—from tiny rooms rented by the elderly poor to temporary quarters taken by state legislators and staffers during legislative sessions. These residents did not leave strong traces in the historical record. Property acquisition files named owner-occupiers and tenants with leases but merely labeled rooming house residents as roomers or boarders, irrespective of how long they had lived in their rooms. Capturing the experiences of displaced rooming house residents remains a major challenge for urban renewal researchers.[49]

Churches were some of the most prominent institutions that promoted community and neighborhood stability. But demographic shifts in the inner city posed financial and spiritual challenges for congregations in the years before urban renewal. Church records show how particular congregations responded to these challenges. Three of the four churches displaced for the Empire State Plaza graciously granted access to their records, which greatly expanded this chapter's archival research base.[50]

St. Sophia Greek Orthodox Church, founded in 1923, is one of the only churches of this faith community in the Albany area. Its congregants came (and continue to come to its new location) from a wide area to attend services and take part in social activities and Greek language classes. As a result, it was somewhat insulated from the changing neighborhood around it. In fact, it had finished a major expansion campaign to build a new school and community center just two years before the state seized the area in 1962.[51]

First Methodist Church experienced the area's changing demographics much differently. It traced its roots back to the late eighteenth century and was the spiritual home of Albany's elite for much of its history. As affluent whites moved out of their elegant downtown rowhouses in the mid-twentieth century, the area became blacker, poorer, and denser. By 1949, First Methodist's leaders were aware that its future was in jeopardy. A "religious census" that year concluded that many of its congregants had moved out of the area and that whites who remained were predominantly Catholic. At the same time, an influx of African American migrants from the South were moving into the area. Might outreach to these newcomers be an "opportunity" to rejuvenate the church?[52]

Church leaders were reluctant to seize this opportunity. Instead, over the next decade, the congregation continued to dwindle. By 1958, only 320 congregants remained. Leadership called an emergency meeting on June 16 to determine the church's future. The forty-nine who showed up agreed that the church's location was the main reason for its declining numbers. The alternatives they debated were to close the church outright, merge with another Methodist congregation, or transform the church into an inner-city mission.[53]

The congregation chose the last option. Two years later, the church set up a nearby storefront ministry and hired Rev. Angelo Mongiore, a fiery advocate for the poor, to lead it. Soon afterward, in July 1961, the church brought in a second clergyman, Rev. Randolph Nugent, a twenty-six-year-old black minister from Queens. Nugent's hire was too much for some church leaders. One trustee resigned immediately, explicitly stating that this had "convinced me that the day is not far off when First Methodist will be predominantly colored. I cannot go along with this." The church congregation merged with a nearby Methodist congregation in 1963, when New York State demolished the area. But its inner-city mission relocated nearby and continues its work today.[54]

The community records described here are important sources for building richly textured social histories of urban renewal in particular places. They reveal the experiences of people and neighborhood institutions directly affected by urban renewal and show how they responded to wrenching changes. However, they cannot tell the whole story. Sensitivity to local contexts must be central to our understanding of urban renewal, but we must also connect individual and community experiences to larger scales of analysis.

## Conclusion

A key element of President Richard M. Nixon's "New Federalism" was the return of federal activities, including urban renewal, to state and local control. In a radio address on January 28, 1973, he charged that urban renewal had cost "billions of dollars, with very disappointing results. How can a committee of Federal bureaucrats, hundreds or thousands of miles away, decide intelligently where building should take place?" Nixon was mistaken that federal officials decided where demolition, rehabilitation, and new construction occurred—local elected officials, planners, and urban renewal agencies did so, subject to federal oversight. Although Nixon's motives were far different from those of the National Commission on Urban Problems, he had essentially reached the same conclusion they had five years earlier—local context matters.[55]

Urban renewal fell out of public favor because of shortcomings at all levels of the program. The National Commission on Urban Problems attributed much of the blame to the "unconscionable amount of time," between six and nine years, from the start of planning to the end of execution. These delays "greatly increase the monetary and human cost of urban renewal and do serious damage to the people involved, to the neighborhood, and to the city as a whole." The commission concluded that both local officials and federal administrators shared the blame for these delays. Similarly, the 1973 Real Estate Research Corporation's report on Kingston identified four areas that explained a project's success or failure: exogenous factors beyond anyone's control, market forces that explained why redevelopment did or did not occur on cleared land, local factors, and national policy factors.[56]

Records held at the state, local, and community levels are essential to build a layered history of urban renewal. Understanding reasons for local success or failure is important, of course, but this layered approach leads us away from policy questions toward a social history of urban renewal. At the state level, the annual reports of urban renewal agencies reveal the diversity of projects undertaken by various towns and cities, ranging from modest efforts like new motels or sewage treatment plants to huge downtown shopping malls. These reports can serve as jumping-off points for more intensive local investigations. For example, several reports discussed episodes of resistance to urban renewal plans. Local and newspaper research can help us understand the nature and scope of this resistance. Local agency and municipal records, likewise, can help us understand the political and economic factors at work in particular places—factors that often determined the success or failure of urban renewal projects. Records of community institutions like churches permit deep social histories of urban renewal.

These records also give us the opportunity to connect urban history and public history more closely. They point the way to new avenues for public engagement, particularly when used in conjunction with oral histories and community stories. We know that relocation imposed financial and social hardships and that race, age, and the presence of children affected relocation outcomes. But we know far less about how families and communities weathered these disruptions or how they have communicated these experiences to their children and grandchildren.[57]

This research can lead us to a much deeper understanding of urban renewal. They refocus our analysis from the larger cities of the Northeast and Midwest to smaller places in other parts of the country that were more strongly affected by renewal. More important, they offer a promising way to communicate the history and lasting impact of urban renewal projects to both academic and public audiences. This type of research promises to reframe our understanding of this important episode in our nation's history and foster deeper connections between historians and the public whom we serve.

## NOTES

1. National Commission on Urban Problems, *Building the American City: Report of the National Commission on Urban Problems to the Congress and to the President of the United States* (Washington, D.C.: U.S. Government Printing Office, 1968), 1. A biographical list of commission members is at 501–502.

2. For histories of urban renewal at the national and policy levels, see Mark I. Gelfand, *A Nation of Cities: The Federal Government and Urban America, 1933–1965* (New York: Oxford University Press, 1975); Jon Teaford, *The Rough Road to Renaissance: Urban Revitalization in America, 1940–1985* (Baltimore: Johns Hopkins University Press, 1990); Roger Biles, *The Fate of Cities: Urban America and the Federal Government, 1945–2000* (Lawrence: University Press of Kansas, 2011).

Local histories of urban renewal, especially for local audiences, are legion, especially if one includes documentary films, websites, blogs, historical society exhibits and publications, and so on.

One excellent model for using local context to tell a national story was the *Fringe Cities* exhibit, which ran from October 2020 to January 2021 at the Center for Architecture in New York City: see "Fringe Cities: Legacies of Renewal in the Small American City," Center for Architecture, accessed February 18, 2021, available at https://www.centerforarchitecture.org/exhibitions/fringe-cities-legacies-of-renewal-in-the-small-american-city/.

3. This chapter serves as a companion to Ann Pfau, David Hochfelder, and Stacy Sewell, "Urban Renewal," *The Inclusive Historian's Handbook*, November 12, 2019, available at https://inclusivehistorian.com/urban-renewal/. This online resource is a joint publication of the National Council on Public History and the American Association for State and Local History.

4. Department of Housing and Urban Development, *Urban Renewal Directory* (Washington, D.C.: U.S. Government Printing Office, 1974), 2.

5. Douglas R. Appler, "Changing the Scale of Analysis for Urban Renewal Research: Small Cities, the State of Kentucky, and the 1974 Urban Renewal Directory," *Journal of Planning History* 16, no. 3 (2017): 200–221.

6. Department of Housing and Urban Development, *Urban Renewal Directory*, 23–29.

7. Elmira Urban Renewal Agency Annual Report, 1972, Department of Audit and Control, Annual Financial Reports, Urban Renewal Agencies, New York State Archives, Albany (hereafter Annual Financial Reports).

8. Corning Urban Renewal Agency Annual Report, 1974, Annual Financial Reports; New York State Urban Development Corporation, "Annual Report for 1972," New York State Urban Development Corporation Annual Reports, New York State Archives, Albany.

9. On UDC, see Stacy Sewell's chapter in this volume. See also Eleanor Brilliant, *The Urban Development Corporation: Private Interests and Public Authority* (Lexington, MA: Lexington Books, 1975); Nicholas Dagen Bloom, *How States Shaped Postwar America: State Government and Urban Power* (Chicago: University of Chicago Press, 2019).

10. Rochester Urban Renewal Agency Annual Report, 1972, Annual Financial Reports. These community organizations included the Ibero-American Action League, Rochester Northeast Development, and FIGHT. On FIGHT Square, see D.167, boxes 4b and 4c, Franklin Florence Papers, Rare Books, Special Collections, and Preservation, River Campus Libraries, University of Rochester, Rochester, New York.

11. Batavia Urban Renewal Agency Annual Report, 1965, Annual Financial Reports. Emphasis in original.

12. Ellenville Urban Renewal Agency Annual Report, 1965, Annual Financial Reports.

13. Binghamton Urban Renewal Agency Annual Report, 1968, Annual Financial Reports.

14. Ilion Urban Renewal Agency Annual Report, 1973, Annual Financial Reports.

15. Elmira Urban Renewal Agency Annual Report, 1972, Annual Financial Reports.

16. On UDC's failed Nine Towns project, see New York State Urban Development Corporation, *Annual Report*, 1973; Brilliant, *The Urban Development Corporation*; Edward Logue, interview with Ivan Steen, July 11, 1991, Ivan Steen Papers, M. E. Grenander Department of Special Collections and Archives, University at Albany, SUNY (hereafter Grenander). note to editor: University at Albany, SUNY is the formal name of the university.

17. George Vecsey, "Townhouse Plan Splits L.I. Blacks," *New York Times*, September 12, 1973.

18. Rona Kavee, "Blacks Fear Loss of Stake in Spinney Hill Business Project," *New York Times*, October 7, 1979; North Hempstead Urban Renewal Agency Annual Reports, 1972–1982, Annual Financial Reports; Jones v. Tully, 378 F. Supp. 286 (U.S. District Court, Eastern District of New York); Arielle Martinez, "The Historical Information Health of Black Communities on Long Island" (Honors College thesis, Stony Brook University, 2017), available at http://ariellecmartinez.com/honorsthesis/.

19. Plattsburgh Urban Renewal Agency Annual Report, 1971, Annual Financial Reports.

20. Plattsburgh Urban Renewal Agency Annual Reports, 1970–1980, Annual Financial Reports.

21. Peekskill Urban Renewal Agency Annual Report, 1973, Annual Financial Reports.

22. Port Jervis Urban Renewal Agency Annual Report, 1975, Annual Financial Reports.

23. Dunkirk Urban Renewal Agency Annual Reports, 1971–1978, Annual Financial Reports.

24. New York State Urban Development Corporation, *Annual Report of the New York State Urban Development Corporation* (New York: New York State Urban Development Corporation, 1973), 74.

25. Amsterdam Urban Renewal Agency Annual Reports, 1977–1981, Annual Financial Reports.

26. Syracuse Urban Renewal Agency Annual Reports, 1974–1983, Annual Financial Reports.

27. Jamestown Urban Renewal Agency Annual Report, 1982, Annual Financial Reports.

28. Newburgh Urban Renewal Agency Annual Report, 1972, Annual Financial Reports.

29. Charles H. Horan to Albert J. Abrams, March 25, 1959, box 64-C2b, Newburgh Urban Renewal Agency Records, Grenander (hereafter NURA). In 2018, the City of Newburgh transferred about one hundred boxes of NURA records to the University at Albany's M. E. Grenander Department of Special Collections and Archives.

30. Remarks of David M. Rosen, June 27, 1966, Newburgh Common Council Minutes. I am grateful to Orange County historian Johanna Porr Yaun for making available digitized copies of the minutes from 1940 to 2001.

31. Ann Pfau and Stacy Kinlock Sewell, "Newburgh's 'Last Chance': The Elusive Promise of Urban Renewal in a Small and Divided City," *Journal of Planning History* 19, no. 3 (2020): 144–163.

32. "Battle of Newburgh," *Times Hudson Valley*, April 2, 2013, available at http://time shudsonvalley.com/stories/battle-of-newburgh,3131?.

33. Jack Present to Charles J. Horan, December 10, 1970, and WGNY editorial by Gen. Mgr Campbell K. Thompson, December 9, 1970, both NURA.

34. In 1965, James M. Gaynor, state commissioner of housing and community renewal, singled out Newburgh for its "appalling record" of failure in rehousing displaced residents; quoted in "Relocation Delays Renewal in State," *New York Times*, June 15, 1965.

35. "Remedial Action Is Ordered," *Kingston Daily Freeman*, March 29, 1967; Hugh Reynolds, "Press for Stricter Site Inspection of Downtown Demolition Locations," *Kingston Daily Freeman*, May 12, 1967; "UR Obligated to Give Out Data: Resnick," *Kingston Daily Freeman*, June 14, 1967; S. James Matthews, letter to the editor, *Kingston Daily Freeman*, June 17, 1967.

36. Press Release, May 19, 1967, folder "KURA," Joseph Y. Resnick Papers, Grenander.

37. "Report of Congressman Joseph Y. Resnick, Urban Renewal and Related Activities, Kingston, New York," June 30, 1967, folder "KURA," Joseph Y. Resnick Papers, Grenander.

38. "Blasts Farm Bureau, UR," *Kingston Daily Freeman*, July 24, 1967.

39. "Hemphill Statement on Resignation," *Kingston Daily Freeman*, August 28, 1967. "Triangle Project Chronology of Events Extracted from HUD Project Files by the U.S. General Accounting Office," May 5, 1970, GAO document #B-168690, available at https://www.gao.gov/assets/200/192332.pdf.

40. Real Estate Research Corporation, *Urban Renewal Land Disposition Study: Kingston, New York* (Washington, D.C.: Real Estate Research Corporation, 1973), 67–72.

41. Material related to the negotiations and the financing agreement is in box 7, folders 6–11, Erastus Corning 2nd Papers, Albany Institute of History and Art, Albany, New York. See also Paul Grondahl, *Mayor Erastus Corning: Albany Icon, Albany Enigma* (Albany: State University of New York Press, 2007), 465–471.

42. Canvasser's notes, March 29, 1962, with the remarks of Martin, Tropp, and Drake, are in box 7, folder 1, Erastus Corning 2nd Papers, Albany Institute of History and Art, Albany, New York.

43. Alan M. Voorhees and Associates, "Community Planning Survey–Tri-City Area," box 8, folder 30, Temporary State Commission on the Capital City Records, New York State Archives, Albany.

44. For a sample of these photos, see "Picturing Urban Renewal," Flickr, accessed April 14, 2021, available at https://www.flickr.com/photos/14499769@N02/albums.

45. Themis Chronopoulos and Deqah Hussein-Wetzel found that supporters of wholesale site clearance used streetscape photos for the same purpose in New York City and

Cincinnati. Themis Chronopoulos, "Robert Moses and the Visual Dimension of Physical Disorder: Efforts to Demonstrate Urban Blight in the Age of Slum Clearance," *Journal of Planning History* 13, no. 3 (2014): 207–233; Deqah Hussein-Wetzel, "Urban Renewal in Cincinnati's Lower West End: A Deeply Rooted Heritage Story Map," June 17, 2020, available at https://storymaps.arcgis.com/stories/43f1767de26d49a58594e7d14f4eee22.

46. Sid Leavitt, "Couple Willing to Give Up Home Again," *Kingston Daily Freeman*, August 9, 1976.

47. "Paved with Good Intentions," *Kingston Daily Freeman*, August 6, 1976; remarks of Councilman Lawrence Herbst, December 8, 1969, Newburgh Common Council Minutes.

48. Marc Fried, "Grieving for a Lost Home: Psychological Costs of Relocation," in *Urban Renewal: The Record and the Controversy*, ed. James Q. Wilson, 376–379 (Cambridge, MA: MIT Press, 1966); Mindy Thompson Fullilove, *Root Shock: How Tearing Up City Neighborhoods Hurts America, and What We Can Do About It* (New York: One World Books, 2004), 11.

49. On the urban elderly poor, see Joan Hatch Shapiro, *Communities of the Alone: Working with Single Room Occupants in the City* (New York: Association Press, 1971); Joyce Stephens, *Loners, Losers, and Lovers: Elderly Tenants in a Slum Hotel* (Seattle: University of Washington Press, 1976); Charles Hoch and Robert A. Slayton, *New Homeless and Old: Community and the Skid Row Hotel* (Philadelphia, PA: Temple University Press, 1989).

50. Many churches have an archivist or librarian who is the first point of contact for gaining access to church records. On the relationship between Protestant churches and urban renewal, see Mark Wild, *Renewal: Liberal Protestants and the American City after World War II* (Chicago: University of Chicago Press, 2019), 130–136; John R. Scotford, "When to Move and When to Stay Put," typescript excerpt from *Protestant Church Administration*, September 1956, St. Paul's Episcopal Church Records, Albany, New York.

51. C. S. Koutsakis, President, Board of Directors, to "Members and Friends," undated but late 1960, and list of "Operation Demolition" donors, undated 1960, both St. Sophia Greek Orthodox Church, Church Archives and Library Room, Albany, New York.

52. Frederick A. Shippey, "The Religious Census of Downtown Albany," 1949, Board of Missions, Methodist Church, Methodist Archives, Drew University, Madison, New Jersey.

53. "Congregational Meeting Held in Grace Chapel," June 16, 1958, and Minutes, Board of Trustees, October 10, 1960, both First Methodist Church Records, Trinity United Methodist Church, Albany, New York.

54. Albert H. Savage to John Cromie, President, Board of Trustees, July 31, 1961, First Methodist Church Records, Trinity United Methodist Church, Albany, New York; William E. Rowley, "Ex-Barber Shop Deals in Counseling—and Hope," *Knickerbocker News*, December 31, 1960; "Pastor Stresses Need of Program for 'Gut,'" *Knickerbocker News*, April 29, 1961.

55. Richard Nixon, "The New Budget: Charting a New Era of Progress," January 28, 1973, in *Public Papers of the Presidents of the United States, 1973*, 31 (Washington, D.C.: U.S. Government Printing Office, 1975).

56. National Commission on Urban Problems, *Building the American City*, 165–167; Real Estate Research Corporation, *Urban Renewal Land Disposition Study*, 67–78.

57. See, for example, Dolores Hayden, *The Power of Place: Urban Landscapes as Public History* (Cambridge, MA: MIT Press, 1995); Andrew Hurley, *Beyond Preservation: Using Public History to Revitalize Inner Cities* (Philadelphia, PA: Temple University Press, 2010); Gabrielle Bendiner-Viani, *Contested City: Art and Public History as Mediation at New York's Seward Park Urban Renewal Area* (Iowa City: University of Iowa Press, 2018).

# II

# Telling the Stories of Urban Renewal

# 3

# Modernizing the Mill Town

*Space, Power, and Urban Renewal*
*in Waterville, Maine*

Benjamin D. Lisle

George Mitchell and Mintaha Saad met in the Head of Falls neighborhood in Waterville, Maine, in the early 1920s. It was a Lebanese enclave under two acres in size—a cluster of houses and shops flanking the Wyandotte Worsted woolen mill, just feet from the Kennebec River. Mitchell worked a jackhammer, laying gas lines for Central Maine Power. Saad, who had moved from Lebanon to Waterville in 1920, at age eighteen, was becoming a skilled wool weaver, working at various plants in the area—including the one steps from her door. The couple married and lived in Head of Falls at King Court. Their first son, Paul, spent his early years there as one of nearly a hundred children living in the pack of old homes. A few years later, the upwardly mobile Mitchells moved to the other side of the train tracks that pinned the neighborhood to the river.[1] The family grew; among the additions was George Jr., a future U.S. senator. Paul would become executive director of the Waterville Urban Renewal Authority and thus a central figure in the process that would ultimately destroy his old neighborhood in Head of Falls as part of a profound reorganization of the city: economically, politically, materially, spatially, and socially.

Urban renewal in Waterville was marked by a fundamental contradiction. It was intended to save the traditional Main Street, materially and symbolically, by adopting the logics of the suburban shopping center; to beat back the threat of the shopping center, renewal advocates believed, Main Street had to become one. Urban renewal presented an opportunity to symbolically change the city from factory town to modern consumer hub, and downtown business owners jumped at the chance; as one store owner urged, "Let's keep up with the space age and move."[2] Crucial to the city's modernization was the adoption of modern planning practices—a controversial process for a city historically averse to governmental interventions—that concentrated political power in the hands of merchant interest. And to become modern meant erasing markers of old ways of living—the textile mill, the crooked street, the working-class apartment, and the people who lived there: structures and people disproportionately old, economically precarious, and ethnically marginal (particularly the French Canadian working class). Those opposed to urban renewal were cast as relics of the past, opponents of progress. Through dispersal and erasure, the landscape was visually and spatially reordered—sharpening territorial boundaries around use, class, and ethnicity and creating a sense of modern order out of seeming chaos.[3] And so, urban renewal shaped the social and material landscapes of Waterville in ways that echoed those of other communities, large and small, across the country.

But urban renewal also played out differently in different settings, something long acknowledged by scholars but underrepresented in the scholarship—a problem particularly acute when considering questions of scale.[4] Though the scholarship focuses almost exclusively on larger cities, most urban renewal projects actually occurred in smaller communities like Waterville, which had a population of just 18,695 in 1960.[5] In a town of this size, nearly everyone knew each other; the process of urban renewal was immediate and intimate—perhaps best exemplified by the experience of Paul Mitchell himself, who steered the renewal machine that bulldozed his childhood home. Local merchants played a particularly important role in dictating the terms of the projects, unlike in larger cities, where, for example, large corporate interests were more likely to shape the plans.[6] And while the costs and scope of renewal in Waterville might pale in comparison to larger projects in bigger cities, at this small scale, they were profoundly invasive, practically grinding the city to a halt in the mid-1960s while also stoking social conflict.[7] Waterville is a place where residents' families go back generations. The memory of urban renewal is very much a living one: it remains a widely recognized signature moment in the town's history and a touchstone for controversies around development today.

Through its attention to big projects in larger cities, urban renewal scholarship also fittingly focuses much of its attention on the spatialization of racial difference in cities and their suburbs.[8] Again, analyzing a place like Waterville complicates our understanding of urban renewal. Of the town's 18,695 residents in 1960, just 40 were non-white (including a mere 14 black residents).[9] But even within a city deemed almost exclusively white by the census, the contours of that whiteness were shifting. The small Lebanese population rapidly assimilated into Waterville's professional classes after the war.

Some members of the much larger French Canadian community did as well, though as a whole it remained economically and socially secondary to Waterville's dominant "Yankee" class.[10] Urban renewal in Waterville would augment the spatial segregation of this group by forcing them out of affordable rental housing downtown, often into the South End, the traditional working-class Franco stronghold.

A small New England river mill town, fueled by textiles and paper mills and almost entirely white racially—this is not the typical lens through which urban renewal has been examined. But the history of places like Waterville can help us better understand the ways this influential federal program affected a diversity of people and communities across the country—in its local peculiarities and as a shared national experience.

## Waterville in the 1950s

Waterville in the 1950s was a palimpsest of a century of urban development. Its downtown was at the lower end of Main Street, which ran roughly north and south for three-tenths of a mile, flanked by three- and four-story brick buildings. Two blocks to the east of Main Street was the Kennebec River, home to the Wyandotte Worsted woolen mill and the Head of Falls neighborhood, populated largely by Lebanese and French Canadian factory workers. Three bridges reached across the river to the neighboring town of Winslow: one for cars, one for trains, and the "Two-Cent Bridge" for workers crossing over to the Hollingsworth and Whitney paper plant.

Immediately west of Main Street lay a patchwork of angled streets and a hodgepodge of aged but affordable rental housing, light industry, service stations, small shops and offices, parking, a church, the YMCA, and the library. Many of the area's residents were retired or widowed. Those with jobs worked nearby—at the wool mill, paper plant, or Hathaway shirt factory on the southern edge of downtown; as clerks and cashiers at Main Street businesses; or, in true Maine fashion, as "woodsmen."[11] They lived there for its convenience, with easy walks to nearby jobs, downtown shops, and churches; they also lived there because it was inexpensive.[12]

Main Street was a bustling commercial district of small shops and familiar faces. (See Figure 3.1.) At Post Office Square, home to two of the city's four traffic lights, was the century-old Elmwood Hotel, which had just recently turned over its front lawn to an Esso Service Station. From there, a drive south down Main took you past Parks Diner, open round the clock; Leo Diambri's Fruit Stand, a lunch counter known for its plates of spaghetti; LaVerdiere's Drug Store; Bea's Candy Kitchen, where you could look through the window to see taffy being pulled; the Harris Bakery, with its small army of female clerks in starched uniforms; W. B. Arnold's hardware store; Levine's clothing store,

**Figure 3.1** Main Street Waterville, ca. 1950, looking north from Castonguay Square.
(Source: George French, *Main Street Waterville*, n.d., black-and-white acetate negative, 8 × 10 in., George French Collection, Maine State Archives.)

which catered to men and boys; and Alvina and Delia, a shop for fashionable women.[13] Scattered between and above these stores were the offices of dentists, lawyers, jewelers, physicians, bankers, insurance salespeople, and accountants, as well as the shops of barbers, cobblers, tailors, and music teachers; an Alcoholics Anonymous clubhouse; and many apartments.[14]

Main Street's traffic seemed to increase by the day. Though Waterville ranked just eighth in population among Maine cities, its retail sales were the fourth highest. The city was a regional commercial center due to its proximity to many summer recreation areas, its increasingly important role as a regional medical and professional services center, its geographic positioning as a distribution point for freight, and its location at a node of state roads.[15] Local officials, backed by a recently reinvigorated chamber of commerce, jumped on plans to extend the interstate highway system into central Maine, hoping to steer it as close to Waterville as possible.[16] Developers looked eagerly at the possibilities of commercial hubs at the interstate's proposed two exit ramps— one about three miles due west, the other a mile and a half to the north.

As the impact of the automobile raised new questions, Waterville was tested by the first tremors of deindustrialization, which would wreak havoc on its economy—and across the region—over the coming decades. Scott Paper Company purchased the sixty-four-year-old Hollingsworth and Whitney paper plant in 1954, retooled it to produce toilet paper, and shed nearly half its workforce of 1,680. These job losses were compounded by the collapse of the Lockwood Company in 1955. Like many cotton manufacturers in the Northeast, it had been struggling in the decade since the war, as mills in the South and manufacturers abroad drove down prices. Lockwood's closure eliminated 850 jobs—30 percent of the mill workforce in the city.[17]

By the end of the decade, Waterville was staring down what Mayor Albert Bernier called a "host of problems." There was a national recession. The launch of Sputnik in 1957 had provoked a "crisis in confidence" in "the competitive ability of our economy, and in the performance of our educational system." Factory job losses had amounted to the equivalent of nearly one-tenth of the city's population. And with those job losses came nearly three hundred apartment vacancies in the city.[18] Growth in other areas partially compensated for these industrial losses—including the expansion of C. F. Hathaway, a quality shirt maker; the addition of a poultry-processing plant nearby; and the expansion of the professional sector, which added about four hundred new jobs (half of them at Colby College). Altogether, there were about four hundred fewer jobs in 1960 than a decade before.[19] According to Bernier, "Waterville was suffering from growing pains," which were particularly reflected in "the impact of the automobile on downtown." There was a lack of parking on busy shopping days, undesirable traffic patterns, and a subsequent loss of customers to nearby towns. Bernier claimed that these challenges "required an immense amount of fact-gathering and planning. Comprehensive long-range planning was the key."[20]

## Planning for Urban Renewal

One of Bernier's initial moves upon taking office in 1958 was to "reactivate the planning board."[21] Shortly thereafter, the city and the Waterville Merchants Bureau partnered to hire Planning and Renewal Associates—out of Cambridge, Massachusetts—to develop a comprehensive plan.[22] The firm, working with the planning board, laid the groundwork for a new zoning ordinance, urban renewal, and the new "Downtown Improvement Plan," using federal and state assistance from the 701 planning grant program, which provided financial support for creating planning agencies in small cities.[23]

The formation of the Waterville Urban Renewal Authority followed, approved by voters in December 1959. Its goal was to acquire federal grants and loans from the federal HHFA "to eliminate substandard, slum or blighted areas within the city."[24] Mayor Bernier appointed five members to its board of commissioners in February 1960, as well as a fifteen-person citizens advisory board.[25] After a few changes to the commissioners' board in 1961, it remained largely intact throughout the decade, chaired by Bradford Wall, who had recently retired from his position as a superintendent at Scott Paper Company, and vice chaired by Willard Arnold, president of the Maine Merchants Bureau and owner of a Main Street hardware store.[26] They appointed Paul Mitchell as the Waterville Urban Renewal Authority's executive director in January 1962. Waterville native Mitchell had returned to the city in 1958 after working for the Liberty Mutual insurance company in Boston.[27] Wall knew him well: Mitchell was a long-time friend of Wall's son. Local historian Earl Smith called Mitchell "genial, capable, and hard-working"—qualities that would help him navigate the combative politics of urban renewal over the coming years.[28] Mitchell was the public face of urban renewal for over a decade, meeting with civic groups, explaining planning rationale at public meetings, and enduring a constant stream of public criticism. Over the course of a few short years, Waterville integrated professionalized planning into its city governance, and access to urban renewal funds had drawn together a coherent renewal coalition.[29]

As the city built out its planning bureaucracy, over the objections of many small-government conservatives, consultant Morton Braun and his assistants developed a plan for a modernized downtown.[30] (See Figures 3.2 and 3.3.) Released in June 1960, the proposal was animated by the need to link the downtown to the interstate, circulate people within downtown, and add additional parking, which Braun called "the very basis of this Plan."[31] He hoped to separate shopping traffic from through traffic, as "through tourist traffic and local park-and-shop traffic do not mix well."[32] He proposed rerouting through traffic along the perimeter of a rehabilitated downtown shopping district via an extended Charles Street (to the west) and Front Street (to the east). Main Street would be dedicated to shopping traffic exclusively, essentially turning it into "a parking lot along its entire length" and giving it "the effect of a shopping center with parking surrounding the stores."[33] A small common, called Castonguay Square, would be extended across Main Street as a pedestrian mall, physically and visually severing the road to through traffic. Braun's plan echoed proposals for downtown revitalization across the country—most inspired by Victor Gruen's 1956 vision for downtown Fort Worth, which called for a comprehensive reorganization of traffic flows, the integration of new parking, and the creation of pedestrian zones—all strategies to essentially re-create the experience of suburban shopping in the center city.[34]

In the end, this was the real organizing idea behind Braun's proposal: "A downtown business center should provide the physical advantages associ-

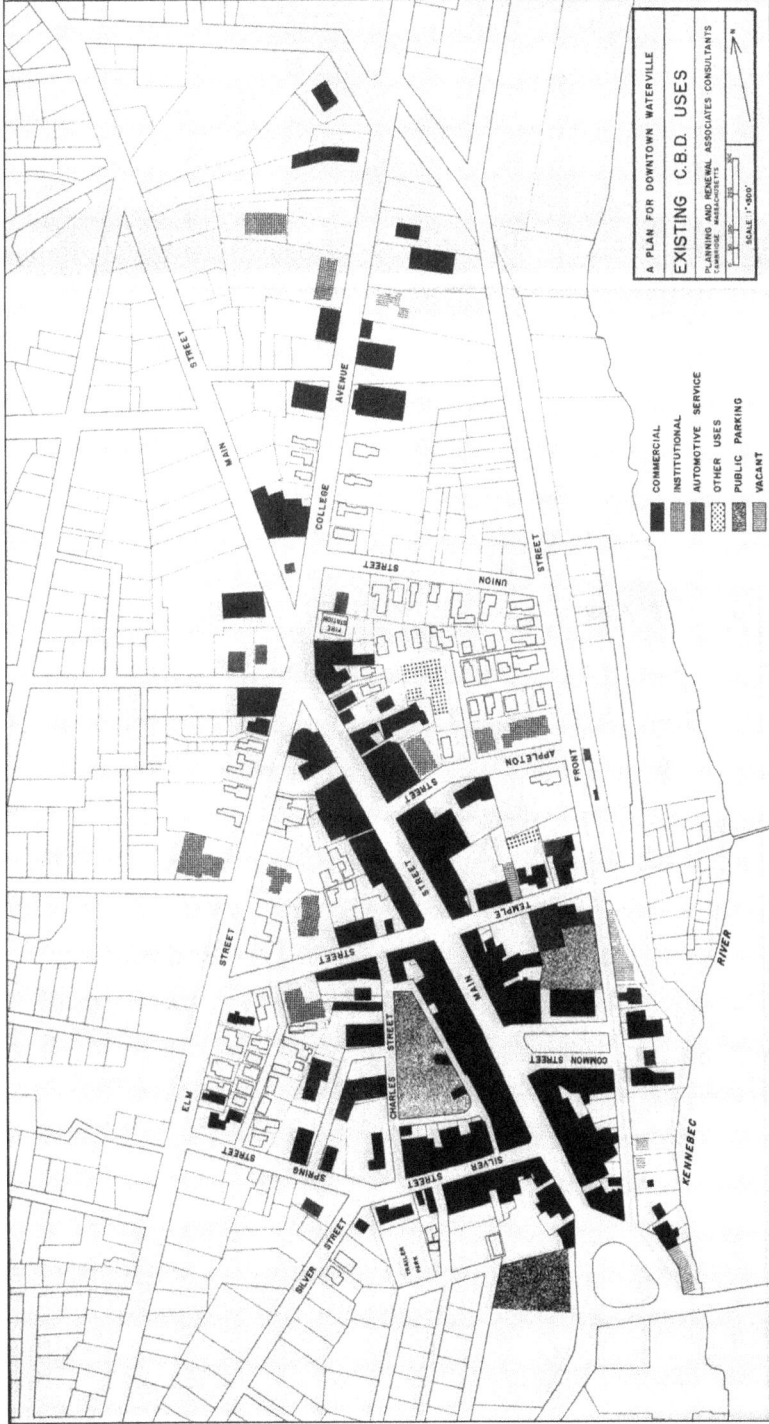

**Figure 3.2** Prerenewal land use in downtown Waterville in 1960.

(Source: Planning and Renewal Associates, *A Plan for Downtown Waterville* [Cambridge, MA: Planning and Renewal Associates, 1960].)

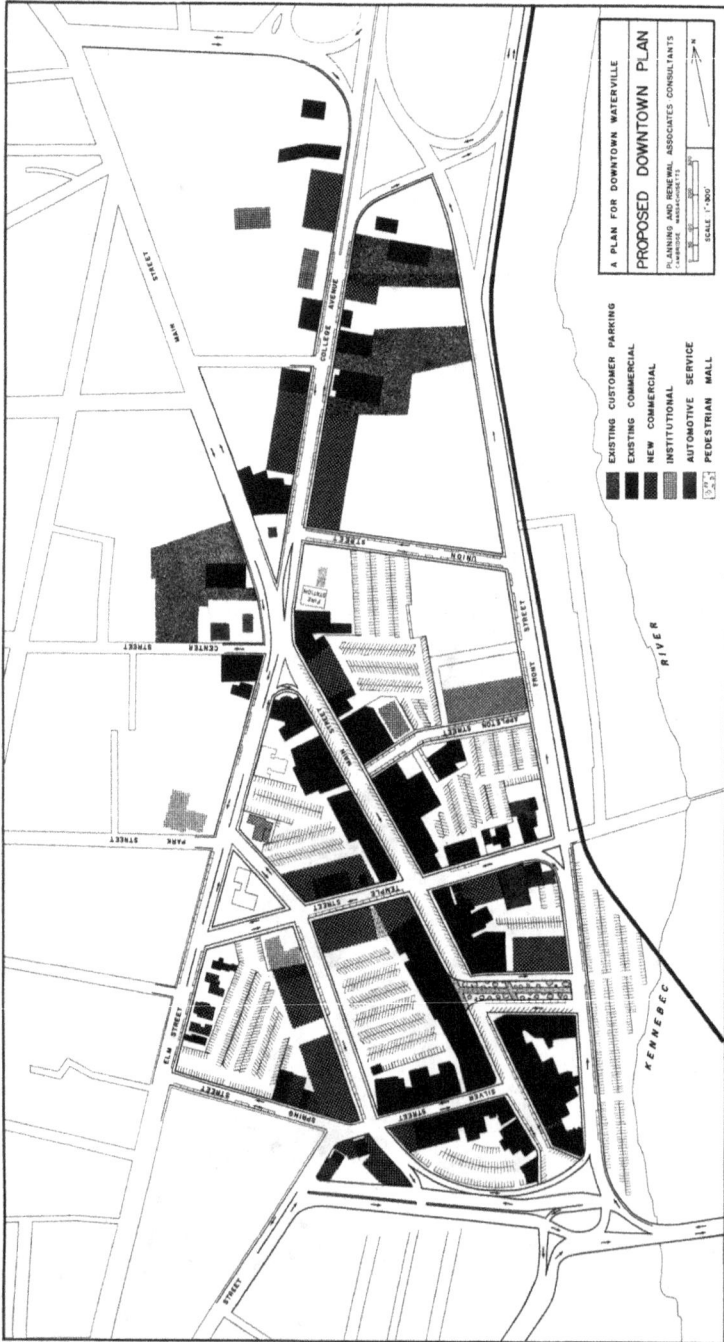

**Figure 3.3** Morton Braun's urban renewal plan for downtown Waterville in 1960, featuring perimeter traffic circulation and a pedestrian mall near the southern end of Main Street.

(Source: Planning and Renewal Associates, *A Plan for Downtown Waterville* [Cambridge, MA: Planning and Renewal Associates, 1960].)

ated with new shopping centers; or to put it another way, downtown should become a shopping center itself."[35] New shopping centers—like those being hatched near the interstate—had many advantages over traditional downtowns: "they are modern and eye-catching; their very newness is a distinct attraction."[36] And that newness was accentuated by downtowns where, "in the absence of an incentive or a counterattack . . . deterioration sets in."[37] Downtown Waterville had not yet passed the point of no return on this front. However, Braun insisted that it needed to improve its appearance in order to create an image of "freshness and attractiveness."[38] The city required a "rational relationship between parking, circulation, and stores . . . which . . . will create order out of much of the present physical and aesthetic clutter."[39]

Waterville's new urban renewal authority was not entirely convinced by Braun's plan—particularly to convert Main Street into a parking lot and pedestrian mall. However, Braun's core concept—to make downtown "a shopping center itself"—clearly captured their imaginations. But rather than extending Charles Street, using it to circulate through traffic around a downtown that would then be solely commercial, the urban renewal authority opted to erase the neighborhood entirely with a suburban-style shopping center and an expansive parking lot essentially grafted onto the western flank of Main Street. They also elected to convert the downtown's two major roads to one-way traffic, hustling cars south along Main Street and north along Front Street, which ran parallel to the river.[40]

This would become known as the "Charles Street" project, and the urban renewal authority, the merchants bureau, and Braun's firm—assisted by the local newspaper, the *Morning Sentinel*—took their sales pitch to the public. Their arguments for renewal mirrored what historian Alison Isenberg termed the "mantras of urban renewal": saving downtown businesses (particularly retail), resolving traffic and parking congestion, rebuilding property values (for the tax base), and replacing shabby, worn-out structures.[41] In a series of explanatory articles in 1961, the *Sentinel* explored the justifications for renewal. One of the first articles allowed Main Street business owners to make their case, focusing on the terrifying economic and symbolic prospects of an abandoned downtown. Saul Mandell, proprietor of Waterville Hardware, asked, "If Urban Renewal doesn't go through and Main Street becomes a ghost street, who will furnish the taxes for the city? With Urban Renewal, the city is improved, property value goes up, thus lessening the chances of the average citizen being forced to pay more taxes."[42] Willard Arnold bristled at suggestions that this was merely a scheme for merchants to get more parking for their businesses while also warning about the tax implications: "Any loss on Main Street would have to be made up through private citizens and industry."[43] Store owner A. W. Larsen offered sympathy to those who would be displaced but argued that clearing out the Charles Street area would be "for the benefit of the whole city."[44] Edward Vlodek, a shop owner and former head of the merchants bureau, invoked a nostalgia for small-town America: "There is still nothing like Main Street, USA, no matter what they say about the shopping centers. I say if there is a place to park, the Main Street is still the place where people want to shop."[45]

Not everyone was impressed by these arguments. Many business owners in the area objected to what they saw as overreaching power. Tailor Robert Guite, whose business was in the targeted area, said he had not been contacted by the urban renewal authority, claiming that "City Hall does as it pleases."[46] Charles Rancourt owned and lived in a building, just inside the proposed project area, that was home to the Elm Street Variety Store and five rental apartments. "I don't see why people in this neighborhood should have to sacrifice homes and business for Main Street," he argued. He complained about the loss of taxable property to the city. He also lamented the loss of his strategic position: "How could they possibly relocate me in as good a place as I am now? Right here, within 1000 feet, there are more than 300 apartments, three schools with about 700 students and 12,000 cars pass right in front of my door every day."[47] Like many in the city, those in the targeted area thought urban renewal should address Head of Falls instead.

Resistance to urban renewal became more organized in the summer of 1962 with the formation of the Citizens Committee for a Better Urban Renewal Plan. The group, fronted by Main Street clothier Julius Levine, requested a more targeted approach to renewal downtown. They proposed more precise spot clearance to create new parking spaces, rather than one enormous lot—aligning them with Braun's original proposal. They also recommended rehabilitation over demolition at Head of Falls.[48] At a public meeting, Levine warned of the "giant gamble" of demolishing 10 percent of the city's wealth in the proposed renewal area. He pointed to the failure of other cities to attract new development in slum clearance areas. He warned of federal control over development, the effect on existing property owners who might be forced to remortgage, the displacement of renters who could not afford FHA loans for home ownership, the threat of large corporations being the only ones who could afford to build in the cleared area, and a seeming absence of concern with the "human costs" of appropriating cultural institutions like the Congregational Church. "If this is federal leaf-raking," Levine argued, "we wish they wouldn't burn down the buildings to rake the leaves." He claimed that the group was not antirenewal but rather urged a more cautious and "democratic" approach.[49] Mitchell was unmoved: in the margins of a *Sentinel* article recounting Levine's positions, he wrote, "Good intelligent opposition is helpful, but this [is] pure slop."[50]

Mitchell's margin notes might have revealed something about the private attitudes of the renewal authority and its board, but in public, advocates were more diplomatic. A *Sentinel* profile of Temple Court—the main concentration of housing in the proposed renewal zone—suggests the intricate and complicated mess of economic priorities, political power, and human concerns at play on this small stage. The author sets the scene with a portrait of age and poverty at odds with imaginaries of postwar, suburban prosperity: "Kids were playing in the narrow street. Only a few had bicycles: the rest amused themselves with broken toys and by jostling with one another. Occasionally a mother would scold a child from one of the many porches."[51] A six-year-old boy "shoved an unpainted scooter down the worn wooden steps of an apartment house."[52] His mother, Mary Dumont, explained her relief that he was even outside, as "whooping cough during the summer . . . had left him thin and pale." Her husband too had been "recently ill" and was unemployed. Dumont also had four other children to tend to.[53] The physical decay of the congested block, it seemed, went hand in hand with illness and economic precarity.

But the *Sentinel* also allowed some residents to express their concerns about renewal. Dumont, who had lived on Temple Court her entire life, noted the difficulties of finding an affordable apartment with five kids and the need to live in town because they did not own a car.[54] Pensioner Anne Thibodeau, who had lived in the same apartment there for thirty years, said, "I can't move. It would cost too much elsewhere."[55] Mabel Smith, who had lived there for forty-four years, also expected that she would "have to pay more somewhere else."[56] Theresa Chizy—whose retired parents, the Bouchers, lived two doors down—noted that she could walk to work. Widow Virginia Vigue told the reporter, "I like to be near the church and downtown. I don't want to move because I can't afford a higher rent. I don't have a big pension."[57] Joseph Paradis, who had raised six children there, said, "I have lived here for 40 years and I want to go on living here."[58] The block was the "urban village" in microcosm—a resilient community of working-class French Canadian Watervillians, many of whom had lived there for decades.[59]

The *Sentinel* portrait provided a forum for this airing of grievances. It also massaged in popular arguments for renewal, framing the project as an effort to "remove substandard property and eliminate blight and traffic congestion."[60] It would be "self-liquidating at no out-of-pocket cost to Waterville taxpayers."[61] And the article cited a number of residents who appeared to be taking the potential changes in stride—particularly property owners willing to take their buyouts and move elsewhere. Altogether, the article crystallized many of the competing discourses around urban renewal in Waterville and elsewhere: it both pathologized and humanized the area while subtly depicting it as a relic of the past and implicitly rendering it as a barrier to the city's modern future. This was consistent with much of the *Sentinel*'s coverage of renewal—a furrowed brow of concern giving way to a "there is no alternative" logic of development as progress. The newspaper's position was clarified by its relentless series of editorials fretting over the slow pace of development.[62]

Anxieties over the slow pace of development were colored by fears of competing development at the interstate exits. Privately and publicly, renewal advocates advanced the idea that Waterville faced an either/or prospect—either suburban shopping centers *or* a robust Main Street, but not both. Early in the planning process, a memo from the chamber of commerce to downtown businesses tried to enlist support by claiming, "This project is the only thing that will help discourage an edge-of-town shopping center."[63] Welton Farrow, chairman of the planning board and member of the urban renewal citizens advisory committee, asserted that there was "not enough population in and around Waterville to guarantee the success of both a shopping center and downtown."[64] But really, renewal advocates implied that this was a false choice: Waterville residents could have it all, preserving the charm and historic meaning of Main Street *and* enjoying the comfort and convenience of a modern suburban shopping center in the very same space at the city center. According to the *Sentinel*, "The Urban Renewal project proposed for Waterville's downtown envisions a downtown shopping center that would retain the best of Waterville's downtown shopping area while adding the best features of a suburban shopping center."[65] Another *Sentinel* article teased, "Extensive plastic surgery may soon be performed on Waterville's downtown profile, making the central commercial district one of the most modern in Maine."[66] According to Paul Mitchell, echoing Braun's original plan, urban renewal would result in "the creation of a large shopping center in the heart of Waterville. . . . Downtown Waterville will become, essentially, a shopping center."[67] Regarding the threat of new shopping centers at the interstate, a *Sentinel* editorial mused in June of 1962, "One strongly suspects that there won't be any serious digging for buildings at either proposed shopping center until there is a final decision on the downtown renewal program."[68]

Such predictions were proven wrong barely two months later, when contracts were awarded to construct the new Elm Plaza Shopping Center in August. The complex opened the following summer on upper Main Street at its junction with the interstate. It hosted 155,000 square feet of retail space— laid out in expansive and adjoining low-slung, flat-roofed, glass-faced utilitarian structures—fronted by a massive parking field for 1,500 cars. It was advertised as the largest shopping center in central Maine.[69] The development was anchored by a W. T. Grant department store, a First National supermarket, and the discount department store, Mammoth Mart; both First National and Mammoth Mart had closed stores near downtown to reopen at the interstate.[70] And as Elm Plaza was being built, two additional shopping centers were being planned for the southern interstate intersection at Oakland Road.[71] The downtown merchants had presumably lost the race, though they had no intention of turning back.

## Urban Renewal: Charles Street

With construction on Elm Plaza underway, the Charles Street project (Me. R-6) was approved in December 1962. The news came from Senator Edmund Muskie, who just years before had been practicing law in Waterville and was part of the group that revived the chamber of commerce. The city received a capital grant of $1.6 million and a loan of $2.6 million. The following month, the urban renewal authority hosted a public meeting in the Opera House to present Morton Braun's revised plan.[72] Despite vocal opposition from many in the crowd, the board of aldermen approved the plan five to two.[73] The city began acquiring properties later that year, after funding was executed in August.[74]

The project limped along slowly. Some landowners objected to the compensation being offered for their properties. The whole process dragged to a halt when Rose Warren, who owned six apartment buildings on Temple Court, sued the urban renewal authority. She was supported by many of her tenants, who were mostly elderly, did not own cars, and worried about finding other affordable housing in the city.[75] Warren claimed that the condemnation procedures had illegally invalidated the eminent domain process. The urban renewal authority argued that her buildings were "old, deteriorating, and dilapidated" and thus it was necessary that they be demolished for the sake of "public health" and the "safety" and "morals" of the residents.[76] In May 1965, the Maine Supreme Court ruled in the urban renewal authority's favor.[77]

The Charles Street area was finally cleared out by September of the following year, and downtown shoppers began using the yet-to-be-paved parking area. Eighty-two buildings were destroyed overall.[78] Among them were the 130-year-old First Congregational Church and the YMCA, which occupied an elegant, Italianate home built in 1842. A dizzying array of buildings were leveled: Temple Court's affordable housing—an architectural mixture of old wooden two- and three-story temple-front houses, four squares, and roughed-up colonials; two- and three-story brick boxes that were home to shops and professional offices along Main Street between Appleton and Temple; the blocky, utilitarian structures of service stations, car dealers, and repair shops; and even some old wooden storage sheds. Among the demolished businesses were restaurants like the beloved old Parks Diner, Spauldy's Lobster Grill, Leo's Lunch Bar, and Barney's Hot Dog Stand; small stores like Huard's Radio Shop, Page's Key Shop, Central Auto Parts, Waterville Auto Sales, and Leo's New and Used Furniture; services like Colby Drive-In Cleaners, Silver Street

Laundromat, Arbo's Garage, and Joseph's Pool and Billiard Parlor. The sur-names of those displaced from their homes—Cloutier, Theriault, Laplante, Roy, Voisine, LeClair, Dacoteau, and Bourque, among many others—spoke to the French Canadian roots of half the city.[79]

The many were replaced by a few in the new downtown shopping center named "the Concourse." In August 1967, discount chain Zayre moved in, join-ing Cottle's Market—relocated from its demolished home on nearby Main Street—in a seventy-four-thousand-square-foot structure echoing the no-frills modernism of a suburban strip mall. An adjacent complex flanked this larg-er building; called "the Forum," it housed five other relocating businesses from the project area.[80] The much-celebrated parking lot could fit 725 cars. By the end of 1967, the project was considered nearly complete, though it would not be officially finished until 1971.[81]

As the Concourse took shape, Waterville's economic prospects dimmed. Population growth was slower than anticipated in the 1962 plan, due in part to the loss of several hundred manufacturing jobs.[82] Birth rates declined, as did the number of building permits for new homes—both negative indica-tors.[83] Even so, a revised city plan looked optimistically at the "program of self-improvement" represented by urban renewal. Many looked hopefully to the city's old Head of Falls area—the city's second urban renewal project—as a potential site for new industrial and commercial development.[84]

## Urban Renewal: Head of Falls

The second phase of urban renewal in Waterville centered on the old Head of Falls neighborhood: the project site ran along the Kennebec River, just a long city block from Main Street and the edge of the Concourse. (See Figure 3.4.) Officially named R-17, it received planning approval in 1964. The city council signed off on it in April 1968, the regional office of HUD approved the plan in June 1969, and funding was delivered in October 1969. Some proper-ties had already been optioned, and demolition began in spring 1970.[85] In the end, $4,751,032 in federal grants were approved.[86]

For many, Head of Falls had long been the obvious starting point for ur-ban renewal in Waterville. It was one of the town's oldest areas and was home to Lebanese and French Canadian factory workers as well as the Wyandotte Worsted woolen mill. The urban renewal authority justified its selection of the area for renewal in language nearly identical to that used for Charles Street, arguing, "The area is adjacent to the Central Business District and has long been a source of blighting influence. One of the most vital entrances into Wa-terville is through the Head-of-Falls section, and the present blight often cre-ates a depressing effect upon the visitor or shopper."[87] The prospect of "de-pressed" shoppers threatened to unravel all the previous work. Slum clearance at Head of Falls, the urban renewal authority noted, would align the space with the new downtown, providing parking, improved traffic flows, and green areas.[88]

Though the original site was eighty acres—four times the size of the Charles Street project—it would gradually be scaled back to thirty acres directly on the waterfront.[89] There were fewer than twenty families living in the cluster of houses when project work was initiated—most houses had been vacant for years, as residents anticipated their displacement.[90] Many of those still living in the area were homeowners, and according to Mitchell—whose father, as well as Rose Warren, were among those property owners—they "did quite well," given federal reimbursement.[91] The most complex component of the project was the relocation of the large Wyandotte Worsted woolen mill to the outskirts of the city; at the time, it was the largest single HUD-financed industrial relocation.[92] Unlike Charles Street, the work at Head of Falls proceeded quickly, without impediments to property acquisition.[93] By project

**Figure 3.4** Aerial photo of downtown Waterville, looking north, ca. 1969. The completed Charles Street project, marked by its vast new parking lots, is just west of Main Street. The Heads of Falls area sits between Front Street and the Kennebec River. Demolition there would begin in 1970.

(Source: Unpublished photo of Waterville Business District, *Morning Sentinel*, n.d. Urban Renewal Scrapbooks, Waterville Historical Society, Waterville, Maine.)

completion, all that remained was the historic "Two-Cent Bridge"—the foot-bridge that since 1901 had been used by mill workers crossing the river to the paper factory in Winslow.[94] Planners hoped to combine open green space with some industrial or commercial development in the future, but those dreams crashed into the reality of a city with stagnant growth and rising taxes.[95] Head of Falls became a makeshift parking lot and a dumping ground for snow re-moval—another empty lot left by the federal bulldozer.[96]

## After Renewal: Meaning and Memory

Willard Arnold championed urban renewal in Waterville but rejected the term. "The real objective is modernization," he claimed.[97] In Waterville, to become modern required the erasure of the past—the removal of the people and build-ings haunting downtown like ghosts of the Depression. But modernization was not simply the erasure of the past; after all, the modernity that Arnold and others envisioned would include the historic Main Street. Main Street has long been an important symbol: its mythology has played a significant role in the ways we think about community—particularly in times of per-ceived social disruption.[98] But Main Street, as a physical place and an idea, is also a site of contention and invention—and, at times, even a symbol of decay.[99] The remaking of Waterville's Main Street revealed a mess of contra-dictions. Its champions invoked both the romantic appeals of a historic Main Street *and* dismissed it as obsolete. The names they chose to mark this hybrid spatial form—"the Concourse" and "the Forum"—signal democratic spaces of convergence; however, this democratic signaling occurred simultaneously with the class-based streamlining of those very urban spaces.[100] These des-ignations read like elegies for the very mixed spaces they replaced—swap-ping the poor, the elderly, the well-worn heterogeneity of old urban life for the motorized and consumerist homogeneity of the postwar suburban ideal. It was a form of democracy figured through the citizen-consumer.[101]

To become modern in this sense—to rewrite the landscape in the image of white, middle-class, suburbanized consumption—was something Water-ville shared with communities across the country. As elsewhere, urban re-newal in Waterville was a response to changes wreaked by the car, as it jammed up downtowns and enabled development on the urban periphery. It was a tool to clear out "blight." It was used to spatially reorganize the community, dis-locating working-class renters and industry from spaces of speculative com-mercial value and solidifying middle-class claims on it. It introduced profes-sional planning practices to the city, and in doing so, it concentrated planning power in a Main Street merchant class.

But urban renewal in Waterville was also shaped by the specific social, economic, and geographic qualities of this small, relatively remote mill town.

There was no racial other to be contained in new public housing; rather, there were working-class white ethnics, whose affordable and convenient housing was sacrificed for the sake of downtown property values. Though to some urban renewal felt like a program imposed from on high and inevitable, this drama unfolded quite personally on a small stage in which all involved worked, ate, slept, and shopped. The material legacy of those changes and the memory of the conflicts remain central to the city's sense of itself and what is possible.

Deindustrialization darkened the horizon in the late 1950s and stalled growth in the 1960s, effectively wrecking Waterville's economy over the following decades. But today, downtown Waterville is in the midst of a renaissance, stemming from large investments along Main Street from Colby College—new development that, in many ways, both undoes some of the work of urban renewal while also potentially fulfilling some of its unrealized goals. The college, which had once been located directly north of downtown, had relocated in 1952 to Mayflower Hill, nearly two miles west, on farmland bought and gifted to the college by city residents as an incentive for staying in town.[102] Over the decades the college and town had increasingly grown apart, a gap accentuated by the relative prosperity of the school and its students and the crushing impacts of industrial downsizing on the town and its full-time residents. An ambitious new college president arrived in 2014, set on marshaling college resources to reinvigorate downtown—viewed as crucial to new student and faculty recruitment. And so, the college began buying up Main Street properties. The largest and most visible intervention has been a new downtown dorm built atop a section of Main Street demolished under renewal. The college is constructing a new arts center a block south of the dorm on Castonguay Square. And just yards past that, at the south end of Main, the college has constructed a boutique hotel where renewal opponent Julius Levine's clothing store once stood. Colby has also renovated buildings across Main from the hotel, converting them into studios for artists. A new streetscape with tree plantings and bump outs is being planned to transform the pedestrian experience along Main.[103] Front and Main Streets, which were converted to one-way traffic in association with urban renewal plans, has been changed back to two-way traffic, thanks to a $7.37 million federal BUILD grant, with an additional $1.9 million from private investment (including Colby).[104] Directly east of Front Street, the $1.5 million RiverWalk opened in 2018, on the site of the former Head of Falls neighborhood and Wyandotte Worsted plant, which had sat empty for decades. The dedication ceremony was highlighted by a speech from George Mitchell, whose parents and brother Paul had lived in a house there eighty years earlier.[105] Private investment has chased the college's investments; one of the major private investors is Bill Mitchell, Paul's son.[106] Over the course of a mere half decade, Waterville's Main Street has been transformed immensely—and in a way that reverses many of changes wrought by urban renewal: returning residents to downtown, increasing density, embracing pedestrianism, slowing down traffic, and—most controversially—eliminating parking. And just as opponents of urban renewal bristled at the sense that their city was being irretrievably altered under their feet, to the benefit of a few, today some residents feel equally alienated from these rapid changes, as Waterville becomes "Colbyville," according to critics.[107] If there was a certain irony to the new shopping spaces created by urban renewal—"the Concourse" and "the Forum"—invoking democratic togetherness, it is perhaps fitting that the most visible space in the new college dorm, at the corner of Appleton and Main, is dubbed "the Commons." It is a name more aspirational than descriptive as the downtown undergoes what is arguably another round of class sorting, invoking the specter of urban renewal and the social fractures it generated.

## NOTES

1. "Interview with Paul Mitchell by Mike Hastings," George J. Mitchell Oral History Project, July 31, 2008, available at https://digitalcommons.bowdoin.edu/mitchelloralhistory/62/.

2. "Urban Renewal: Answer to Problems?" *Morning Sentinel*, August 31, 1961.

3. Edward Relph outlines this tendency in modern planning in *The Modern Urban Landscape* (Baltimore: Johns Hopkins University Press, 1987), 139. Relph cites Jane Jacobs's evocative critique: "An all too familiar sort of mind is obviously at work here, a mind seeing only disorder where a most intricate and unique order exists; the same kind of mind that sees only disorder in the life of city streets, and itches to erase, standardize, suburbanize it."

4. Jon C. Teaford, *The Rough Road to Renaissance: Urban Revitalization in America, 1940–1985* (Baltimore: Johns Hopkins University Press, 1990), 3; Douglas R. Appler, "Changing the Scale of Analysis for Urban Renewal Research: Small Cities, the State of Kentucky, and the 1974 Urban Renewal Directory," *Journal of Planning History* 16, no. 3 (2017): 200–221.

5. United States Census Bureau, *U.S. Census of Population: 1960*, vol. 1, *Characteristics of the Population*, part 21, *Maine* (Washington, D.C.: U.S. Government Printing Office, 1963), 21–11; Appler, "Changing the Scale of Analysis," 203–204.

6. Alison Isenberg, *Downtown America* (Chicago: University of Chicago Press, 2005), 195.

7. Waterville's two urban renewal projects were approved for federal grants of roughly $7.7 million; Boston's Government Center project was approved for nearly $40 million in federal grants. Department of Housing and Urban Development, *Urban Renewal Directory: June 30, 1974* (Washington, D.C.: U.S. Government Printing Office, 1974), 6–7.

8. For overviews on race and urban renewal, see Eric Avila and Mark H. Rose, "Race, Culture, Politics, and Urban Renewal: An Introduction," *Journal of Urban History* 35, no. 3 (2009): 335–347; Michael Carriere and Samuel Zipp, "Introduction: Thinking through Urban Renewal," *Journal of Urban History* 39, no. 3 (2013): 359–365.

9. United States Census Bureau, *U.S. Census of Population: 1960*, 21–38.

10. Amy E. Rowe, "An Exploration of Immigration, Industrialization and Ethnicity in Waterville, Maine" (honors thesis, Colby College, 1999), 145–164.

11. *Manning's Waterville, Fairfield, and Winslow Directory* (Boston: H. A. Manning, 1960). Thank you to Henry Thomas for compiling much of this data.

12. "Most Temple Court Folk Are Reluctant to Move," *Morning Sentinel*, September 1, 1961.

13. Earl H. Smith, *Water Village: The Story of Waterville, Maine* (Unity, ME: North Country Press, 2018), 105–107.

14. *Manning's Waterville Directory*, 1960.

15. Planning and Renewal Associates, *A Comprehensive Plan: Waterville, Maine* (Cambridge, MA: Planning and Renewal Associates, 1962), 32.

16. Smith, *Water Village*, 117–118.

17. Smith, 115–116.

18. *Annual Report of the City of Waterville, Maine for the Year Ending December 31, 1961* (City of Waterville: Waterville, ME, 1962).

19. Planning and Renewal Associates, *Comprehensive Plan: Waterville, Maine*, 8–9.

20. *Annual Report of the City of Waterville, Maine for the Year Ending December 31, 1961*, 17–18.

21. *Annual Report of the City of Waterville, Maine for the Year Ending December 31, 1961*, 21.

22. The merchants bureau formed in 1958 as a branch of the chamber of commerce. It focused on the interests of downtown retailers. Smith, *Water Village*, 121. Planning and Renewal Associates worked with cities across New England, helping them initiate and navigate urban development projects. Planning Services Group, "Planning Services Group Records, 1956–1986 Finding Aid," accessed January 4, 2023, available at http://findingaids.library.umass.edu/ead/mums335.

23. *Annual Report of the City of Waterville, Maine for the Year Ending December 31, 1961*, 21.

24. *Annual Report of the City of Waterville, Maine for the Year Ending December 31, 1961*, 133.

25. Smith, *Water Village*, 121.

26. Waterville's annual reports, throughout the decade, list the makeup of the board and other city committees.

27. "Interview with Paul Mitchell by Mike Hastings."

28. Smith, *Water Village*, 122.

29. Appler argues, "Engaging with the bureaucratic framework that preceded participation in the federal urban renewal program led many small communities to develop, for the first time, professional planning practices." Appler, "Changing the Scale of Analysis," 208–209. See also Nicholas Bauroth, "The Reluctant Rise of an Urban Regime: The Exercise of Power in Fargo, North Dakota," *Journal of Urban History* 37, no. 4 (2011): 522, 533.

30. Planning and Renewal Associates, *A Plan for Downtown Waterville* (Cambridge, MA: Planning and Renewal Associates, 1960).

31. Planning and Renewal Associates, 20.

32. Planning and Renewal Associates, 5.

33. Planning and Renewal Associates, 13.

34. Kelly Gregg, "Placing the North American Pedestrian Mall Concept within the Legacy of Downtown Urban Renewal" (18th National Conference on Planning History, Society for American City and Regional Planning History, Arlington, Virginia, November 1, 2019).

35. Planning and Renewal Associates, *Plan for Downtown Waterville*, 8.

36. Planning and Renewal Associates, 10.

37. Planning and Renewal Associates, 12.

38. Planning and Renewal Associates, 12.

39. Planning and Renewal Associates, 25. See also Planning and Renewal Associates, *Comprehensive Plan: Waterville, Maine*, 42. Relph notes postwar planning's compulsion for the "segregation of activities . . . an indication of the obsession with orderliness that grips all modern planning." Relph, *The Modern Urban Landscape*, 165.

40. This followed the State Highway Commission's recommendations in 1957—a plan opposed by most citizens and members of the Waterville Merchants Bureau (who figured potential shoppers would just speed through town, one way or the other). But the bureau's chairman, Willard Arnold, supported the change—along with the city council and the local newspaper, the *Sentinel*. Smith, *Water Village*, 121–122.

41. Isenberg, *Downtown America*, 170.

42. "Many Downtown Merchants Favor Urban Renewal Plan," *Morning Sentinel*, September 8, 1961.

43. "Many Downtown Merchants Favor Urban Renewal Plan."

44. "Many Downtown Merchants Favor Urban Renewal Plan."

45. "Many Downtown Merchants Favor Urban Renewal Plan."

46. "Area Businessmen See Project as Not Needed, Involving Wrong Site," *Morning Sentinel*, September 2, 1961.

47. "Area Businessmen See Project as Not Needed."

48. "Financing of Renewal," *Morning Sentinel*, August 8, 1962.

49. David Marr, "Charles St. Urban Renewal Plan Attacked at Meeting," *Morning Sentinel*, August 31, 1962. See also "New Citizens Committee on Renewal Plan Meets," *Morning Sentinel*, July 20, 1962; David Marr, "Waterville Urban Renewal Plan Opposed at Meeting," *Morning Sentinel*, July 18, 1962.

50. The clipping is from Mitchell's papers at the Waterville Historical Society.

51. "Most Temple Court Folk," *Morning Sentinel*, September 1, 1961.

52. "Most Temple Court Folk."

53. "Most Temple Court Folk."

54. "Most Temple Court Folk."

55. "Most Temple Court Folk."

56. "Most Temple Court Folk."

57. "Most Temple Court Folk."

58. "Most Temple Court Folk."

59. Herbert Gans, *The Urban Villagers: Group and Class in the Life of Italian-Americans* (New York: Free Press, 1982).

60. "Most Temple Court Folk."

61. "Most Temple Court Folk."

62. For a few of the many examples, see "Time Is Wasting," *Morning Sentinel*, May 2, 1962; "UR Should Stop Fiddling," *Morning Sentinel*, April 11, 1964; "Action, Not Promises, Needed," *Morning Sentinel*, November 20, 1964; "Let's Get Moving," *Morning Sentinel*, May 22, 1965.

63. Merchants Division, Waterville Area Chamber of Commerce, "Urban Renewal Poses Challenge to Waterville Merchants," Urban Renewal Scrapbook, Waterville Historical Society.

64. "Many Downtown Merchants Favor Urban Renewal Plan."

65. "For Better or Worse," *Morning Sentinel*, June 16, 1962.

66. As elsewhere, advocates for urban renewal in Waterville often used medical and pathological metaphors in describing "blighted" areas. See Relph, *The Modern Urban Landscape*, 147; Isenberg, *Downtown America*, 193–194.

67. Everett W. Webb, "Urban Renewal Project Could Give Waterville New Face," *Morning Sentinel*, February 28, 1962.

68. "For Better or Worse."

69. "Mart to Open Today in New Shopping Center," *Morning Sentinel*, August 7, 1963.

70. "Mart to Open Today in New Shopping Center"; "Verrier Awarded Contract for Elm Plaza Construction," *Morning Sentinel*, August 25, 1962.

71. "Verrier Awarded Contract for Elm Plaza Construction."

72. Smith, *Water Village*, 122. Planning and Renewal Associates, *Comprehensive Plan: Waterville, Maine*.

73. Smith, *Water Village*, 122.

74. *Annual Report of the City of Waterville, Maine for the Year Ending December 31, 1962* (City of Waterville: Waterville, ME, June 1963), 136.

75. "Most Temple Court Folk."

76. Smith, *Water Village*, 125–126.

77. Warren v. Waterville Urban Renewal Authority, 210 A.2d 41 (1965).

78. Elliott Potter, "Urban Renewal," *Morning Sentinel*, June 20, 2002.

79. *Manning's Waterville Directory*, 1960.

80. Smith, *Water Village*, 126, 128, 129.

81. *Annual Report of the City of Waterville, Maine for the Year Ending December 31, 1967* (City of Waterville: Waterville, ME, 1968), 136–37.

82. James W. Sewall Company, *Waterville Maine: Comprehensive Plan 1967–1969* (J. W. Sewall Co.: Old Town, ME, 1969), 2, 9.

83. James W. Sewall Company, 4.

84. James W. Sewall Company, 5.

85. *Annual Report of the City of Waterville, Maine for the Year Ending December 31, 1969* (City of Waterville: Waterville, ME, 1970), 33.

86. Department of Housing and Urban Development, *Urban Renewal Directory*, 6.

87. *Annual Report of the City of Waterville, Maine for the Year Ending December 31, 1964* (City of Waterville: Waterville, ME, 1965), 102.

88. *Annual Report of the City of Waterville, Maine for the Year Ending December 31, 1964*, 102.

89. Smith, *Water Village*, 129.

90. Smith, 129.

91. Potter, "Urban Renewal."

92. Potter.

93. Smith, *Water Village*, 129.

94. Smith, 129.

95. James W. Sewall Company, *Waterville Maine*, 30.

96. Smith, *Water Village*, 129.

97. "Urban Renewal: Answer to Problems?"

98. Miles Orvell, *The Death and Life of Main Street: Small Towns in American Memory, Space and Community* (Chapel Hill: University of North Carolina Press, 2012), xi, 38, 139, 240.

99. Isenberg, *Downtown America*, 308, 316.

100. The *Oxford English Dictionary* defines "concourse" as "the condition or state of being so gathered together" and "an open space or a central hall in a large building." "Forum" is "the public place or market-place of a city" or "the place of public discussion."

101. Lizabeth Cohen, *A Consumer's Republic: The Politics of Mass Consumption in Postwar America* (New York: Vintage, 2003).

102. Smith, *Water Village*, 78–80, 109. The college had threatened to move to Augusta.

103. "Downtown Waterville: Rich History, Promising Future" (New York: Beyer Blinder Belle Architects & Planners LLC and BFJ Planning, 2017). For a rundown of college investments in downtown Waterville, see "The Revitalization of Downtown Waterville," Colby News, accessed January 4, 2023, available at https://news.colby.edu/story/the-re vitalization-of-downtown-waterville/.

104. Amy Calder, "$9.14M Downtown Plans Unveiled," *Kennebec Journal*, September 12, 2019.

105. Amy Calder, "$1.5 Million RiverWalk Opens Up to Public," *Kennebec Journal*, September 18, 2018.

106. Smith, *Water Village*, 200n.

107. Smith, 200; Amy Calder, "Some Residents Want Waterville to Take Its Business Elsewhere," *Kennebec Journal*, February 21, 2019; Douglas Rooks, "Waterville Finding Its Future," *Kennebec Journal*, December 20, 2018.

# 4

# Slums as a Problem, Not an Excuse

*Urban Renewal in Growing Texas Towns*

ROBERT B. FAIRBANKS

The history of the federal government's urban renewal program created in 1954 has received rough treatment by historians. Much of the recent scholarship has emphasized that the program—which, among other things, was supposed to provide and improve the housing of the poor (especially minorities)—was hijacked by civic leaders and city officials who wanted to save their downtowns. As a result, urban renewal is most remembered for destroying stable communities and uprooting black residents and other minorities who lived near the central business districts. Failure to provide adequate housing for those displaced, especially African Americans, pushed many into aging white neighborhoods and encouraged increased white flight even while such programs were supposed to be saving the city from the allure of the suburbs. Historians have also critiqued how the superblock and other manifestations of modernism replaced the dynamic and pluralistic settings that had characterized cities and accelerated the trend away from vibrant downtowns.[1] Special attention has also been given to the racist motives of the supporters of much urban renewal.

Although these are important histories of urban renewal, there are other stories that need to be told. For instance, African-American and Mexican-American communities in several Texas cities faced a serious housing shortage during and after World War II, accelerated by their low wages, segregation, and the high costs of housing materials. In response, they often found unregulated and available land beyond city limits and erected primitive, jerry-built dwellings without plumbing and other basic necessities associated with acceptable housing. These unsanitary settings that serviced a transient population were unlike the neighborhood communities that Robert Moses leveled for New York City's Lincoln Square and other large-scale developments.

At a time when planners and academics emphasized the importance of well-designed neighborhoods in shaping healthy families and promoting good citizenship, these instant slums outside of municipal corporations were seen as a danger not only to their residents but also to the nearby city. Understanding that the development of appropriate living space for their minority populations (primarily African Americans and Mexican Americans) was critical for successful city building, some Texas cities used the state's liberal annexation laws and the federal government's urban renewal program to eradicate these slums and develop better neighborhoods. Because of the color line, as well as economic factors that limited where minorities could relocate, civic leaders often opted to annex and salvage those outlying areas that minorities inhabited through rehabilitation of some dwellings and spot clearance of decrepit shacks. That meant not only improving the housing of slum dwellers through the repair of decaying and unhealthy abodes, as well as connecting utilities to the homes of the poor, but also providing parks, playgrounds, libraries, and schools as well as adequate infrastructure for the larger neighborhood. These areas of decline, then, would be transformed into healthy and more attractive neighborhoods. Such action, officials hoped, would also transform those living in the renewed neighborhood, whether white, brown, or black residents.

Although several large Texas cities, such as Dallas, Houston, and Fort Worth, refused to participate in the urban renewal program, smaller towns and cities embraced the new program as a viable way to better the housing situations of African Americans and Mexican Americans by providing improved shelter and better neighborhoods for people who were in desperate need for just that. These small cities and towns also employed urban renewal to reinforce the color line. Their inability to furnish adequate housing, especially for black people during and after World War II, challenged the viability of their segregated housing markets. They therefore used urban renewal as a tool to keep races apart, maintain segregation, and, they hoped, avoid increased racial tensions.

In some Texas cities, urban renewal became attractive to civic leaders as African Americans carved out new neighborhoods in areas beyond the municipal boundaries and free from city regulation. Drawn by inexpensive and underdeveloped land, these newcomers had few other options, so they often located near those areas in lieu of established, crowded black neighborhoods within city limits. Despite the conservative nature of many Texas cities civic leaders understood the need to improve the housing conditions of black residents, whether in the older traditional neighborhoods or those located on the outskirts of municipalities. To do that, local officials in some Texas towns turned to the federal urban renewal program for help. This study focuses on the experiences of two very different Texas communities: one was the small but rapidly growing community of Grand Prairie, an industrial suburb of Dallas, and the other was Lubbock, a mid-sized booming agricultural processing center in West Texas. Despite the dissimilarities of the two places, they shared a commitment to improve housing for their neediest populations, especially minority newcomers, through federal urban renewal. This story provides an alternative to the more common urban renewal narrative that historians have embraced.

## Grand Prairie

Grand Prairie, located thirteen miles west of Dallas, had been a small agricultural community of about 1,600 residents before World War II. That would change in 1940, after North American Aviation (NAA) built a federally funded aircraft manufacturing plant nearby that produced airplanes for World War II. Not only did the factory employ more than thirty-five thousand workers after the government erected a second NAA plant there in 1943, but Grand Prairie also attracted additional businesses that provided ancillary services. In addition, the United States Navy established a flight training school near Grand Prairie at Hensley Field, bordering the North American Aviation plant. The base served naval, marine, and coast guard cadets who took their flight training there. It also housed a radial engine repair center that overhauled thousands of airplane engines.[2]

As a result of the increase of available jobs, Grand Prairie's population climbed to 14,594 by 1950, as it became the fastest growing city in Texas.[3] In a very short period, Grand Prairie went from being a small, quiet, and rural community to an industrial suburb. African American newcomers appeared particularly frustrated as they found it difficult to find adequate housing in segregated Grand Prairie. Indeed, most black people resided in the southwestern fringe of Grand Prairie known as South Dalworth.

Wartime and afterward resulted in significant economic growth for the industrial suburb, even with a short recession after the closing of its large airplane factories. Soon, city officials helped secure Chance Vought in 1948 to share the abandoned aircraft complex with the newly formed Texas Engineering and Manufacturing Company (TEMCO). By 1950 the city's black population, drawn by job opportunities, increased to 641. Although the early African American population in South Dalworth had built modest but sturdy housing in the segregated area, later African American arrivals who came searching for jobs arrived at a time when they had limited access to building supplies, forcing them to rely on whatever materials were available. According to one report, newcomers during and after the war who lived beyond the boundaries of South Dalworth stayed "in lean-to shacks, bus bodies, large boxes and crates discarded by the airplane manufacturer."[4]

Fearful that such growth outside the city limits threatened Grand Prairie's welfare, officials initiated annexation proceedings in 1952 for those areas and completed the process in 1954, expanding its municipal boundaries beyond South Dalworth.[5] As a result of that annexation, the city's black population more than tripled.[6] This also extended the city's legal responsibility to improve the area, which was overwhelmed by the wartime migration.

Meanwhile, thanks to a continued housing shortage, working-class white people moved just northeast of Grand Prairie, where they secured primitive shelter in another unregulated and unincorporated area. The Dallas suburb eventually annexed this area in 1954 and responded to its rapid and chaotic growth on the city's fringes by hiring a city planning firm. Overwhelmed by the wartime surge, the city commission had established a planning commission in 1949 and employed Powell and Powell from Dallas as plan consulting engineers. They not only completed a comprehensive zoning ordinance the following year but provided the city its first comprehensive plan in 1954.[7] One section of the plan, entitled "Provision for Expansion of the Negro Population," addressed the needs of the South Dalworth subdivision with its inadequate infrastructure and unsafe dwellings. Because the crowded South Dalworth area had all the trappings of a suburban slum, the plan called for its re-creation as "an orderly and well-rounded congenial neighborhood section." It went on to suggest that the areas surrounding South Dalworth could "accommodate a considerable expansion of the negro population." The plan called for a "diversity of housing for the negro neighborhood section," including "the better types of homes" along with "minimum cost housing." The plan pointed out that "few if any negroes desire indiscriminate intermingling in white residential areas" but rather that they desire decent neighborhoods. This meant not only improved dwellings but infrastructure, such as new schools, parks, paved street, and utilities, so the area could attract middle-class African Americans as well as promote middle-class sensibilities to the working poor. Such a development would also "avoid conflict with whites." The plan also thought that the city should "furnish schools, parks, shopping districts, and other neighborhood features in proper relationship to population and the area served." It concluded that infrastructure should be provided in South Dalworth as elsewhere throughout the Grand Prairie area.[8]

Convinced that Grand Prairie could benefit from participating in urban renewal, officials contacted the regional office of the HHFA in Fort Worth to find out more about the urban renewal program. When told that a Workable Program was necessary for participation, officials responded to the requirement and submitted a proposal for one in January of 1957.[9] It focused on the prevention of further housing decay through a variety of tactics such as housing and building codes, neighborhood analysis, citizen participation, and community planning.[10] After federal officials approved it, Grand Prairie became eligible to participate in the urban renewal program.

Unable to proceed immediately because the state of Texas had not passed the necessary enabling legislation that would allow cities to carry out urban renewal, the city manager appointed a fifteen-member citizen committee (including two African Americans) to investigate blighted areas throughout the entire city and designate several areas that needed the renewal program, including South Dalworth.[11] That committee also played an important role educating the community about urban renewal. Understanding that black residents who had limited housing options lived in one of the targeted areas, Grand Prairie officials opted to focus on rehabilitation rather than large-scale slum clearance.[12] When state legislators finally passed the necessary enabling legislation in March of 1957, civic leaders appeared ready to proceed.[13] But because the state required an open hearing before the city could hold a referendum on urban renewal, city officials postponed their original February date for the vote until May 31, 1958.[14]

Despite the delay, the HHFA set aside $232,000 for the planning and development of the South Dalworth project and forwarded $17,000 to help with the initial planning.[15] Before the final referendum on urban renewal, the city held a hearing on April 18 that allowed citizens to share their views on the federal program. According to city manager Larry Crow, "not a single person voiced opposition to the urban renewal proposal."[16] Although the newly annexed and larger white slums of northeast Grand Prairie, known as Lakeview, had many similar problems to those of South Dalworth, Crow told reporters that South Dalworth, with its 2,500 black residents, would be the suburb's top priority for urban renewal because its residents "required the benefits of Federal Housing Administration loans more than any other people in our city"[17] and "because there were few other places uprooted blacks could go."[18]

Before the referendum vote, there appeared to be little organized opposition to urban renewal even though neighboring Dallas and Fort Worth would later vote against it. Only several South Dalworth slumlords and ultraconservative Dallas congressman Bruce Alger publicly opposed it.[19] Despite the limited opposition, advocates for urban renewal campaigned hard and spoke at various organizations. For instance, Mayor C. R. Sargent told the Grand Prairie Real Estate Board that the city was "morally bound to spend money on South Dalworth since it had annexed the area."[20] The mayor explained how the improved black neighborhood would not only better residents' living conditions but would provide more tax dollars to the city.[21] The *Grand Prairie Texan* editorialized that "this is probably Grand Prairie's last chance to get rid of blight in S. Dalworth and its surroundings. The task is already insurmountable without outside assistance." It asked, "Why stick our heads in the sand when we have a chance to make the colored residential section an asset instead of a liability?"[22] Another proponent of urban renewal reminded voters that the South Dalworth project was not a slum clearance effort but rather one emphasizing rehabilitation. Those whose homes did not meet the city's housing code standards could renovate them with the help of FHA mortgage insurance, which allowed borrowers to secure loans with no money down and forty years to repay their debt. Indeed, as early as May 8, 1959, the FHA notified Grand Prairie's urban renewal agency that it would accept applications for Section 221 housing loans for the Dalworth rehabilitation project.[23] City Manager Crow was so confident that the referendum would pass that he hired Eugene W. Hill, former urban renewal director at Harlington, Texas, to do a preliminary project plan before the referendum.[24]

Despite the strong support of civic leaders, including the chamber of commerce and the city's newspaper, the final vote on urban renewal was closer than anticipated. At the May 31 special election only 550 voters turned out as 290 people voted for urban renewal and 260 voters opposed it. Black residents from South Dalworth had cast 117 votes in their precinct for urban renewal. The following week, after the referendum, the newly appointed nine-member board of directors for the urban renewal agency formally selected Hill as their executive director.[25] In early July, he hired Carter and Burgess of Fort Worth to draw up a final plan for the renewal of South Dalworth.[26] While waiting for that, residents of the targeted area had initiated their own clean-up and fix-up drives to make their dwellings compatible with the city's new housing code. Commenting on these activities, Hill observed that currently, "the most noticeable effect of urban renewal has been the change of attitude among residents of the area. They've been removing the structures that give the neighborhoods a run-down look."[27] Federal officials informed local urban renewal advocates that the city's cost for urban renewal could be met by in-kind expenditures for the targeted area. Using bond money, the city participated in South Dalworth's renewal not only by providing storm sewers, sidewalks, and curbs but also by furnishing streetlights and water lines. In addition, by combining money from federal and local government, the urban renewal agency erected a recreation center, which became the focal point of the neighborhood with its gymnasium and game room. Urban renewal funds also helped develop a seventeen-acre park and built a school extension for the area's residents. Federal moneys were used to align and pave ten miles of streets and clear 108 structures (some of which were vacant) that could not be restored. Over 150 dwellings would be improved thanks to the FHA's helpful rehabilitation loan insurance, with some of these dwellings even converted from wood to a brick frame.[28] By 1968 all dwellings in the urban renewal area met city housing code requirements, and the fifty-six displaced families were relocated in housing that met the city's standards.[29] Despite the fact that Hill thought the area had "grown like Topsy," it appeared that his claim of how the renewal of South Dalworth had not been a "bulldozer operation" was true, although he did admit that some dwellings had been cleared away, "either for the right of way to make room for a planned shopping center," or because present owners had been unable to finance repairs that "would have brought their structures up to standard." Indeed, when the city manager made reference to the clearance of "151 shaky shacks, crates and boxes that used to be called homes," it appears that he referred to prior abodes abandoned after the war when many left the area to return to their homes. Still, the Grand Prairie Urban Renewal Agency statement that finding replacement housing for the displaced would be the agency's "biggest single job" was true, since many of those uprooted were elderly or disabled with incomes of $200 per month.[30] This underscored the unavailability of adequate housing for the city's black population.

Despite these challenges, the agency completed the suburb's first urban renewal effort by January of 1968. It eventually covered 296 acres and cleared 108 structures, while it also rehabilitated or rebuilt an additional 153 dwellings. Fifty-six families were relocated into housing that met city standards. Just as important, urban renewal improved South Dalworth's infrastructure and provided many amenities expected of a standard neighborhood. Indeed, the city's mayor praised the completed project in South Dalworth, concluding that "for some people living out there this will offer their opportunity for the first time to live as human beings."[31] It is hard to dispute that African Americans experienced a better neighborhood after urban renewal then they had in the 1950s.[32] Indeed, when the National Commission on Urban Problems visited Grand Prairie in 1967, it concluded that the Dallas suburb provided "the finest example urban renewal in the country."[33]

Based on its success with South Dalworth, the Grand Prairie Urban Renewal Agency decided to try once again to use the federal urban renewal program to improve a suburban slum. This time it focused on Lakeview, a massive shantytown created in the southeastern part of Grand Prairie during World War II. Unlike South Dalworth, which had been occupied by African Americans since the 1920s, Lakeview emerged as a temporary housing option for white defense workers employed by North American Aviation. Although some workers were fortunate to secure federal defense housing in places such as Avion Village, the majority of job seekers hired at North American Aviation had little opportunity to find decent shelter as thousands poured into southeastern Grand Prairie seeking defense jobs.[34] House-hungry workers bought undeveloped lots and used whatever materials were available to build dwellings. Others erected rental properties, and less ambitious workers transformed old wooden packing crates or large cardboard boxes into their shelter on untitled land. A few plant employees bought land and erected more stable wood houses on undeveloped subdivisions that still had no sewer or water connections and depended on shallow wells and primitive outhouses. After North American Aviation erected a second plant next to the original one in 1943, crowding got even worse as more workers sought out temporary places to live. By then, Lakeview had earned the nickname Cardboard City, and the area's reputation as a dangerous, chaotic place with bars and brothels cemented its reputation as a suburban slum.

When the war ended in 1945, the housing problems of Lakeview unfortunately did not. During its heyday, the unincorporated land had experienced very little oversight. After the closure of the plants in 1945, many former employees abandoned the area, leaving deteriorating housing with little infrastructure and an ugly and partially abandoned landscape. Those with nowhere else to go continued to live in shacks and temporary housing often not connected to plumbing or electricity. Without housing codes or zoning ordinances, the area continued to deteriorate and soon threatened Grand Prairie's social and physical well-being. Lakeview provided a significant challenge for the city's urban renewal agency after the war. Fearful that the continued deterioration of the suburban slum would create serious social and medical problems if not addressed soon, city commissioners annexed the land and then approved an application for urban renewal in the sum of $162,243 in federal funds to finance surveys and plan the rehabilitation of the Lakeview area.[35] The city eventually received a final commitment of $4,356,928, with the federal government being responsible for three-fourths of the total cost.

The area included 558 structures, including 531 dwellings, and urban renewal officials believed 481 units would need either rehabilitation or clearance.[36] Unsightly, dilapidated housing would be removed to improve the appearance of the neighborhood, while dwellings that could be rehabilitated would benefit from the city's commitment to provide infrastructure. According to Pat Svacina of the *Dallas Morning News*, the urban renewal site was "a no-man's land of 3,755 lots fronting on dirt streets and without city water or sewer facilities."[37] Since the area had always been unincorporated, it had no city services or utilities and not much infrastructure. As a result, the Grand Prairie Urban Renewal Agency initially focused on installing water and sanitary sewer lines and drainage storm sewers. Later the agency designed new streets and paved existing dirt roads while constructing sidewalks and curb guttering for the first time.[38] Before that could happen, renewal officials pushed for the removal of debris and abandoned buildings left from the postwar exodus of the area's former residents.

Incompatible businesses, such as automobile junkyards or chicken farms, were not allowed in most sections of Lakeview now zoned for housing. Anything else that was not appropriate for the residential area was also forced to move. The addition of new zoning restrictions protected the area from future decline. Although the local newspaper claimed that this urban renewal effort would be another rehabilitation project, it would eventually uproot approximately 209 families.

Although destruction of slums through total clearance and rehabilitation of the area's decaying housing stock were significant contributions made by urban renewal efforts, they were not the only factors. According to one source, 328 substandard structures (including those that were no longer occupied) were demolished, and another 200 dwellings experienced significant rehabilitation.[39] Those displaced were rehoused in other sections of the city that met appropriate housing standards. Thanks to FHA Section 221 loans, clearing unoccupied dwellings and improving numerous houses in the area started to attract investors and builders ready to construct housing for working- and middle-class residents. As early as 1969, the Grand Prairie Urban Renewal Agency had sold 110 residential lots (including some buybacks), thanks to successful efforts to improve the Lakeview area in Grand Prairie; 93 others kept their land titles but allowed the city to demolish their weathered dwellings and then built new housing on the improved lots. The combination of rehabilitation along with the erection of various apartment buildings and livable houses along with improved infrastructure and new shopping centers, helped make Lakeview a place to visit rather than an area to avoid. Not only did it have access to a lake, but developers provided a new and attractive golf course too. Lakeview mirrored South Dalworth by receiving new parks and playgrounds and schools along with a community center paid for by Grand Prairie bonds.[40] Although President Nixon's cutbacks in urban renewal money in the early 1970s brought a premature ending to the Lakeview project, it was a success. Once again, as in South Dalworth, the federal government's urban renewal program had not destroyed a viable neighborhood but had created a stable and attractive new residential setting.

Urban renewal in Grand Prairie had achieved its chief goals for both its projects by providing improved housing and more attractive neighborhoods for black and white residents. Despite this achievement, urban renewal in Lakeview reinforced the color line and refused to allow the city's growing number of African Americans access to the Lakeview renewal area. As a result, it provided new opportunities for whites to distance themselves from black neighborhoods. Unfortunately, the few urban renewal efforts that took place in Texas continued to reflect the bigotry of local residents and helped promote segregated cities as a way to avoid racial tensions by distancing the projects that had been built for each race.

## Lubbock

Like Grand Prairie, Lubbock's population increased rapidly thanks to defense spending during the war and a growing agribusiness economy. Not only did its white population surge, but its African American population increased from 2,229 to 10,287 between 1940 and 1960.[41] Because black newcomers faced restrictive laws including racial zoning and planning strategies to limit their living spaces, many ended up in the eastern portion of Lubbock near the city's industrial facilities, often outside the municipal limits. Mexican Americans experienced similar pressure to segregate themselves from Anglo neighborhoods, not from the city council, but from whites in nearby neighborhoods. Low wages and unsafe, unhealthy, housing made the city's black and Mexican American citizens some of its most vulnerable residents.[42]

In response to this housing crisis, urban renewal efforts focused on improving housing opportunities for the city's black and Mexican-American populations, who had come to the metropolitan region in search of jobs.[43] Despite the real need to maintain adequate housing for black workers, civic leaders feared the consequences of this migration. During the war African Americans had found cheap land on the city's fringe and built primitive makeshift housing. Without adequate infrastructure and absent city housing and health codes, this area deteriorated quickly. By 1956, city officials feared the consequences of slum conditions and worried that they not only threatened their occupants but posed health and financial risks for the larger city too. As a result, they decided to include these slum areas as part of a massive annexation package (44.9 square miles) that doubled the city's size. Shortly after annexation, city officials turned to the federal government's urban renewal program to improve these impoverished black neighborhoods that had existed without city services or regulations, some since the 1920s.

It was not the first time Lubbock officials had approached the federal government for housing help. In 1950, city officials had become concerned with serious slum conditions found in an all-black neighborhood known as Queen City nestled between two railroad tracks in southeast Lubbock. They proposed to eradicate the slum area by building a public housing project for African Americans. Although the city had completed a public housing project for Mexican Americans and a few white Anglos, the new effort to build a public housing project failed when the Lubbock Citizens' League, dominated by real estate interests, campaigned hard against it, labeling public housing as socialist. Civic leaders also split over the issue, and despite the support of the *Lubbock Avalanche-Journal*, voters defeated the public housing proposal by an opposition vote of 4045 against the 3941 who supported public housing.[44]

As the problem of inadequate housing continued for a rapidly increasing black population, realtors worked out a deal with local government officials to address the black housing shortage by developing a subdivision for them on city-owned land. The mayor appointed twelve individuals (including three African Americans) to serve in the newly created Southeast Lubbock Development Corporation, whose job was to subdivide and oversee the selling of needed land. Developed in 1954 in the city's southeast section, the one hundred improved lots created on previously unused city-owned land would be available to black buyers for the cost of water, sewers, and street paving. Manhattan Heights, as it was called, became one of the first black residential subdivisions to secure FHA approval for mortgage insurance. Promoters of the project believed this carefully planned neighborhood setting would attract black newcomers as well as African Americans from the slums in Queen City and other underdeveloped areas. Despite the FHA's stamp of approval, African Americans still found it difficult to secure loans from local banks, since many applying had low incomes that made it difficult to save enough for even the minimum down payment needed for the lot and/or dwelling.[45] Others simply faced the prejudice of some bankers. As a result, the development grew slowly. Many house-hungry African Americans found cheaper lots in the same area but with less infrastructure.[46] Unable to build or secure good housing, they turned to less attractive options far short of the city's expectations.

Frustrated by their inability to get the kind of outcomes promoted by the private sector, city officials turned to urban renewal in the mid-1950s, even before the state had passed the necessary enabling legislation for slum clearance. Toward that end, the city's planning board started the process required to participate in the federal urban renewal program. It developed a Workable Program that the HHFA approved on October 16, 1956.[47] Now it just needed the state's enabling legislation that would allow Texas cities to employ all the aspects of urban renewal, including slum clearance.[48]

Although Lubbock's effort shared some characteristics with Grand Prairie's program in that its ultimate goal was to provide proper housing for African Americans in a decent neighborhood, its initial emphasis on slum clearance differed from Grand Prairie's focus on rehabilitation. Lubbock officials had expressed concern about the inexcusable conditions of black housing in the southeast portion of their city when they proposed building a public housing project to replace the Queen City area as early as 1950.[49]

Not only did city officials target the black slum areas for improvement, but they called for the betterment of a blighted Mexican American neighborhood known as Guadalupe, located north of downtown near one of the city's industrial areas. Indeed, city officials secured a planning grant from federal urban renewal officials to clean up this so-called blighted Mexican American area in November of 1956.[50] Lubbock's planners surveyed residents of that district who appeared supportive of the city's apparent plans for rehabilitation of their deteriorating neighborhood. But that changed after city officials proposed to replace its rehabilitation plan with a new emphasis on slum clearance. Upset at how clearance would fracture their community, residents rejected that plan so strongly that urban renewal officials feared the Mexican-Americans opposing slum clearance might resort to litigation.[51] As a result, urban renewal supporters abandoned the Guadalupe project and focused on the slum and blight problems found in the black residential areas, the worst housing in Lubbock. Under the guidance of the planning department, the city secured a federal planning grant not only for the Coronado pilot project (including Queen City and the area around it) but also for the much larger Yellowhouse neighborhood.[52]

As a result of the city's findings from its survey of the thirty-five-acre slum area, Lubbock secured the state's first loan and grant contract for urban renewal in Texas on May 26, 1958.[53] Planning officials targeted the Queen City slum area agreeing it should be cleared and repurposed for industrial use.[54] As a result, the city's first urban renewal program focused not on rehabilitation but on total clearance of the Queen City area, home to many of the city's neediest African Americans. According to the *Lubbock Avalanche-Journal*, this decision made sense because the area "furnished the city with many of its problems of health, overcrowding, public safety and sanitation."[55]

The city had already held a referendum required by state law on November 26, 1957, where voters had shown, by a margin of 1,181 to 160, their willingness for the city to participate in the federal government's urban renewal program. Although urban renewal was already a controversial issue in Texas, both white and black voters supported it decisively, and African Americans who participated in the election voted for it by an eight-to-one margin, knowing full well that their inadequate housing was the focus of the program. The promise of better housing and healthier neighborhoods helped sway their vote. Shortly after the referendum, city commissioners approved the creation of a nine-member Lubbock Urban Renewal Agency, and the city manager selected H. O. Alderson to head that body. Alderson had played a key role in the preliminary work for the planning department's efforts to determine how the city should proceed.

As noted previously, renewal officials debated if recently annexed Queen City should be cleared (because it was inappropriate for housing and could be reused for light industry) or spared the bulldozer since there existed so little housing for African Americans at the time.[56] Not only did its terrain make it difficult to provide adequate housing, but most of the dwellings there were in such poor shape that rehabilitation would not be possible. Of the 238 places of residence in this part of the Coronado project area, only seven met the city's minimum housing standards. Over 100 dwellings were overcrowded, and almost 200 had inadequate plumbing. Indeed, 93 dwellings only had access to a community toilet and a shared shallow well. About 280 dwellings housed approximately 1,174 people, many living in small (288 square feet) dilapidated units often called shotgun houses. Others erected makeshift shacks using scrap lumber, cardboard, tin and used whatever other discarded material they could find. Before long, these small houses had "sagging roofs, little or no foundation, flimsy and leaking walls, along with cracked and warped floors."[57] Like many dwellings found in these areas, most were unfit for habitation, but they remained the only option for impoverished African Americans living in a segregated society. Although the neighborhood included some small businesses and churches, it was riddled with crime and deep poverty. The area's so-called hotel featured prostitution and gambling. Since the area had no paved streets or adequate drainage, it was a mess during rainstorms.[58] It is safe to conclude that this was not the type of neighborhood planners had imagined.

The decision to clear the Queen City area might have explained why the city embraced another adjacent urban renewal project known as the Yellowhouse area (near a canyon with the same name). Black residents had already bought lots in several of its underdeveloped subdivisions. Some were Depression-era shacks in this blighted housing development covering 380 acres, but there appeared to be enough space in Yellowhouse for additional houses and apartments for those displaced through spot clearance.[59] Some dwellings already located there were code compliant, but the area was in need of infrastructure for those houses and was initially designated as a rehabilitation project. Housing officials believed the Yellowhouse urban renewal project area could be converted into decent living space through rehabilitation and spot clearance for the city's growing working-class African American population.[60] Eventually, in 1970, the federal Urban Renewal Agency mandated that the city merge Coronado and Yellowhouse together as Coronado. (See Figure 4.1.) One reason for this was that combining the two adjacent projects, which were soon to be connected by an overpass, would allow the city to take more financial credit for its public works, such as the expenses associated with a new high school, that would help fulfill some of the city's urban renewal financial obligations.[61]

But even with this potential "solution," the renewal agency faced real problems finding adequate housing for those too poor to live in rental housing. According to LURA, "probably no other phase of the Agency's required activities has caused as much initial and continuing concerns as relocation."[62] Because absentee landlords owned much of the land in the Coronado urban renewal area, there were very few places for renters with little money to relocate until the Yellowhouse section of Coronado was rehabilitated and the private sector started erecting relocation housing. As a result, LURA allowed

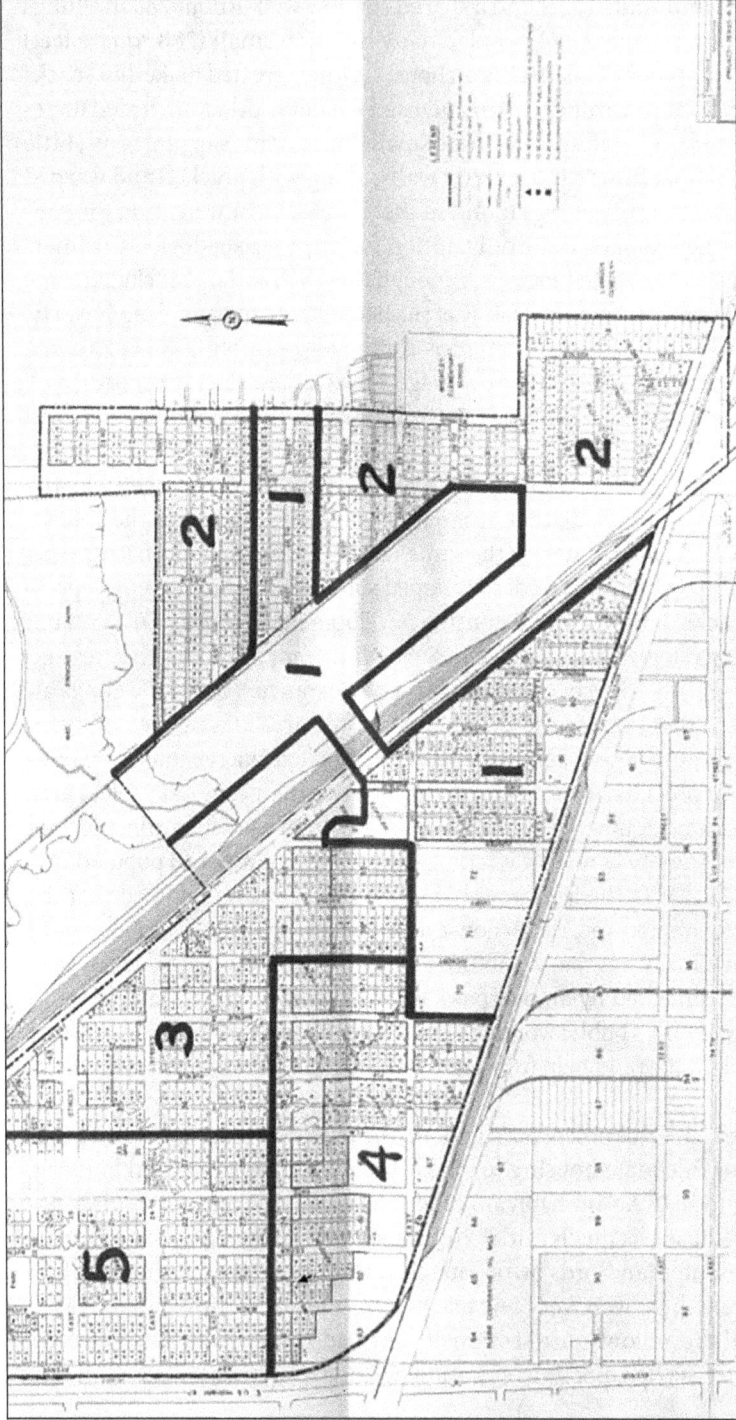

**Figure 4.1** The map of the combined Coronado urban renewal project located in southeast Lubbock, the designated black residential area. It includes area 1, Queen City (the wedge-shaped section isolated by the railroads). Much of the rest of the area on the map was designated as Yellowhouse and was where most uprooted residents were relocated.

(Source: Photo courtesy of Southwest Collection/Special Collections Library, Texas Tech University, Lubbock.)

between one hundred and two hundred families to stay in their slum dwellings and pay their rent to LURA, which had purchased the land marked for clearance.[63]

But many tenants had already lost their dwellings from the larger Yellowhouse area, where a number of homes had been marked for clearance or significant rehabilitation. As a result, the need for replacement housing increased and complicated the relocation issue. Many of the poorer tenants were unable to pay even the little rent required and faced eviction. But realizing that tenants had no other place to go, renewal officials again allowed large families and others to stay in the temporary housing without paying any rent. One renewal official claimed that an out-of-state-landlord was "not collecting rent with any regularity and it appeared that she was either operating a charity housing establishment through an extremely good heart or poor management."[64] Clearance was actually delayed by the federal government until LURA could prove that it had found the necessary housing for those uprooted by urban renewal.[65]

Although the nearby Manhattan Heights addition for African Americans had numerous vacant lots, it required buyers to purchase a single-family lot. but most tenants from the Coronado site simply did not have the resources (either equity in a house or a savings account) to purchase the land or build a house even with the FHA's generous mortgage terms for displaced home homeowners. Had Texas allowed public housing on urban renewal land, finding homes for those displaced from their dwellings would have been much easier.

Although some nonprofit organizations attempted to produce relocation housing, fewer did than anticipated. They also discovered that the process was slower than they had planned. For instance, the Southeast Lubbock Development Corporation, the nonprofit organization and developer of Manhattan Heights, agreed to erect Green Fair Manor, a 236-apartment complex developed for slum clearance relocatees. It promised a completion date near the end of 1963, but the building was not finished until 1965.[66] By then other apartments had begun to appear—including the Coronado Apartments, a low-cost, two-hundred-unit FHA Section 221 apartment complex funded by the Lubbock Masonic Lodge—that would also alleviate the housing shortage.[67] Other groups constructed smaller apartment complexes using FHA mortgage insurance. Finally, over one hundred houses were rehabilitated, and a growing number of dwellings were completed and sold thanks to the efforts of the LURA. Despite the serious problems associated with relocation, the final development of the Coronado renewal project had succeeded in creating vastly improved neighborhoods for the city's African American population.

Although relocation of the displaced had been a serious problem, LURA succeeded in eliminating the Queen City slum and also eradicated blight and slum conditions in parts of Yellowhouse as well as other sections of Coronado by enforcing housing and building codes while providing the necessary infrastructure that made some subdivisions attractive to African-American house hunters. Moreover, the city's noncash grants-in-aid, its share of the urban renewal program, had provided a junior-senior high school as well as two newly enlarged elementary schools with playgrounds. Another urban renewal contribution resulted in the East 26th Street overpass connecting the east side of Coronado with its west side, allowing students to avoid crossing the heavily used railroad tracks to get to school. Thanks to additional urban renewal money, the Coronado project also secured additional parks and paved roads. In addition, that money added a fire station, storm sewers, and water lines and developed new streets for the area, including a paved road to the new high school.[68] This all followed the advice of Koch and Fowler in their City Plan of Lubbock, Texas, 1943.[69] Finally, with the help of FHA mortgage insurance for relocation housing and rehabilitation efforts, builders had completed 335 units of Section 221 housing in the Coronado site and an additional one hundred dwellings had been rehabilitated to meet housing code standards. Urban renewal had provided a variety of quality housing options for residents of the area and developed infrastructure that provided a better neighborhood setting than most residents had ever experienced before.

Although the experiences of urban renewal in South Dalworth, Lakeview, and the Coronado projects differed, they all shared an emphasis on residential improvement as the ultimate goal. Black residents were uprooted for sure, and many were inconvenienced. But with the exception of the original Queen City slum area, part of the Coronado project, these urban renewal projects employed rehabilitation not only by requiring residents to bring their dwellings up to code but by providing necessary utilities and the infrastructure needed to create complete neighborhoods. Schools, parks, and community centers as well as swimming pools were just some of these types of improvements. For these two cities, poor white and African American residents often ended up in better living conditions than they had previously experienced and were not simply sacrificed to slum clearance, as was the case in many larger cities. In these Texas cities, simply clearing out slums and dispersing black residents throughout the area was unacceptable, so officials, committed to segregation, believed that the only way to maintain the status quo of segregation was to improve black neighborhoods through rehabilitation and spot clearance and replacing black areas in decline with better housing and neighborhoods. For them, providing better neighborhoods for black and poor white residents had been the goal, not an excuse to claim the land for other uses such as upscale housing or fancy office buildings.

## NOTES

1. Christopher Klemek, *The Transnational Collapse of Urban Renewal: Post War Urbanism from New York to Berlin* (Chicago: University of Chicago Press, 2011); Samuel Zipp, *Manhattan Projects: The Rise and Fall of Urban Renewal in Cold War New York* (New York: Oxford University Press, 2010); Arnold R. Hirsch, *The Making of a Second Ghetto: Race and Housing in Chicago, 1940–1960* (New York: Cambridge University Press, 1983).

2. Art Leatherwood, "Naval Air Station," in *Handbook of Texas*, Texas State Historical Association, last updated November 1, 1995, available at https://www.tshaonline.org/handbook/entries/naval-air-station-dallas; Robert B. Fairbanks, "Dallas in the 1940s: The Challenges and Opportunities of Defense Mobilization," in *Urban Texas: Politics and Development*, ed. Char Miller and Heywood T. Sanders, 145–147 (College Station: Texas A&M University Press, 1990).

3. United States Census Bureau, *Census of Population 1950, Vol. 2, Characteristics of the Population, Part 43 Texas* (Washington, D.C.; Government Printing Office, 1953), Table 10; Marvin Springer and Associates. *Comprehensive Plan Report City of Grand Prairie 1966*, Archives, Grand Prairie Memorial Library, Texas.

4. "151 Shacks Taken from Blight Areas," *Dallas Morning News*, February 2, 1962, 4.

5. "Annexation Made by Grand Prairie," *Dallas Morning News*, April 11, 1954, 12.

6. United States Census Bureau, *Census of Population 1960, Vol. 2, Characteristics of the Population, Part 43 Texas* (Washington, D.C.; Government Printing Office, 1963), 43–119.

7. R. L. Powell, Letter of Transmission in Powell and Powell, Consulting Engineers, Dallas, Texas in *The City Plan for Greater Grand Prairie, Texas 1954*, Archives, Grand Prairie Memorial Library, Texas.

8. *City Plan for Greater Grand Prairie, Texas*, 1–5.

9. "Town Plan Razing of 636 Houses," *Dallas Morning News*, January 31, 1957.

10. For more on the Workable Program, see Charles S. Rhyne, "The Workable Program: A Challenge for Community Improvement," *Law and Contemporary Problems* 25 (Autumn 1960): 685–704.

11. "G. P. Committee to Inspect Blighted Areas," *Dallas Morning News*, March 21, 1957, 41; "Citizens Endorse Dalworth 'Facelift,'" *Grand Prairie Texan*, n.d., Urban Renewal Scrapbook, Archives, Grand Prairie Memorial Library, Texas. Several months later two African Americans were appointed to the committee, and this helped secure support from the South Dalworth community; "2 Negro Members Added to Renewal Committee," Grand Prairie Texan, May 12, 1957, 9.

12. Grand Prairie Urban Renewal Agency, "Report of Activities for Calendar Year Ending in Dec. 31, 1958," "No Clearance Needed in Plan," *Grand Prairie Texan*, May 19, 1957; both in Urban Renewal Scrapbook, Archives, Grand Prairie Memorial Library, Texas; "South Dalworth Program Planned," *Dallas Morning News*, May 8, 1957, 14.

13. "Slum Clearance Bill," *Dallas Morning News*, May 15, 1957, 3.

14. "Grand Prairie Vote Set on Urban Renewal Plan," *Dallas Morning News*, January 17, 1958, 4; Don Freeman, "Renewal Voting Set by Grand Prairie," *Dallas Morning News*, May 15, 1958, 2.

15. "Grand Prairie Request for Slum Funds Okayed," *Dallas Morning News*, March 27, 1958, 15.

16. "Town Sets Vote for Urban Plan," *Dallas Morning News*, April 25, 1958, 3.

17. "Peek Heads U.R Agency," *Grand Prairie Texan*, n.d., Urban Renewal Scrapbook, Urban Renewal Collection, Grand Prairie Memorial Library, Texas.

18. "Renewal Program Survey," *Dallas Morning News*, May 7, 1958, 3.

19. "Town Snipes at Dallas Congressman," *Dallas Morning News*, May 15, 1958, 35.

20. "Mayor Tells Realtors of Urban Renewal Goals," *Grand Prairie Texan*, n.d., Urban Renewal Scrapbook, Archives. Grand Prairie Memorial Library, Texas.

21. "Mayor Tells Realtors"; "Slum Seen as a Tax Drain," *Grand Prairie Texan*, May 18, 1958, 1.

22. "We Can Be Proud of South Dalworth," editorial, *Grand Prairie Texan*, May 29, 1958, Urban Renewal Scrapbook, Archives, Grand Prairie Memorial Library, Texas.

23. "Minutes," 1958 Grand Prairie Urban Renewal Agency, June 24, 1958 Urban Renewal Scrapbook, Grand Prairie Memorial Library, Texas, Archives; "Home Repairs Seen as Big Part of Urban Renewal," *Grand Prairie Texan*, May 4, 1959, 29.

24. "Dallas Manager Hired at Grand Prairie," *Dallas Morning News*, April 1955, 1.

25. "Renewal to Begin in Grand Prairie," *Dallas Morning News*, June 8, 1958, 5.

26. "Grand Prairie Urban Study Is Launched," *Dallas Morning News*, July 10, 1958, 10.

27. "Grand Prairie Maps Plans for Renewal," *Dallas Morning News*, December 21, 1958, 20.

28. The role of FHA home repair and property development loans in urban renewal have not received the attention they deserve by students of urban renewal. See Judge Glock, "How the Federal Housing Administration Tried to Save America's Cities, 1934–1960," *Journal of Policy History*, April 20, 2016, 303–304.

29. "Minutes, Urban Renewal Agency of Grand Prairie," June 14, 1958, 35–48, Grand Prairie Memorial Library, Texas; "Renewal to Begin in Grand Prairie," *Dallas Morning News*, June 8, 1958, 5.

30. "Relocation Job Looms," *Grand Prairie Texan*, n.d., Urban Renewal Scrapbook, Archives, Grand Prairie Memorial Library, Texas; "Grand Prairie Acts to Expand Renewal," *Dallas Morning News*, December 28, 1958, 10; "Renewal Area Is Enlarged," *Dallas Morning News*, March 12, 1959, 7.

31. Larry Grove, "Grand Prairie Mayor Calls for UR Meeting," *Dallas Morning News*, February 4, 1961, 1.

32. "Renewal Project Completed in Suburb," *Dallas Morning News*, January 13, 1968, 4.

33. "Area Cited for Effort in Renewal," *Dallas Morning News*, October 21, 1967. President Lyndon Johnson appointed the National Commission on Urban Problems (Kerner Commission) to investigate the root causes of the urban riots in 1967.

34. Kristin Szylvian, "Avion Village: Texas' World War II Housing Laboratory," *Legacies: A History Journal of Dallas and North Texas* 4 (Fall 1992): 28–34.

35. "G. P. Committee to Inspect Blighted Areas," *Dallas Morning News*, March 21, 1957; "More Urban Renewal," *Dallas Morning News*, October 31, 1963, 18.

36. Dorothie Erin, "Grand Prairie, Lubbock Tackling Blight," *Dallas Morning News*, May 5, 1966, 3.

37. Pat Svacina, "Urban Renewal Feeling Pinch," *Dallas Morning News*, March 11, 1973, 37.

38. Mike Kingston, "Uphill Road for the Cleanest City," *Dallas Morning News*, February 26, 1971, 2.

39. Kay Crosby, "Urban Renewal Project in Suburb 50% Complete," *Dallas Morning News*, December 1, 1969, 3. The online website on family displacements through urban renewal, 1950–1966, had a lower figure for displacements at the Lakeview view project than what was reported in the newspaper. See Digital Scholarship Lab, *Renewing Inequality*, in *American Panorama*, ed. Robert K. Nelson and Edward L. Ayers, accessed January 4,

2023, available at https://dsl.richmond.edu/panorama/renewal/#view=0/0/1&viz=map
&city=grandprairieTX&loc=14/32.7148/-96.9722&project=3643.

40. "Tradition Continues," *Dallas Morning News*, December 18, 1966, 16.

41. Sixteenth Census of the United States, Characteristics of the Population, Texas,
1040; "Data for Lubbock, Texas Studies in Economics and Business," Vernon T. Clover.
"Some Analytical Tabulations of Census Tract Data in 1960," United State Census Data
for Lubbock, Department of Economics, School of Business Administration, Texas Technological College, 2

42. In 1923, the Lubbock City Council passed an ordinance that kept African Americans from owning or renting property anywhere outside south of 16th street and east of
Avenue C, from Lubbock Fair Housing Complaint 12-9-2019 HUD Form 903, 7. As late
as 1960, 93.8 percent of all black residents in Lubbock lived in the areas defined by the
racial zoning ordinance, 8. Later in 1943 after the court had voided the earlier city ordinance the city's first comprehensive plan called for an industrial buffer zones that separated communities of color from the city's white population.

43. Quote from Lubbock Fair Housing Complaint 12-9-2019 HUD Form 903, 7. As late
as 1960, 93.8 percent of all black residents in Lubbock lived in the areas defined by the
racial zoning ordinance, 8. (M.A. thesis, Texas Tech University, 1966), 22.

44. Roger Schaefer, "Law and Politics in Lubbock: 1945 to the Present," in *Lubbock,
from Town to City*, ed. Lawrence L. Graves (Lubbock, TX: West Texas Museum, 1986) 137.

45. Carl Aaron McNeece, "Family Relocation in the Coronado Urban Renewal Project"
(M.A. Thesis, Texas Technological College 1966), available at http://hdl.handle.net/2346
/20029; Lubbock Urban Renewal Agency, *Draft Environmental Impact Statement for Ma-
hon School Area Housing Rehabilitation Program* (Lubbock: Lubbock Urban Renewal
Agency, October 1975), A-4, available at https://www.google.com/books/edition/Lubbock
_Mahon_School_Area_Rehabilitation/Aeg3AQAAMAAJ?hl=en&gbpv=1&pg=PP6&pri
ntsec=frontcover.

46. John Overton Burford, "The Development of the Coronado Urban Renewal Project," (M.B.A. Thesis, Texas Technological College, 1966) 21–22, accessed January 23, 2023,
available at http://hdl.handle.net/2346/13637.

47. C. W. Ratliff, "A Declining City Area Spurs Plans for Urban Renewal," *Lubbock
Avalanche-Journal*, October 23, 1957, Urban Renewal clipping File, Southwest Collection/
Special Collections Library, Texas Tech University.

48. Urban Redevelopment Enabling Act, H.B. 70, 55th R.S. Leg. Tx., 1957, chap. 98.

49. Schaefer, "Law and Politics in Lubbock," 133–191.

50. Billy George York, "Development of the Urban Renewal Program" (M.A. Thesis,
Texas Technological College, 1959), 49–51.

51. York, 45–57. Ironically, it was R. Davis, owner of land in Coronado, who sued the
city of Lubbock and its suburban renewal agency to enjoin them from taking his land,
accessed January 23, 2023, available at https://www.google.com/books/edition/Lubbock
_Mahon_School_Area_Rehabilitation/Aeg3AQAAMAAJ?hl=en s. His lawsuit also challenged the constitutionality of the state's law allowing urban renewal in the redevelopment
of that slum area. The case was not resolved until 1959, which delayed slum clearance under
the urban renewal act in Texas until the Texas Supreme Court ruled against the suit in 1959.
See Davis v. City of Lubbock, 326 S.W.2d 699 (1959), JUSTIA US Law, accessed January 23,
2023, available at https://law.justia.com/cases/texas/supreme-court/1959/a-7072-0.html.

52. York, "Development of the Urban Renewal Program," 49–51; Burford, "The Development of the Coronado Urban Renewal Project," 35.

53. Burford, 33–34.

54. York, "Development of the Urban Renewal Program in Lubbock," 45–57.

55. C. W. Ratliff, "Two Areas in the City Border of 'Slum' Classification," *Lubbock Avalanche-Journal*, n.d.; Urban Renewal Board Minutes (Lubbock, Texas) Records, 1956–1962, Southwest Collection/Special Collections Library, Texas Tech University.

56. Burford, "The Development of the Coronado Urban Renewal Project," 18.

57. Paul Carlson, "Caprock Chronicles: Lubbock's Queen City Neighborhood," *Lubbock Avalanche-Journal*, March 6, 2020, available at https://www.lubbockonline.com/story/news/local/2020/03/06/caprock-chronicles-lubbocks-queen-city-neighborhood/1569188007/.

58. Carlson, "Caprock Chronicles."

59. "A Report on the Relocation Plan, Coronado Area, Texas R-33," January 15, 1960, Urban Renewal Board (Lubbock, Texas) Records, 1956–1962, Southwest Collection/Special Collections Library, Texas Tech University; Burford, "The Development of the Coronado Urban Renewal Project," 33.

60. "A Report on the Relocation Plan, Coronado Area."

61. "Schedule of Execution Coronado Urban Renewal Area Including Yellowhouse Urban Renewal Area," Urban Renewal Board (Lubbock, Texas) Records, 1956–1962, Southwest Collection, Special Collections Library, Texas Tech University.

62. Relocation document, Urban Renewal Board (Lubbock, Texas) Records, 1956–1952, Southwest Collection/Special Collections Library, Texas Tech University.

63. Urban Renewal Annual Report, March 1962, Southwest Collection/Special Collections Library, Texas Tech University.

64. Lubbock Urban Renewal Minutes, August 18, 1961, (Lubbock, Texas) Records, Southwest Collection/Special Collections Library, Texas Tech University.

65. "Understanding Said Urban Renewal Key," *Dallas Morning News*, October 21, 1967, 20.

66. Charles K. Edgely, W. G. Steglich, and Walter J. Cartwright, "Rent Subsidy and Housing Satisfaction: The Case of Urban Renewal in Lubbock Texas," *American Journal of Economics and Sociology* 27, no. 2 (1968): 113–124.

67. Burford, "The Development of the Coronado Urban Renewal Project," 81.

68. Burford, 65.

69. Koch and Fowler, *City Plan of Lubbock, Texas, 1943* (Lubbock: City Planning Commission, 1943) 9, accessed January 23, 2023, available at http://hdl.handle.net/2346/48575.

# 5

# Three Views of Urban Renewal in Puerto Rico

Douglas R. Appler

E xamining how urban renewal funds were used in U.S. territories and commonwealths creates an opportunity to highlight and understand the historical, political, and cultural circumstances of locations that in many respects have been defined by their marginality. They are part of the United States but do not enjoy the political status or influence of states. Their residents are U.S. citizens, but they cannot vote in presidential elections.[1] Their populations are much more likely to be Hispanic, Native American and Pacific Islander, or black than is the case for most of the mainland United States. Yet for all these differences, they have been, and continue to be, shaped by many of the same policies created with states in mind. This allowed U.S. territories and commonwealths to participate in the federal urban renewal program and use urban renewal funds subject to largely the same rules and restrictions as U.S. states. And while the overwhelming majority of communities to have used urban renewal funds were, of course, in the continental United States, U.S. territories and commonwealths made significant use of the program as well.

With a handful of exceptions, most of the scholarship that examines urban renewal in territories or commonwealths might be described as "urban renewal adjacent" in that it discusses housing, land reform, architecture, or the consequences of urban renewal for diasporic communities.[2] It does not generally approach urban renewal as the main subject of the research. It often helps provide context for the subject but rarely examines the consequences of urban renewal in the territory or commonwealth itself. The lack of awareness of these histories represents a significant missed opportunity for those seeking to understand both who used the urban renewal program and why they used it. For example, the motivations and circumstances driving Puerto Rico to use urban renewal funds bore little resemblance to those that drove many postindustrial cities in the Northeast and Midwest that were struggling to regain their former economic and social centrality. And they were very different from those of the fast-growing cities in the Southwest, where the presence of a large Anglo community was able to establish the parameters of how urban renewal funds would be used.[3] Puerto Rico's land reform efforts in the years preceding and during urban renewal were the result of profoundly different historical forces than those that shaped the majority of the continental United States, and those differences guided its use of urban renewal. In this context, understanding Puerto Rico's use of urban renewal funds invites scholars to learn more about the labor, agricultural, and economic history of the Caribbean Basin, among many other topics, bringing larger regional narratives into the mainstream planning literature. In addition to these differences, even the most cursory examination of how urban renewal shaped the landscape in Puerto Rico begs a discussion of the island's design traditions and influences. Three of these traditions—the casita, the central plaza, and tropical modernism—are addressed in this chapter.

Each of these three topics offers something novel to our understanding of the history of urban renewal in the United States. The casita, the Creole cottage as articulated in Puerto Rico, has been the subject of significant academic attention, although its relationship with urban renewal has not.[4] In many Puerto Rican cities, urban renewal projects were responsible for clearing this building type while, at roughly the same time, casitas were becoming a symbol of home for members of the Puerto Rican diaspora in major U.S. cities.[5] Central plazas, a design tradition associated with the island's long history as a Spanish colony, represent a second area of focus for this chapter. Puerto Rico's central plazas largely managed to avoid the clearance and redevelopment efforts that often characterized comparable downtown districts in other U.S. cities, making its cities anomalous in this regard. Finally, including Puerto Rico in this discussion also presents an opportunity for scholars of high design because urban renewal served as a vector for the introduction of design ideas from throughout the world. This allowed architects working on the island to shape and make a significant contribution to the architectural discourses of the day, including the development of tropical modernism.

By exploring the consequences of urban renewal for Puerto Rico—and, to a much lesser extent, for the U.S. Virgin Islands, Guam, Alaska, and Hawaii—this chapter provides urban renewal scholars with a better understanding of how the program affected a more geographically diverse area.[6] It also helps link conversations about urban renewal to broader, more globally relevant themes. To begin the process of making these connections, this chapter uses data from the 1974 *Urban Renewal Directory*, as well as historic aerial photographs and neighborhood photographs submitted by local governments and housing authorities to either the HHFA or HUD, along with their applications for urban renewal funds. These sources of data, along with other archival publications, help draw attention to Puerto Rico during this period as a place where different histories and theories of architecture, urbanism, and economic development intersected and combined in ways that simply did not happen in other parts of the country, with or without the "helping hand" of urban renewal.

## Urban Renewal in the U.S. Territories

In all, the 1974 *Urban Renewal Directory* identifies eighty-one urban renewal projects of one form or another as having been approved for Puerto Rico, the Virgin Islands, Guam, and the territories of Alaska and Hawaii.[7] Of those eighty-one projects, Puerto Rico accounted for the lion's share with sixty-six projects. The Virgin Islands were approved for seven projects, Guam was approved for two, and Alaska and Hawaii each had three projects approved for planning prior to statehood.[8] Given Puerto Rico's primacy within this group, as well as its almost total absence from conversations about urban renewal, this chapter situates the territory of Puerto Rico at the center of the discussion.

The Commonwealth of Puerto Rico received funding for more urban renewal projects or programs than did thirty-four states.[9] The amount approved for its projects was over $94 million.[10] The project that was approved for the largest amount of federal funding was R-41, the Concordia-Marina project in the city of Mayagüez, which received its approval for planning in 1950 for the amount of $11,704,770.[11] Even on a relatively small island, urban renewal projects in Puerto Rico were not limited to the capital city of San Juan. Rather, Puerto Rico experienced a project distribution pattern similar to that found in most states, where the major central city received more projects than any other city but the number of projects going to outlying areas vastly outnumbered those approved for the major central city.[12] One noteworthy characteristic of Puerto Rico's urban renewal program is that it began very early on, with seven projects approved for planning by the HHFA in 1950.[13] By contrast, the state that ultimately made the heaviest use of urban renewal, Pennsylvania, had only six projects approved for planning in that year.[14] This early start was the result of a number of factors that resulted in a political climate favorable to modernization policies and the intentional production of affordable housing.

## Political Context for Urban Renewal in Puerto Rico

It would be difficult to understand Puerto Rico's heavy use of urban renewal funds without first recognizing that its history is very different from most of the continental United States, particularly as it relates to property ownership and housing. To begin, there has been a European presence in Puerto Rico since 1508, when Juan Ponce de Leon established a settlement at Caparra. This settlement was moved to the modern location of San Juan in 1521, which makes San Juan the oldest European-founded city in the United States, predating St. Augustine, Florida (1565); Jamestown, Virginia (1607); Santa Fe, New Mexico (1608); and Plymouth, Massachusetts (1620).[15] For over three and a half centuries, Puerto Rico was ruled by Spain, and its economy was largely extractive in nature. During the first half of the nineteenth century, Puerto Rico's sugar industry developed, and by the late nineteenth century, it was a major exporter of coffee as well.[16] It is worth noting, however, that Spanish influence over Puerto Rico's economic circumstances slowed the development of strong economic ties with the United States. As an example, during the last ten years of Spanish control over the island, only 2 percent of the coffee exported from Puerto Rico was sold in the United States. Instead, the overwhelming majority went to Spain, Cuba, and non-Spanish European countries.[17] This changed in 1898, when Spain ceded Puerto Rico to the United States at the conclusion of the Spanish-American War. U.S. sugar interests quickly inserted themselves into Puerto Rico's economy, and although the U.S. Congress had passed a joint resolution in 1900 limiting corporations to land holdings of five hundred acres or less in Puerto Rico, many sugar producers simply ignored this law. Farms were quickly consolidated, and property ownership became concentrated in the hands of a few major producers. According to one report, by 1934, 0.4 percent of the farms growing sugarcane produced more than half the island's crop.[18]

Because of the island's heavy reliance on industrial sugar production for its economic base, the inadequate wages and living conditions for workers in these environments, and the sudden consolidation of land ownership taking place in the early twentieth century, there was broad support among the Puerto Rican population for some kind of land reform in the years leading up to urban renewal. The United States Department of the Interior was responsible for administering Puerto Rican affairs, and when it began enforcing the five-hundred-acre rule in 1935, it opened the door for more significant land reform initiatives on the part of Puerto Rico's populist political leaders.[19] It helped that, beginning in 1941, the island's appointed governor was Rexford G. Tugwell. Tugwell was one of the intellectual leaders of the New Deal, and as an administrator, he was responsible for directing some of Franklin Roosevelt's most progressive policy efforts, including the Resettlement Administration.[20]

The years between 1941 and 1964 were described by Henry Wells as the "Muñoz Era" based on the political and ideological leadership provided by Luis Muñoz Marín.[21] The party founded by Muñoz in 1940, the Popular Democratic Party, would adopt as its slogan "Bread, Land, Liberty," and early on it squarely aligned itself with Roosevelt and his New Deal policies.[22] Given the outbreak of World War II and the explosion of federal spending that occurred in Puerto Rico during the war, it could hardly have been otherwise, but there was more to the relationship than simple military necessity.[23] In 1941 Muñoz became president of the senate, and in 1949 he became the first elected governor of Puerto Rico.[24] Muñoz was a progressive populist, and the hallmarks of this era were his efforts to modernize the public infrastructure of the island, provide better employment opportunities by diversifying its economy beyond its historical basis in sugar production, and improve the living conditions of its working population.[25]

Policies launched by Muñoz and the Popular Democratic Party facilitated housing reform efforts in the years leading up to and during the urban renewal era and helped give Puerto Rico significant experience in the process of housing production. The Land Reform Act of 1941 stopped short of taking control of the island's sugar industry, but among its major reforms, it allowed the Land Authority of Puerto Rico to create new settlements on lands unsuitable for industrial agriculture to house those working in the agricultural sector.[26] The Land Authority retained title to the land itself, and the workers were given the right to live on this land, build houses, and use it as they saw fit. The government of Puerto Rico also established a program where it provided plans, materials, and financing for a home, built of concrete, that cost the would-be homebuyer $300 to build, and it developed a variety of other programs to improve the quality of homes and increase homeownership levels.[27] This effort turned workers into homeowners instead of tenants and allowed the Land Authority to at least begin the process of replacing the substandard housing of rural workers with modern homes and small communities. These policies reflect a cultural phenomenon noted by Zaire Dinzey-Flores in which home ownership, even of modest dwellings, was prioritized both by individuals and by the government housing agencies.[28]

While its passage slightly predates the Muñoz era, the Housing Act of 1937 created the Puerto Rico Housing Authority, which became an early vehicle for addressing the island's housing issues and gave Puerto Rico significant experience in the development of public housing. Between 1937 and 1948, the Puerto Rico Housing Authority oversaw the construction of twenty-seven public housing developments designed to house more than 5,700 families.[29] Though its construction was actually initiated by the Puerto Rico Relief Administration, the building that became known as El Falansterio was built in 1937 in San Juan and was Puerto Rico's first public housing project.[30] In addition, as a result of the Housing Act of 1937, the municipalities of San Juan, Ponce, and Mayagüez, the island's largest cities, had oversight of their own housing production programs.[31] It is not surprising, given their prior experience, that the first urban renewal projects approved in 1950 were for San Juan, Ponce, and Mayagüez.[32]

Thus, by the time the Housing Act of 1949 was passed, Puerto Rico was more administratively prepared than most states to put federal funds to work clearing problem neighborhoods. It had maintained much of the progressive political culture that had been common during the New Deal era and was accustomed to encouraging a large government role in making the infrastructural improvements necessary to promote economic development.

## Urban Renewal and Design in Puerto Rico

There are ways in which Puerto Rico's experiences with urban renewal mirrored those of communities in the continental United States. The range of projects undertaken cleared the way for the development of public housing, infrastructural improvements, private development, and public or institutional uses, for example. In other respects, the differences are readily apparent, and few areas provide more visible evidence of those differences than the relationship between urban renewal and design. "Design," as used in this chapter, is inclusive of vernacular architecture, architecture, and urban design. Vernacular architecture might be thought of as the buildings and structures planned and built by people without formal architectural training to serve a specific function.[33] It includes the structures, often very basic, that provide space for people of the world to live, work, and meet their daily needs. It typically reflects local culture, resource availability, and climate demands. To borrow a line from Henry Glassie, "We call buildings 'vernacular' because they embody values alien to those cherished in the academy."[34]

The term "architecture," on the other hand, implies structures that were designed squarely in accordance with those academic values. Architecture in this sense requires a formally trained architect who possesses an understanding of design that has been informed by the developments that gave rise to the modern profession. From Benjamin Henry Latrobe to Louis Sullivan to Zaha Hadid, the appearance, materials, and function of the structure may be radically different from place to place and era to era, but the key ingredient is that the structure is the product of an individual, or group of individuals, with formal architectural training.[35]

As used in this chapter, "urban design," or "urban form," deals with the arrangement and use of buildings and, more specifically, public space. Streetscapes, plazas, public squares, and the parts of cities that, generally speaking, are "outside of the building" are included in these terms. While this defi-nition could be expanded in a number of ways, for the purposes of this anal-ysis, the traditional perspective fits well.[36]

## Urban Renewal and Vernacular Architecture in Puerto Rico

In Puerto Rico, one of the traits that becomes immediately apparent to some-one interested in the history of urban renewal is how radically different the "blighted" urban environments were from what was typically encountered in the continental United States. The neighborhoods cleared were obviously home to high-poverty households, and in that respect, they are similar to many other sites across the United States. But images of these environments also reflect significant differences in the social history of the neighborhoods, a different planning history, and different architectural traditions than typi-cally encountered through urban renewal research. (See Figure 5.1.) The de-molished tenement houses and urban landscapes of Boston's West End, for example, tell the tale of immigration from southern Europe, the formation of urban ethnic enclaves in the new country, and the subsequent loss of com-munity that resulted after clearance. The buildings, streets, and landscapes cleared in Puerto Rico, however, reflected different stories.[37] The vernacular architecture found in Puerto Rico's urban renewal sites was the product of the cultural and economic influences present on a Caribbean island with sig-nificant population pressures, an industrial agricultural base that required large numbers of low-wage workers, and a population that was increasingly moving away from the countryside and becoming more urban. As formerly rural populations migrated in increasing numbers to the cities, formal and informal settlements saw the expanded use of a particular type of house, the casita, adapted to urban environments in increasing numbers. Photographs documenting neighborhoods cleared through urban renewal consistently show casitas in the process of clearance and removal.

Casitas are a variant of the Creole cottage, which has a long history in the Caribbean Basin.[38] In Puerto Rico, casitas reflect the influences of various ethnic groups, including Africans, the Taíno, the Spanish, and others whose cultural traditions have guided decisions about form, style, desired construc-tion materials, building orientation, and the building's relationship to the landscape.[39] Casitas are rectangular structures typically, although not always, made of wood-frame construction, with a gabled roof, and are usually ori-ented so the gable faces the street. They are commonly raised off the ground on stilts to improve airflow and in some cases to elevate the building above

**Figure 5.1** Bayamon, UR-PR-5-12, 1954. A modest casita before demolition.
(Source: RG 207-UR, Photographic Archives, Department of Housing and Urban Development, 1951–1967, Urban Renewal, box 29 of 33: Aibonito, PR-Columbia, SC, National Archives II, College Park, MD.)

wet conditions. They may be one or two bays wide and are typically two or three rooms deep.[40] Urban renewal sites within Puerto Rico frequently included neighborhoods and settlements that were made up of casitas. With that said, however, it is important to remember that these urban renewal projects were initiated because the neighborhoods were perceived to be "blighted." The images included here should perhaps be seen as providing evidence of how this particular building type was interpreted in high-poverty neighborhoods, rather than how they appeared throughout Puerto Rico as a whole.

The city of Arecibo, on the northern coast of Puerto Rico and about an hour's drive west of San Juan, provides an excellent opportunity to examine the vernacular architectural traditions and urban forms present in an area characterized as blighted in order to secure federal urban renewal funds. It also provides a vehicle for understanding some of the challenges facing users of those funds in Puerto Rico and how they differed from those typically encountered in the mainland United States.

In a 2015 piece in *Planning Perspectives*, Florian Urban described a pattern of informal settlement in the San Juan neighborhood of La Perla, sandwiched between Old San Juan to the south and the Atlantic Ocean to the north. In La Perla, throughout most of the twentieth century, differences between privately and publicly owned lands guided the level of formality of the dwellings that were built within the same settlement. In Puerto Rico, the beach itself was (and is) publicly owned, but there is nothing preventing land adjacent to the beach from being privately owned.[41] These private lands could be rented to low-income households for the purpose of constructing a home, with the understanding that the tenant owned the home but not the land.[42] This arrangement is essentially a ground lease, similar in some respects to what many community land trusts use today to keep housing prices low while allowing low-income households to build equity in the house itself. This system facilitated the production of housing that was reasonably substantial but hardly permanent. On the other hand, areas closer to the water—on public land where residents did not enjoy the right of occupancy resulting from having paid the owner a monthly rent and where hazards from the ocean were more pronounced—were much less desirable for obvious reasons. These areas were more perilous and were occupied by squatters. These distinctions had an effect on the shape and condition of the structures built near the beach. In contrast to the more substantial houses built on private lands that were being rented, the houses on the beach were clearly less substantial, less expensive to build, and more exposed to catastrophic damage from the ocean.[43]

Four urban renewal projects took place in Arecibo, and in-progress images from various urban renewal projects in the city of Arecibo can be used to provide additional support for Urban's observations about casita form and location as a spatial representation of poverty. (See Figure 5.2.)

Images of Arecibo's "La Playa" urban renewal projects show that the buildings closest to the water had the smallest footprints, suggesting that they were occupied by squatters and lower-income households, while the building footprints gradually became larger as the distance from the water increased. Further demonstrating the spatial preferences of those with even slightly great-

**Figure 5.2** Arecibo, UR-PR-5-5, 1957. Aerial image of the urban renewal area at Arecibo showing the shrinking size of casitas based on proximity to the water.
(Source: RG 207-UR, Photographic Archives, Department of Housing and Urban Development, 1951–1967, Urban Renewal, box 29 of 33: Aibonito, PR-Columbia, SC, National Archives II, College Park, MD.)

er access to resources, while all of these images show very modest housing, the structures at the top of the hill, in Figure 5.3, provide evidence of concrete walls, stone or slab foundations, and electrical service, while houses closer to the water, in Figure 5.4, appear to be made of found materials, are raised off the ground to accommodate the tides, and do not appear to be connected to electricity, even though power lines are visible in the background. The overall impression of the area presented in the photographs is one of extreme fragility and vulnerability to the elements. This is obviously a part of the city where residents are living at the literal and figurative edge of the community. According to the *Urban Renewal Characteristics Report*, just over 1,700 families were displaced by the first three phases of the La Playa project.[44]

While the form of blighted neighborhoods may differ from many found in the continental United States and may reflect very different social forces, the subsequent reuse of the spaces cleared should be quite familiar to urban renewal researchers. For all intents and purposes, everything in Figures 5.3 and 5.4 that looks remotely like a residential structure was cleared through one of Arecibo's urban renewal projects. Everything that was rebuilt was made

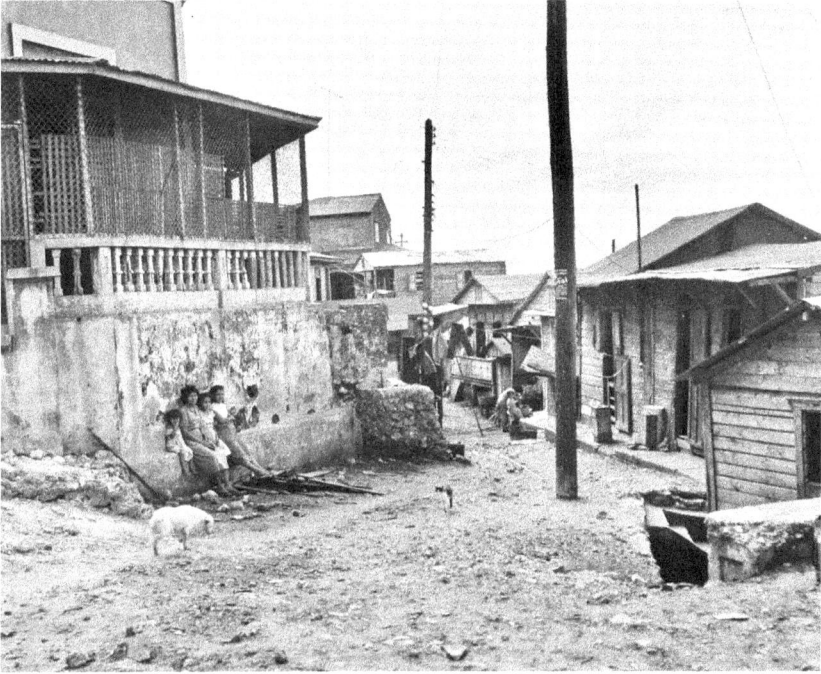

**Figure 5.3** Arecibo, UR-PR-5-26, 1957. While still a high-poverty neighborhood, houses at the top of the hill have concrete foundations and electricity.
(Source: RG 207-UR, Photographic Archives, Department of Housing and Urban Development, 1951–1967, Urban Renewal, box 29 of 33: Aibonito, PR-Columbia, SC, National Archives II, College Park, MD.)

of concrete. An admittedly informal survey completed by the author found only one residential structure in the urban renewal area that reflected this earlier architectural tradition. In place of a neighborhood of extremely modest residential structures, this section of the modern city now has a divided highway separating the city from the ocean, a concrete and boulder seawall instead of a beach, and large concrete commercial and institutional spaces that include a hospital, a technical school, a major chain retail store, and houses and small-scale commercial buildings with flat roofs made of concrete instead of the traditional casita.

Without further research to try to track the fates of the individual householders affected by Arecibo's urban renewal projects, it is difficult to say how closely the experiences of the residents of the "blighted" area mirrored the experiences of their counterparts in the continental United States. Whether they ultimately moved to private housing in a different neighborhood, for example, or were provided with housing in a newly constructed public housing project is presently unknown. From the perspective of architectural tra-

**Figure 5.4** Arecibo, UR-PR-5-26, 1957. The houses closest to the water appear to lack electricity and are much more precariously situated.
(Source: RG 207-UR, Photographic Archives, Department of Housing and Urban Development, 1951–1967, Urban Renewal, box 29 of 33: Aibonito, PR-Columbia, SC, National Archives II, College Park, MD.)

ditions in this neighborhood, however, it is easy to see that urban renewal hastened Arecibo's transition away from one traditional vernacular architectural form and toward another form that was made possible by the industrial production capabilities of the mid-twentieth century. The replacement of traditional casitas with new building types that took advantage of the properties of concrete is also emblematic of Puerto Rico's embrace of a design language that was being adopted by many other Caribbean locations. It was still vernacular, and was still shaped by the local climate, geography, and cultural norms, but it did so with very different forms and materials.

The town of Toa Baja, between San Juan and Arecibo, was also shaped by urban renewal, but through a much smaller project. And, like Arecibo, it was primarily a clearance project. Project number UR-PR-5-22, known as the "Jalisco" project, was approved for planning in January of 1954 and completed in April of 1961.[45] The project cleared a neighborhood of modest but tidy casitas. According to the *Renewing Inequality* map, eighty-eight families were displaced by this project. One part of the neighborhood consisted of houses that were evenly spaced and aligned by a uniform "build to" line, shown prior to demolition in Figure 5.5. The other part had a looser connection to the existing street pattern but also included small, tidy houses. The houses were primarily made of wood and were one or two bays wide and one or two rooms deep. The site was adjacent to an existing public housing project that had been recently completed (though it was not, strictly speaking, an urban renewal project). As a result of the Jalisco project, the dirt road in front of the houses was paved and the houses were cleared and subsequently replaced with a smaller number of much larger, two-story, flat-roofed concrete houses that are not radically different in style from the concrete structures found in Arecibo or the public housing projects that were just built on site. Differences among the newly constructed houses on this street, however, suggest that they may have been developed privately rather than publicly as a group. The redevelopment itself was not part of the urban renewal project, only the clearance and street infrastructure.

In Mayagüez, on Puerto Rico's west coast, casitas again were by far the dominant form of housing that was present in the neighborhood, and that

**Figure 5.5** Toa Baja, UR-PR-5-22, c. 1956. Casitas cleared for the Jalisco project in Toa Baja.
(Source: RG 207-UR, Photographic Archives, Department of Housing and Urban Development, 1951–1967, Urban Renewal, box 29 of 33: Aibonito, PR–Columbia, SC, National Archives II, College Park, MD.)

was what was cleared for urban renewal. (See Figure 5.6.) In this case, however, the site was used for the North Concordia public housing projects. The North Concordia projects, from the outside at least, have a great deal in common with the "tower in the park" philosophy driving the design of public housing developments in the continental United States during this period. (See Figure 5.7.) The shade-creating concrete latticework of the brise-soleil, however, suggests a small nod to the climate as was common in tropical modernist architecture of the period. Though originally a form of vernacular architecture, this practice had been adopted by western architects and entered the architectural mainstream in Brazil, India, and other tropical climates worldwide.[46]

Despite their frequent destruction through urban renewal projects, casitas have had an enduring legacy, particularly for Puerto Ricans who left the island and established homes and communities in the radically different urban environment of New York City. These diasporic communities have had their own experience with urban renewal, and the casita has played a role

**Figure 5.6** Mayagüez, UR-PR-3-3, 1957. Disassembly of a casita in Mayagüez. Photo by Arturo Cifuentes.

(Source: RG 207-UR, Photographic Archives, Department of Housing and Urban Development, 1951–1967, Urban Renewal, box 29 of 33: Aibonito, PR-Columbia, SC, National Archives II, College Park, MD.)

**Figure 5.7** Mayagüez, North Concordia public housing.
(Source: Google Street View, May 2016.)

there as well. Rather than being destroyed and replaced, they became symbols of resilience. As has been noted by Luis Aponte-Pares and others, large parts of Puerto Rican neighborhoods in Harlem, the Lower East Side of Manhattan, and the South Bronx were cleared by urban renewal projects. The residents who remained often built casitas in the vacant lots that were left behind as a way of maintaining the neighborhood's cultural traditions and creating community spaces.[47] Though threatened by more recent development, several of these casitas still exist in New York City, honoring a vernacular architectural form and transplanting it into a new environment.

## Urban Renewal and Urban Design in Puerto Rico: The Central Plaza

One aspect of Puerto Rico's experience with urban renewal that is immediately apparent from the aerial views of in-progress urban renewal projects, and that may help distinguish Puerto Rico's experience from its mainland counterparts, is the relationship of any given city's urban renewal project to its historic central plaza. Puerto Rico experienced roughly four hundred years of Spanish colonial rule prior to being ceded to the United States in 1898, and as a result, its urban environment was shaped by roughly four hundred years of Spanish colonial city planning traditions. The government of Spain was much more involved in dictating the form of its colonial cities than were other European powers, and its expectations can be found in a set of documents commonly known as the Laws of the Indies. The Laws of the Indies offer incredibly detailed instructions for anyone establishing a permanent settlement in the New World under the authority of the Spanish crown. The influence of the laws can be seen throughout South America and Central America, to a more limited extent in North America, and in Spain's former colonies in Asia as well. Though many of Puerto Rico's cities predate the codification of the Laws of the Indies by King Philip II of Spain in 1573, the laws' guiding principles had largely been standard planning practice for as long as Spain had been colonizing the New World.[48] One of the most enduring legacies of that tradition is the organization of small cities and towns around a central plaza.

In some respects, the central plaza might be seen as occupying a place of honor similar to the courthouse square in county seat towns across the continental United States. It is a public space of at least some elevated social significance, it is a landmark, and it provides a location where certain civic activities and transactions take place. But while there is a great deal of variety in the layout and arrangement of courthouse squares, only one ingredient is truly essential: the courthouse. Courthouse squares can exist with a variety of other land uses adjoining, whether they be commercial, institutional, or religious; they may be bordered by hotels, train stations, public parks, libraries, schools, parking lots, private property, or other facilities. They may or may not actually be square. And, of course, communities that do not hold the county seat may simply possess a city hall or municipal building with no particular distinguishing characteristics from a planning or urban design perspective.

The formula for a Spanish colonial central plaza is much more rigid, and it reflects the central role the Catholic Church played in Spanish government and in the process of conquest and colonization. Law 126 of the Laws of the Indies declares that when laying out a new settlement, "In the plaza no lots shall be assigned to private individuals; instead they shall be used for the buildings of the Church and royal houses, and for city use,"[49] though it does recommend establishing public buildings on the plaza for commercial and retail activity. Other laws more specifically define the nature of the urban fabric itself, drawing attention to desired dimensions, how the plaza is oriented to cardinal points, how the streets should meet the plaza, the desire for an arcaded colonnade to protect pedestrians, and so forth.[50] While practical circumstances required some variation in how these regulations were applied, the basic ingredients were the same. As a result, the central plaza remains present in the cities of many of Spain's former colonies and, particularly in smaller communities, continues to serve its historical function as a social and administrative center. In two of the oldest European cities in the continental United States, St. Augustine and Santa Fe, the historic central plazas still follow this pattern to varying degrees, though with some significant modern intrusions. In the small cities and towns of Puerto Rico that initiated urban renewal projects, the plaza typically contained the same mix of land uses and design language as proscribed by the Laws of the Indies. They were almost universally rectangular, they contained a church or cathedral in the most prominent location, there was a municipal building, and while there was some flexibility, there was often a market building, armory, police station, school, or other public building occupying the other sides of the rectangle.

In the continental United States, the downtown urban core was often the target of urban renewal projects, and public officials were only too happy to reshuffle the proverbial deck, introducing new land uses, new people, and new forms of urbanism to replace the old. In contrast, in Puerto Rico, a collection of aerial photos from twenty-six different urban renewal projects shows a different pattern. They do not show a single project taking place that affected a building on the central plaza. While whole residential neighborhoods might be cleared and rebuilt as superblocks, creating an interesting juxtaposition of planning traditions, central plazas remained untouched. (See Figure 5.8.) In some respects, this is a surprise, given the high concentration of public buildings surrounding the central plaza and the fact that the center of town would typically be expected to be the most congested and would likely have the oldest and most problematic real estate. From this sample, however, the central plaza seems to have been kept entirely off limits for urban renewal projects. There could be a number of reasons for this. One might be that the presence of so many religious structures fronting the plaza made the prospect of condemnation for an urban renewal project politically unappealing. Another possibility is simply the required connection between urban renewal projects and housing. The Housing Act of 1949 and its successors stipulated that urban renewal funds could be used for projects that were either predominantly residential in character before the project took place or would become predominantly residential after the project was completed, but there had to be some type of connection to residential use. Because of the planning histories of these cities, there was not a pattern of privately held residential land surrounding the plaza, and the introduction of housing onto the plaza through an urban renewal project would have been a significant deviation from centuries of planning tradition. These land use patterns and practices may have simply made it more logical for planners and public officials to look elsewhere for land that could take advantage of these funds.

Of course, it is also possible that the twenty-six projects included in this analysis do not accurately reflect the experiences of each of Puerto Rico's other forty urban renewal projects. Performing an analysis based on archival sources does have its limitations, as records are never as complete as one would like. The one project the author knows of that took place on a central plaza in Puerto Rico was nondestructive and occurred in Old San Juan, which devel-

**Figure 5.8** Utuado, UR-PR-5-14, c. 1956. This image shows some of the richness of Puerto Rico's city planning history. Visible are Spanish colonial city-planning practices as reflected in the central plaza and grid, a modernist housing project from the late 1930s/early 1940s, and an informal settlement on the banks of the river. The urban renewal project cleared the informal settlement.

oped a general neighborhood renewal plan intended to support the newly implemented local historic district.[51] Clearly this remains an area that would benefit from future research.

## Urban Renewal and Architecture
## in Puerto Rico: Tropical Modernism

While casitas reflect the vernacular architectural form most heavily affected by urban renewal projects in Puerto Rico, and central plazas seemed to have survived relatively unscathed, it is worth recognizing that the structures built as a result of urban renewal demonstrate Puerto Rico's engagement with a variety of design discourses taking place throughout the United States and the world during the mid-twentieth century. In Puerto Rico, one of the most visible modernist products of the urban renewal era was project UR-PR-5-2. Better known as "El Monte," this residential and commercial complex was constructed in Hato Rey, on the perimeter of San Juan. El Monte was approved for planning in 1950, and it is pictured, apparently complete, in publications from the mid-1960s, although the 1974 *Urban Renewal Directory* does not list it as being completed until 1970.[52]

El Monte is significant in one sense because it provides a clear example of a high-poverty neighborhood being cleared and subsequently redeveloped for higher-income housing—a trend that links it with many early urban renewal projects in the continental United States. El Monte is probably most significant, however, because of the design for the complex that was built once the site was cleared. Like the North Concordia housing projects in Mayagüez, though on a much larger scale, the community that became known as El Monte can be seen as a place where multiple threads of design history intersected, representing a significant contribution to the development of tropical modernism. It also demonstrates how the study of urban renewal in uncommon geographic locations can lead scholars and students to discover unexpected, but important, aspects of both design and social history.

To begin, the design pedigree of El Monte places it comfortably in any conversation about postwar modernist architecture created with or without the influence of the federal urban renewal program. The first phase of El Monte was designed by Edward Larrabee Barnes, with a landscape design by Hideo Sasaki, and the firm Reed, Basora and Menendez.[53] The second phase was designed by the firm Torres, Beauchamp, and Marvel and landscape architect Hunter Randolph.[54] Barnes and Sasaki are both recognized as belonging to the upper echelon of mid-to-late-twentieth-century designers.[55] A student of Walter Gropius and Marcel Breuer at Harvard prior to World War II,

Barnes had a long and distinguished career and was known for embracing the relationship between the building and its social and physical context.[56] Some of his better-known works include the Haystack Mountain School of Crafts, the Walker Art Center, and the Dallas Museum of Art, among others. For his part, Sasaki was chair of the Landscape Architecture Department at Harvard's Graduate School of Design from 1958 to 1968, and he was responsible for the design of many of the corporate campuses that defined suburbia as established companies left dense urban areas for greener, more auto-friendly pastures.[57] Marvel was a mid-1950s graduate of Harvard's Graduate School of Design who built his career in Puerto Rico and worked throughout the Caribbean, designing the U.S. Embassy buildings in Guatemala and Costa Rica, the Federal Courthouse in the U.S. Virgin Islands, and the Education Building at the University of Puerto Rico, where he also taught.[58] El Monte suited the skills of these designers well in the sense that the two crescent-shaped towers demonstrate an awareness of the tropical context by including shaded outdoor spaces that were integral to each apartment and in that the landscape and facilities planned by Sasaki were an essential part of the complex, meant to be part of how residents enjoyed outdoor life at El Monte. (See Figure 5.9.) In addition to the towers, the complex includes a series of 124 concrete townhouses, a swimming pool, and an extensive network of pedestrian paths that take residents through what is now a mature landscape of native and exotic flora.[59] It is comparable in many respects to contemporary urban renewal–related work, such as Mies van der Rohe's Lafayette Park

**Figure 5.9** El Monte, UR-PR 5-2, 2019. First phase designed by Edward Larrabee Barnes, Hideo Sasaki, Reed Basora, and Menendez; second phase designed by the firm of Torres, Beauchamp, and Marvel and by Hunter Randolph. (Source: Author's collection.)

in Detroit or the towers designed by I. M. Pei for the Society Hill project in Philadelphia. In 2008 El Monte was recognized by the Cultural Landscape Foundation as one of its Marvels of Modernism.[60]

El Monte is important to this discussion because of its connection to urban renewal, but it is also important because it calls attention to Puerto Rico's significant history with the modernist movement and the role that movement played during the dawning of the postcolonial era worldwide. As Europe's empires crumbled following World War II, many former colonies looked to modern architecture to provide a break from the imagery associated with a colonial past while expressing a desire to engage with the global community on equal terms.[61] Even in Brazil, which shed its colonial status in 1822, modernism, including architecture, became a vehicle for transcending the country's European past and forming a new national identity.[62]

Modern architecture meshed well with the progressive vision articulated by Luis Muñoz Marín and the Popular Democratic Party. Established in the mid-1940s, the Comité de Diseño de Obras Públicas helped Muñoz and the island's appointed governor, Rex Tugwell, distance modern Puerto Rico from the political connotations of its Spanish design traditions and the generic colonial revival fantasies that had been pushed by U.S. interests on the island since the early twentieth century.[63] It also helped launch the careers of some of Puerto Rico's most significant architects. The Comité de Diseño de Obras Públicas consisted of Henry Klumb, Osvaldo Toro, Miguel Ferrer, and Luis Torreregosa, with Richard Neutra acting as a consultant.[64] While Puerto Rico remained a U.S. territory, the years immediately following the war saw a major shift in Puerto Rico's status and level of political autonomy. It began electing its own governor, Muñoz, in 1948 rather than having one appointed by the federal government, and it obtained its status as a commonwealth (*estado libre asociado*) in 1952.[65] Within this environment, two members of the Comité de Diseño de Obras Públicas, Toro and Ferrer, became arguably the most visible Puerto Rican architecture firm of the era. Through their modernist design for the Puerto Rico Supreme Court Building, they made a clear argument for a government and judicial apparatus that looked forward toward the future, rather than one that relied heavily on the architectural symbols of its colonial past. Their work on other buildings, particularly the Hotel La Concha, has also been recognized as presenting a uniquely Puerto Rican use of space and "yielding a building specific to the island."[66]

## Conclusion

Puerto Rico had a fascinating relationship with urban renewal that helps demonstrate the many potential benefits of trying to understand the program from a range of geographic perspectives. Its progressive postwar political environment contrasted starkly with the conservatism that defined the mid-century political environment on the mainland. Its rapidly urbanizing population differed from the experience of Rust Belt cities being abandoned for the suburbs. Its long history as a Spanish colony, and then as a U.S. territory, shaped its urban form, its politics, its economic circumstances, and many other aspects of life on the island. Recognizing these differences helps connect Puerto Rico, and the United States as a whole, to a variety of regional and global stories that are rarely, if ever, seen as part of the story of urban renewal.

## NOTES

1. Tom C. W. Lin, "Americans, Almost and Forgotten," *California Law Review* 107, no. 4 (August 2019): 1249–1302.

2. For examples relevant to Puerto Rico, see generally Zaire Z. Dinzey-Flores, "Temporary Housing, Permanent Communities: Public Housing Policy and Design in Puerto Rico," *Journal of Urban History* 33, no. 3 (2007): 467–492; Florian Urban, "La Perla—100 Years of Informal Architecture in San Juan, Puerto Rico," *Planning Perspectives* 30, no. 4 (2015): 495–536; Jose A. Fernandez, *Architecture in Puerto Rico* (New York: Architectural Book Publishing, 1965); Rose Muzio, "The Struggle against 'Urban Renewal' in Manhattan's Upper West Side and the Emergence of El Comité," *Centro Journal* 21, no. 2 (2009): 108–141.

3. Lydia R. Otero, *La Calle: Spatial Conflicts and Urban Renewal in a Southwest City* (Tucson: University of Arizona Press, 2010); see also Fairbanks, this volume.

4. Urban, "La Perla"; Luis Aponte-Pares, "Casitas Place and Culture: Appropriating Place in Puerto Rican Barrios," *Places* 11, no. 1 (1997): 52–61; Joseph Sciorra and Martha Cooper, "'I Feel Like I'm in My Country': Puerto Rican Casitas in New York City," *Drama Review* 34, no. 4 (1990): 156–168.

5. Sciorra and Cooper, "'I Feel Like I'm in My Country.'"

6. Alaska and Hawaii did not achieve statehood until 1959, and both participated in the federal urban renewal program while territories.

7. Department of Housing and Urban Development, *Urban Renewal Directory: June 30, 1974* (Washington, D.C.: U.S. Government Printing Office, 1974), 2–5.

8. Department of Housing and Urban Development.

9. According to the 1974 *Urban Renewal Directory*, Puerto Rico received more funding than did Maine, New Hampshire, Vermont, Rhode Island, Delaware, Maryland, West Virginia, Florida, Kentucky, Mississippi, South Carolina, Minnesota, Wisconsin, Arkansas, Louisiana, New Mexico, Oklahoma, Iowa, Kansas, Nebraska, Colorado, Montana, North Dakota, South Dakota, Utah, Wyoming, Arizona, Hawaii, Nevada, Alaska, Idaho, Oregon, and Washington State.

10. Department of Housing and Urban Development, *Urban Renewal Directory: June 30, 1974*, 2.

11. Department of Housing and Urban Development, 34.

12. Department of Housing and Urban Development, 33–36.

13. Department of Housing and Urban Development.

14. Department of Housing and Urban Development, 39–57.

15. John W. Reps, *The Making of Urban America: A History of City Planning in the United States* (Princeton, NJ: Princeton University Press, 1965), 33, 90; David J. Weber,

*The Spanish Frontier in North America: The Brief Edition* (New Haven, CT: Yale University Press, 2009), 48, 59; David D. Hall, *Puritans in the New World: A Critical Anthology* (Princeton, NJ: Princeton University Press, 2004), 9.

16. Laird W. Bergad, "Agrarian History of Puerto Rico, 1870–1930," *Latin American Research Review* 13, no. 3 (1978): 63–94.

17. Bergad, 69.

18. S. L. Descartes, "Land Reform in Puerto Rico," *Journal of Land and Public Utility Economics* 19, no. 4 (1943): 397–417.

19. Descartes, 399, 400.

20. Henry Wells, *The Modernization of Puerto Rico: A Political Study of Changing Values and Institutions* (Cambridge, MA: Harvard University Press, 1969), 142–146; Louis C. Gawthrop, "Images of the Common Good," *Public Administration Review* 53, no. 6 (1993): 508–515.

21. Wells, *Modernization of Puerto Rico*, 17.

22. "New Party Formed in Puerto Rico," *New York Times*, July 22, 1940, 8.

23. José L. Bolivar Fresneda, "The War Economy of Puerto Rico: 1939–1945," in *Island at War: Puerto Rico and the Crucible of the Second World War*, ed. Jorge Rodriguez Beruff and José L. Bolivar Fresneda, 111–138 (Jackson: University Press of Mississippi, 2015).

24. Wells, *Modernization of Puerto Rico*, 17, 198.

25. Perhaps the most well-known aspect of this postwar push for modernization was Operation Bootstrap, an approach that used a favorable tax structure and low wages to attract industrial investment from the mainland in hopes of developing the island's industrial base. See generally A. W. Maldonado, *Teodoro Moscoso and Puerto Rico's Operation Bootstrap* (Gainesville: University Press of Florida, 1997); Deborah Berman Santana, "Puerto Rico's Operation Bootstrap: Colonial Roots of a Persistent Model for 'Third World' Development," *Revista Geographica* 124 (1998): 87–116; William W. Goldsmith and Tomas Vietorisz, "Operation Bootstrap, Industrial Autonomy, and a Parallel Economy for Puerto Rico," *International Regional Science Review* 4, no. 1 (1979): 1–22.

26. Wells, *Modernization of Puerto Rico*, 137.

27. Wells, 174.

28. Dinzey-Flores, "Temporary Housing, Permanent Communities."

29. Dinzey-Flores, 474.

30. Dinzey-Flores, 471, 472.

31. Wells, *Modernization of Puerto Rico*, 174.

32. Department of Housing and Urban Development, *Urban Renewal Directory: June 30, 1974*, 33–36.

33. See generally Henry Glassie, *Vernacular Architecture* (Bloomington: Indiana University Press, 2000); Thomas Carter and Elizabeth C. Cromley, *Invitation to Vernacular Architecture: A Guide to the Study of Ordinary Buildings and Landscapes* (Knoxville: University of Tennessee Press, 2005).

34. Glassie, *Vernacular Architecture*, 20.

35. Being hired as an architect in the United States, for example, typically requires possessing a license to practice architecture. A case can be made that anything designed by someone without that license is not, in fact, architecture.

36. Lance J. Brown and David Dixon, *Urban Design for an Urban Century: Shaping More Livable, Equitable, and Resilient Cities* (Hoboken, NJ: Wiley & Sons, 2014), xi.

37. Herbert Gans, *The Urban Villagers: Group and Class in the Life of Italian Villagers* (New York: Free Press of Glencoe, 1962).

38. Aponte-Pares, "Casitas Place and Culture."

39. Urban, "La Perla," 511; Aponte-Pares, "Casitas Place and Culture."

40. Urban, "La Perla," 511–515; Aponte-Pares, "Casitas Place and Culture"; Sciorra and Cooper, "'I Feel Like I'm in My Country.'"

41. Urban, "La Perla," 502.

42. Urban.

43. Urban.

44. Housing and Home Finance Agency, Urban Renewal Administration, *Urban Renewal Project Characteristics: December 31, 1965* (Washington, D.C.: U.S. Government Printing Office, 1967), 61.

45. Department of Housing and Urban Development, *Urban Renewal Directory: June 30, 1974*, 35.

46. Harris J. Sobin, "Veils and Shadows: Le Corbusier in North Africa, 1928–1936," *Proceedings of the Meeting of the French Colonial Historical Society* 19 (1994): 187–199; Daniel A. Barber, "Le Corbusier, the Brise-Soleil, and the Socio-Climatic Project of Modern Architecture 1929–1963," *Thresholds* 40 (2012): 21–32; Christopher Mackenzie, "Le Corbusier in the Sun," *Architectural Review* 193 (February 1993): 71–74.

47. Sciorra and Cooper, "'I Feel Like I'm in My Country'"; Aponte-Pares, "Casitas Place and Culture."

48. Axel I. Mundigo and Dora P. Crouch, "The City Planning Ordinances of the Laws of the Indies Revisited. Part I: Their Philosophy and Implications," *Town Planning Review* 48, no. 3 (1977): 247–268.

49. Mundigo and Crouch, 256.

50. Mundigo and Crouch, 254, 255.

51. Urban Renewal and Housing Administration of Puerto Rico, *Old San Juan and Puerta de Tierra: A General Neighborhood Renewal Plan* (Rio Piedras, Puerto Rico: Urban Renewal and Housing Corporation, 1964).

52. Jose Antonio Fernandez, *Architecture in Puerto Rico* (New York: Architectural Book Publishing, 1965); Department of Housing and Urban Development, *Urban Renewal Directory: June 30, 1974*, 34.

53. "El Monte," Cultural Landscape Foundation, accessed September 23, 2019, available at https://www.tclf.org/sites/default/files/landslide/2008/elmonte/history.html.

54. "El Monte."

55. Douglas Martin, "Edward Larrabee Barnes, Modern Architect, Dead at 89," *New York Times*, September 23, 2004, sec. A, 25; Anne Raver, "Hideo Sasaki, 80, Influential Landscape Architect, Dies," *New York Times*, September 25, 2000, sec. B, 9.

56. James Stevens Curl and Susan Wilson, *The Oxford Dictionary of Architecture* (Oxford: Oxford University Press, 2016); Larry Speck, "Edward Larrabee Barnes," September 1, 2003, available at https://larryspeck.com/writing/edward-larrabee-barnes/.

57. Raver, "Hideo Sasaki, 80, Influential Landscape Architect, Dies," sec. B, 9.

58. Deacon Marvel, "Thomas S. Marvel, 1935–2015," *Architect's Newspaper*, February 12, 2016, available at https://www.archpaper.com/2016/02/thomas-s-marvel-1935-2015/.

59. Marvel; David Kaufman, "Modern Times—San Juan," *Monocle* 66, no. 7 (2013): 196–202.

60. "El Monte," Cultural Landscape Foundation.

61. Siddartha Sen, *Colonizing, Decolonizing, and Globalizing Kolkata: From a Colonial to a Post-Marxist City* (Amsterdam: Amsterdam University Press, 2017), 133–190.

62. Styliane Philippou, "Modernism and National Identity in Brazil, or How to Brew a Brazilian Stew," *National Identities* 7, no. 3 (September 2005): 245–264.

63. John B. Hertz, "Authenticity, Colonialism, and the Struggle with Modernity." *Journal of Architectural Education* 55, no. 4 (May 2002): 220–227.

64. Hertz, "Authenticity, Colonialism, and the Struggle with Modernity," 222–223.

65. Wells, *Modernization of Puerto Rico*, 198, 231, 232.

66. Hertz, "Authenticity, Colonialism, and the Struggle with Modernity," 224.

# 6

# The "Developer of Last Resort"

*The New York State Urban
Development Corporation*

Stacy Kinlock Sewell

taff members of the New York State Urban Development Corporation
have variously described how local officials reacted when they arrived
at small cities around the state. Stephen Lefkowitz, the UDC's chief counsel, remembered landing in one upstate city in 1968 "like paratroopers into
this place." Robert Litke, just hired as a UDC regional director, recalls that
in Utica, "they all came racing out onto the lawn, it was probably the biggest
event ever." Alan Talbot, UDC's program director, compared their helicopter to that in the Fellini film *La Dolce Vita*. The opening sequence depicts a
helicopter carrying a large hanging statue of Christ that is cheered by construction workers and sunbathers and others throughout Rome as it flew over
the metropolis. Upon landing, Talbot recalled that local officials would "take
us to these pathetic piles of urban renewal inactivity and plead with us for
help."[1]

The recollections from the UDC staffers are somewhat at odds with the
perspectives of the officials who were still hopeful about redevelopment in
their cities. As desperate as Utica may have been, the city's mayor expressed
confidence that his city might provide the right short-term investment opportunity the UDC needed.[2] Deindustrializing cities like Utica and Newburgh
may have had tremendous hopes for development, particularly for the urban
renewal projects that had been stalled for years if not decades. But they also
had reservations about the new agency, which seemed to overpromise. It was
"a good idea but something of a dream," stated the mayor of Kingston. Yonkers's mayor quipped, "We'll be in there the next day with our problems."

Their caution stemmed from deep knowledge of their local communities' sabotaged renewal plans that resulted from political feuds, racial tensions, or defaulting developers.[3]

The brief years from the late 1960s to the early 1970s presented New York State with a moment to initiate bold plans that would solve local government logjams and secure deep-pocketed developers. The UDC, created by Governor Nelson Rockefeller and approved by the state legislature in the wake of Martin Luther King Jr.'s assassination, was designed as a means to facilitate private investment in the development of downtowns, industrial sites, civic and private structures, and housing. The public-private agency was a solution to city officials' frustration with the political fallout, loss of developers, and languishing downtowns that stemmed from decades-long urban renewal projects. The UDC solution was attractive because it held out hope that the cosmopolitan and technocratic UDC men might smooth over the long-standing partisan squabbles and racial tensions. Our helicopter passengers were to wade into the political ragweed grown from a decade of urban renewal.

This chapter discusses the UDC as "the developer of last resort," the moniker invoked by Edward J. Logue, the UDC's president and CEO. He was referring to the agency's primary role of cleaning up after urban renewal by developing sites and assuming risk that the private sector avoided.[4] Rockefeller, who touted himself as the nation's "buildingest governor," established the agency to burnish his record and create redevelopment opportunities in the wake of urban crisis.[5] As the developer of last resort, the UDC had a platform from which it could challenge assumptions held by small cities about affordable housing and the future of their downtowns. The UDC's moment came when support for urban renewal was on the wane and local leaders were potentially more willing to invite to their cities this entrepreneurial agency that brandished equal parts state power and market-oriented development solutions.[6] Logue explained how the UDC married urban renewal cleanup with a social vision: "The priorities were in housing, to build projects, basically on urban renewal land. Why? Because it didn't cost anything. . . . There was a fairly significant inventory of unbuilt urban renewal land across the state."[7] The UDC stood as an acknowledgment that clearing land and displacing residents was a mistake, and so it built mostly on vacant parcels. The agency's expansive and progressive agenda resulted in the creation of thirty-three thousand units of middle- and low-income housing, three New Towns, among them Roosevelt Island in New York City, and dozens of commercial and civic structures throughout the state.[8]

As a state agency empowered by Governor Rockefeller to be accountable first to the state and its investors, the UDC was, by design, remarkably independent from the localities in which it ultimately worked. It was a public authority, and according to Nicholas Dagen Bloom, it was in the forefront of a movement by states to develop independent authorities with enormous powers to plan and develop projects.[9] But by its own method, the UDC had to be "invited" by local communities to deflect skepticism and embrace co-operation from the outset.[10] Nevertheless, as an entity that surveyed local markets; secured architects, developers, and builders; and then usually exited, the agency never created deep local roots. Even though a city's leaders had invited the UDC, the local community often remained guarded about the agency because it was exempt from local zoning and building codes. But the state's small and midsize deindustrializing cities had few other options, and the UDC built more than nine thousand housing units in these communities.[11]

The UDC was also financially independent, stemming from what Eric David Petersen has called an "imaginative" use of credit by which the agency issued its own bonds to finance its projects. It did not have to seek approval from the legislature or voters. In this way the UDC could develop projects and assume risk that a private developer would not bear and investors had a safe investment. The agency's bonds sold well, and thus the UDC had tremendous leverage with which to go about its work.[12]

It is worth remembering that federal and state urban renewal dollars were disbursed to tear down structures, not to build new ones. Private developers relied upon public subsidies to rebuild, aiming for profit. Inflation in the construction industry for financing, materials, and labor steadily rose throughout the 1960s. Premature clearance and thousands of tenants in need of new housing haunted redevelopment outcomes nationwide. Ghost projects typically served as parking lots for years, and rebuilding might not occur at all when cities could not sell their parcels or find willing developers.[13]

New York State received more urban renewal dollars than almost any other state, and under Governor Rockefeller, these funds had been dispersed widely to small and medium-sized cities, as well as the larger cities. New York's Housing Finance Agency and Division of Housing and Community Renewal were mobilized to assist in the state's building frenzy. These agencies provided small cities and even villages with assistance they could not refuse, so while federal grants made urban renewal happen, the state also contributed tremendous sums. When the federal program was just beginning, small cities and towns could not meet the federal obligation to provide one-third or one-fourth (for cities under fifty thousand) of the costs. To rectify this shortfall, New York voters approved a 1958 bond initiative so the state would cover one-half of a locality's urban renewal share, as well as provide technical assistance. Mayors and city councils jumped at the chance to start or restart programs that had stalled, and dozens of places—some with only a few thousand people—rapidly created renewal agencies and community advisory groups, designated blighted areas, and applied for state money to assist them in their bid for even greater funds to carry out renewal. For example, the state's contribution to a multimillion-dollar project in Nyack (population six thousand) reduced that village's contribution to a scant $100,000.[14]

Because New York was so prolific in its urban renewal projects, it had a sizable problem with rebuilding, a predicament the UDC was designed to remedy. The UDC held many roles as developer and financier, architect and planner. It was not, however, an urban renewal agency. Most of its projects were built upon land that was already cleared; either the land never contained structures in the first place or, very likely, urban renewal demolition had rendered it empty for some time. In practice, the UDC's job was to clean up *after* urban renewal. The new agency had a huge canvas upon which to work, since only 7.2 percent of the land that had been cleared by urban renewal had been rebuilt, a mere 198 of 2,741 acres redeveloped. One regional planner reported in 1970 that 44 of the state's 130 urban renewal projects had been underway for nine to eighteen years, "and some have simply been abandoned."[15] Stephen Lefkowitz, who drafted the UDC legislation and was Rockefeller's aide at the time, recalled that "cities in New York State were hemorrhaging, and in particular, they had cleared large chunks of their central business districts. . . . And so, they had nothing to fill it up with and no ability to really build."[16] Logue concurred when he explained that the UDC's mission "was to improve the speed and quality of development of the State's backlog of vacant urban renewal sites."[17]

## The Housing Solution Upstate

For Logue and the UDC, high-density, low-cost housing for middle- and low-income residents and the elderly became an antidote to the problem of rebuilding after renewal. This was for three reasons: (1) housing could redress the harm done to the disproportionately black and poor communities targeted by renewal; (2) rising rents and shortages of housing plagued many urban areas in the state; and (3) federal and state mortgage subsidies made housing construction financially feasible. Approximately 80 percent of UDC projects were in housing. The housing solution perfectly combined the elements of social benefit and market sense. UDC aimed to build in nearby lower-density and suburban areas, as it attempted to do in the areas north of New York City. Though the cities received about 85 percent of the UDC housing, much of it near urban renewal sites, the enabling legislation did not stipulate that the agency limit itself to the dense urban core.[18]

Governor Rockefeller's 1965 message to the legislature regarding housing needs for the state urged a continuation of funding for his administration's endeavors in housing construction. The governor noted the expansion of the middle-income housing program, the low-rent assistance program, and the urban renewal program. His message drew no connection to the fact that it was the very expansion of urban renewal that contributed heavily to the need for the low- and middle-income programs. Housing shortages in the state were just becoming realized in the middle of the decade, first in New York City. Former state rent administrator Charles Abrams noted that the gathering crisis was a result of twenty-five years of demolition. Abrams warned, presciently, that had the city built on vacant land, it would not have this crisis.[19] State housing officials had urged "massive slum drives" in small communities throughout the state, and housing in many areas was alarmingly "worse than anything in big city slums."[20] In the next few years, housing shortages would be reported around the state, spilling over from urban communities.

After a decade of demolition, the state faced an enormous shortage of moderate- and low-income housing.[21] The small and midsize cities and the suburban communities of the state shared the view that the least desirable outcome of urban redevelopment would be to build high-density housing for middle- and low-income residents and families. Given the choice, the communities of upstate New York wanted commercial and high-value projects and the suburbs wanted the convenience of nearby commercial development. They had undeveloped parcels, substandard housing, and growing minority communities, but they were also apprehensive about the mission and methods of the new state entity. Small and midsize cities north of New York City are particularly illustrative of the conundrum faced by local officials who could not say no to the package offered by the UDC, though they bristled at the more progressive notions held by Logue and the agency.[22]

City leaders in upstate communities—scrambling to undo the harm of industrial and commercial decline—were reticent to create new housing. At best, housing was a means to bolster employment in the construction industry. At worst, it would entice low-income families to their cities, draining tax coffers and increasing demands on public services. Kingston officials expressed fear that the city might "overbuild" public housing. Newburgh's "war on welfare" resulted from the belief that migrants from the South came to exploit generous public assistance.[23] Simply put, some cities did not want to build adequate replacement housing, and there was no requirement that they do so. While cities pressed for commercial development, the UDC countered with offers of affordable housing. To illustrate these divergent aspirations, this chapter first turns to Utica and Newburgh before turning to a third urban renewal location, Westchester County. Utica and Newburgh had both experienced industrial decline and population loss, and subsequently, both appealed in earnest for UDC help.

Utica, a city in central New York with approximately one hundred thousand people in 1960, had seen its population and it fortunes decline in the 1950s with the closing of its last textile mill. Outside the city was a vibrant General Electric plant, which contributed to regional but not central city growth. The city's Democratic political machine was the object of scorn in the press for turning a blind eye to corruption and criminality, revealed in the "Sin City" scandals of 1957–1958. The bars and brothels that were in the shadow of city hall became the targets of a vast renewal plan that had the support of bipartisan forces eager to scrub the city's reputation.[24] As approved by the federal Urban Renewal Administration in 1957, Project #1 would demolish a dense cluster of the downtown district's commercial and governmental buildings. Relocation from the twenty-two-acre parcel would be required for 273 households, many of which included rooming house occupants. Utica's share of the $2.28 million plan would be $550,000, one-half of which would be in noncash site improvements. The city believed its share would be recouped by the future disposition of the improved site, which was to include a new city hall, a theater, shopping, and vast parking facilities.[25]

A 1957 headline in Utica's daily paper declared, "Utica Now Tops in Redevelopment," and the city added several more projects during the next decade that included proposals for a parking garage, department stores, and a new city hall. Hundreds more residents and industrial properties would be displaced through code enforcement and a plan to extend an arterial between downtown and the New York State Thruway. The city of Utica lost approximately nine thousand of its residents in the decade of the 1960s, but that number is thought to be inaccurate because it does not count the families that moved to the peripheral areas that had been annexed by the city decades earlier. The outlying suburban districts of New Hartford and Whitesboro were unavailable to the city's black population, who were relegated to a public housing complex that had been built during World War II and set between railroad tracks and the highway.[26]

By the late 1960s, Utica's urban renewal program was stalled. The city had experienced tribulations in the past decade, but one interested observer noted that "psychologically, the most depressing thing for Utica has been the failure of Urban Renewal."[27] The first developer went bankrupt. The mortgage for the second developer was foreclosed upon, and a third developer was found to be unacceptable to HUD. Fraudulent dealings within the city's urban renewal agency were under an FBI investigation, and outside of the new city hall lay "a graying skeleton . . . that has become the biggest source of civic embarrassment."[28] Enlargement of the renewal area might save the project, argued the city planner, if it was connected to Genesee Street, the city's main commercial thoroughfare. Utica's new mayor, a young Democrat, promoted the idea, which included an office tower, a department store, and a hotel. He also included a modest housing proposal, which stunned some Uticans, who rallied in opposition. Housing was "not right for the area," according to the most vocal city council member, a mayoral contender.[29]

Almost as soon as the UDC was established, the mayor of Utica sent the agency its first invite. He wrote Logue that the city's seventeen-year-old urban renewal project "is one of the oldest in the nation."[30] Not long after the UDC's dramatic helicopter landing outside city hall, three hundred units of low- and middle-income housing was proposed smack in the middle of Utica's downtown. It was not the solution Uticans on the city council envisioned, and the proposal was defeated three times by the common council. The mayor implored the UDC to use its override powers and contract directly with the city's urban renewal agency, which caused a predictable firestorm when his secret request was revealed by a political opponent. Meanwhile, some Uticans, such as the Social Workers for Social Action, supported the housing plan and worked to highlight the fact that the city was plagued by substandard housing.[31]

By dangling the carrot of future commercial development, the UDC was able to complete the Kennedy Plaza Apartments, a three-hundred-unit development that included a high-rise tower and low-rise units near city hall and the central business district. The city's revolving door of mayoral administrations made the UDC something of a political football as the UDC's dealings with the city stretched over the course of five years and three mayors. By 1973, Mayor Hanna announced he would no longer deal with the UDC until it paid the $42,300 he said the UDC owed the city to replace tax revenue.[32] A hotel did finally open in the urban renewal area in 1979, but subsequent development fell far short of the city's vision and remains underdeveloped today.[33]

The situation facing Newburgh shared similarities with Utica when Newburgh beseeched the UDC to come to its city in the spring of 1968. And, like Utica, Newburgh would be the unwitting recipient of housing. Newburgh's stalled urban renewal plans had resulted from a bitter dispute about where to site relocation housing following the displacement of approximately six hundred families. As in Utica, the dormant renewal area was enlarged over the course of several years, increasing the number of people to be displaced. Officials in Newburgh recognized that they needed to create replacement housing. The city's Republican leadership favored a site next to the city's existing low-income housing tower. Others wanted the renewal area—with its splendid Hudson River view—reserved for commercial development, including luxury housing and an office tower, and both proposals were met with suspicion by the city's black community.[34]

The UDC could, it seemed, solve the dispute. An outside entity might calm all parties and quell the gathering protest. The UDC opted to build outside of Newburgh's renewal area, away from low-income housing and in proximity to single-family homes. A rezoning battle ensued, but the UDC plan, perceived as Newburgh's "last chance," moved forward. The 375-unit Lake Street Houses, low rise but high density, would become something of a prototype for UDC upstate housing. (See Figure 6.1.) It was with this project that the UDC hit on its standard occupant formula: 70 percent of the units for middle-income residents, 20 percent for low-income residents, and 10 percent for the elderly. Logue proudly called his formula "representative housing." Liza-

**Figure 6.1** Governor Rockefeller and Peter Brennan, member of the UDC Board of Directors and head of the New York Building and Construction Trades Council, arriving in Newburgh for the Lake Street Houses groundbreaking ceremony, October 29, 1969.

(Source: Augusts Upitis.)

beth Cohen has noted that although the UDC paid the most attention to income and age diversity, "it carefully considered race as well." It could be no other way in cities like Newburgh, in which one-third of the black community had been displaced and was in need of housing.[35]

City officials and business leaders repeatedly requested that the UDC accelerate the surveys and studies necessary for downtown development, even as the Lake Street Houses opened to much fanfare in October 1971. The modest housing complex, with the industrial park adjacent, was not all that Newburghers had in mind. With relentless urging by the city council, the UDC spearheaded negotiations with developer William Zeckendorf for a deepwater container port. The city also discussed an office tower, luxury condominiums, and a downtown retail complex with other developers. None of these were feasible or marketable, the UDC contended. In the end the UDC sponsored a municipal building that contained the public library and the board of education offices—again, short of expectations. As in other cities, the UDC was the bearer of bad news to frustrated city officials.[36] And, like in Utica, vast swaths of the downtown remain undeveloped even today.

To officials in these upstate cities, a UDC bait-and-switch maneuver was at work. Utica and Newburgh—along with Buffalo, which had suffered from an undeveloped urban renewal project since 1949—were among the earliest cities to request assistance from the UDC. Leaders in these cities held out hope that their cities could offset tax deficits with grand commercial plans.[37] As a public corporation, the UDC was specially situated to press reality upon local officials. As a statewide entity, the UDC assessed local projects, evaluated their commercial appeal, and understood the potential for securing developers. It could provide unvarnished truth to small-city mayors and urban renewal officials who had received encouragement from local business leaders and grants from the federal and state agencies that had initially funded the renewal programs. Certainly the UDC did build numerous commercial and civic structures (notably the Niagara Falls Civic Center, Uncle Sam Mall in Troy, the 213-acre Outer Loop Industrial Park in Rochester, and the eighteen-story Lincoln National Bank in Syracuse), as these were what upstate mayors most wanted. But from its start, the UDC projects marked for priority in 1968 were those that planned residential units.[38] In the eleven communities where the UDC initiated projects during its first year of operation, all included a residential component.[39] As such, UDC used the "carrot" and held out the possibility that it would develop nonresidential projects in many of the cities in which it worked. In exchange, UDC wanted to build housing, and through 1973 it relied heavily upon federal subsidy to do so. Logue favored this swap, an arrangement that resulted in much needed housing. In the city of Albany, for example, the mayor wanted the UDC's assistance with a Greyhound bus terminal—a project "of limited appeal to me," wrote Logue.

He knew that was all the mayor really wanted. Logue, however, wanted to build housing in the city's impoverished Arbor Hill neighborhood, which was, as he said, "of great appeal to me."[40] Both were developed by the UDC. The swap was part of the UDC's impressive contribution to the state's supply of affordable housing. That these cities ultimately settled for the sure thing—UDC housing—is a modest positive legacy of urban renewal.

## The Housing Solution Downstate

When the UDC was created, legislators had assumed that the "Urban" in its title would confine the agency's work to cities. But there was no stipulation in the legislation that this must remain so. The notion that was emerging by 1970—that multiunit housing construction could proceed on vacant lands in municipalities that had no urban renewal projects—stunned suburban legislators. They had not imagined the UDC would build in their backyards, and now they sensed mission creep. Had not the governor himself extolled the agency's ability to fulfill the state's "urban needs"?[41] Had not newspapers warned of the UDC's potential to "condemn whole sections of a city"?[42]

The UDC's efforts to build housing on already cleared or undeveloped land had brought it to the far reaches of the state and to suburban locations. It should be noted that while much of the UDC housing was to replace that destroyed by urban renewal, small cities and towns that had no urban renewal projects became sites of UDC housing. These efforts formed part of the UDC's regional planning initiatives. A close suburb of Utica, New Hartford, would host a UDC moderate-income development, and a UDC housing cluster would take shape in the suburbs of Rochester, albeit with some local resistance. As part of a seven-county regional planning effort underwritten by the UDC, hundreds of units of high-quality affordable housing were built in Newburgh-area hamlets of the state, far from renewal sites, in the Catskill Mountains' Sullivan County. These areas needed housing, much of which was for the elderly, and the UDC skillfully packaged the development and financing to ease the process.[43]

For the close suburbs in the New York City metropolitan area, the situation looked quite different. Zoning had maintained large lots and prohibited the expansion of the region's urbanized areas. According to a 1969 report by the Regional Plan Association, a housing crisis of "ominous proportions" was taking shape in the suburban counties of New York City, like Rockland and Westchester. The report indicated that the problem could be alleviated by rezoning vacant lands.[44] Early on, Logue had indicated that he might move "quietly and carefully" to override zoning in selected areas. And it is worth restating here that the UDC was the only agency in the country with the power to build housing in communities that did not want it.[45]

Westchester was the perfect laboratory. This small county, where afford-able housing was scarce, had also hosted numerous urban renewal sites. The Hudson River cities of Yonkers and Peekskill, and cities in the east of the coun-ty, among them Mount Vernon, New Rochelle, and White Plains, all had re-newal projects that resulted in considerable numbers of dislocated families. Logue explained to the governor that these cities—some with renewal areas dating back to 1949—were already built up; too little land was available to create significant projects, and vacant land simply was unavailable in or near the renewal areas. Zoning restrictions would prevent the UDC's construc-tion of housing on the county's vacant lands unless the towns and the state agency could reach an agreement. Though the surrounding suburban com-munities had not been directly affected by urban renewal, Logue believed they should provide their fair share of housing in response to the housing crisis in neighboring cities. Logue accepted and acted upon the Kerner Commis-sion's famed assertion that the suburbs were becoming almost exclusively white. He incorporated this notion when he discussed his plans: "you can't just accept the lily-white noose of the suburbs around the neck of the city and make any progress."[46] Logue believed the right approach in Westchester was to move slowly with "the seeding of existing suburban communities with col-onies of 40–50 housing units" that would "fit right in" and would not "imbal-ance any local elementary school."[47]

Westchester's spate of urban renewal had produced this crisis. Demoli-tion of homes in the late 1950s and early 1960s resulted in hundreds of dis-placements without rehousing many of the black residents of New Rochelle and White Plains. A 1967 report by the Urban League of Westchester noted, "When existing urban renewal programs in the county are completed, more housing units will have been demolished than constructed." Of the approx-imately 4,217 units to be demolished countywide, only about 3,000 new units would be constructed, and only 697 of those would be low-rent housing.[48]

The UDC entered a countywide agreement, signed by Westchester Coun-ty executive Edward Michaelian. As a close associate of Rockefeller, the Re-publican had spearheaded growth and development in the county since he began his two terms as mayor of White Plains in the 1950s. Cognizant that nearby counties of Orange and Rockland had been "reluctant to invite UDC assistance,"[49] in January 1970, Michaelian disclosed publicly that he had been conferring with the UDC for months. He affirmed the need for a countywide housing effort and confirmed that his negotiations should put to rest fears that the UDC would override zoning restrictions.[50] The rollout was cautious. "Sure we could go busting into Westchester, as some of the more militant civil rights groups want us do," said Logue. "We're trying to get a consensus."[51] S. J. Schulman, former Westchester County planning director, and the gov-ernor's nephew, William Strawbridge, were selected to lead the UDC's effort in the county. They quietly connected with corporations, higher education institutions, liberal clerics, and social service organizations to organize their support. Rockefeller, whose family home was located in the county, leveraged his connections with Westchester-based corporate concerns like IBM and Reader's Digest to seek funds and support for the UDC's work.[52]

The UDC hammered out agreements for multiple projects in 1970 in nearly every city in Westchester. Yonkers and Peekskill would receive many hundreds of units of housing near renewal and industrial areas. Ossining, New Rochelle, and White Plains also began discussion with the UDC. But negotiations for multiunit housing for residents at New York Medical College in Mt. Pleasant drew opposition from the community. Opponents of the plan fanned opposition, and lawsuits in a neighboring community to the north in Beacon and in the Rochester area combined with the 1972 electoral season to stir the pot. Into the mix the UDC announced its controversial "Nine Towns" plan in June 1972, ostensibly to diffuse the growing opposition and spread costs across the county. Nine Westchester towns—all far from renewal sites—were each to host their "fair share" of publicly subsidized housing, one hundred units per community. Perhaps Logue did believe that some suburban New Yorkers could accept the housing proposal, as Lizabeth Cohen has written. But according to UDC chronicler Eleanor Brilliant, the plan instead prompted the "fear of bringing the Bronx to Westchester."[53] Initially all the towns resisted, and three lodged lawsuits, unsuccessfully, against the UDC. Residents organized United Towns for Home Rule, and they met, rallied—some drawing more than two thousand attendees—and traveled to neighboring counties and Long Island to spread the word about the UDC's unholy plan to override zoning. They argued that any project should be kept within or adjacent to renewal areas, presuming that was the intent of the UDC legislation.[54] Elected officials stepped up their resistance too, although, as Logue informed his board of directors, "each legislator has privately admitted the need for low- and moderate-income housing in his district, regardless of his public posture."[55] Bipartisan opposition resulted in the cosponsorship of several bills to reduce the power of the UDC. Logue objected to the governor, who caved in to the protest and supported legislation, early in 1973, that stripped the UDC's powers to override zoning and building codes.[56] Unfortunately, the Nine Towns controversy sidetracked other UDC housing projects in the county. A large New Rochelle project was pulled, which Logue feared would have lasting repercussions upon the viability of future projects in neighboring counties.[57] The White Plains mayor, echoing the recent controversy, balked at having to build housing "for outsiders" and pulled the town's support for the eight-hundred-plus-unit Battle Hill complex.[58]

The consensus among staff was that the UDC should stay "where we are wanted,"[59] so this is what the agency continued to do in 1973, constructing hundreds of units, all in or near urban renewal areas. With a housing formula that reserved 20 percent of units for low-income residents, it could never remediate the loss for the poorest displaced citizens.[60] Townsend Tower (200 units) in Syracuse and Claremont Gardens (184 units) in Ossining were some of the several complexes built with relocation in mind, but in most cities, the lag time between demolition and replacement housing was too great. In Yonkers, the UDC built housing in the places that resisted least: in the corridor of public housing projects in the southwest portion of the city.[61]

## Conclusion

The UDC was created with the belief that government, as a builder of infrastructure, could improve lives; it was also a victim of the belief that government had overstepped, had both demolished and spent too much. Early in 1973 the governor stripped the UDC's power to override zoning regulations. In exchange, Rockefeller increased the UDC's borrowing capacity from $1.5 to $2 billion. Commentators noted that this may have contributed to the UDC's undoing, as overborrowing led to declining bond ratings and shrinking private investment. Its rapid demise also came as a result of the Nixon administration's moratorium on the mortgage interest subsidy used by the UDC to construct moderate- and low-income housing. The UDC could function with its loss of override power but not its loss of its subsidies and investors.[62] In the years when urban renewal was "collapsing," Logue and his staff promoted a transformative vision that put the question to upstate communities: how can the levers of government facilitate rebuilding, diverse neighborhoods, and affordable housing? New Yorkers in the metropolitan area and beyond were now confronted with the prospect that the complicated problems of urban America were deeply entwined with their own. And some upstate communities began to agree reservedly, and thus the UDC's record in building homes upstate was impressive. As the developer of last resort, the UDC offered an expeditious and affirmative response to bloated and decaying urban renewal, even as communities and suburbs sorted by income and race. UDC's homebuilding in small cities and on the suburban fringe is a significant though unintended consequence of federal urban renewal.

Rebuilding after renewal in New York briefly integrated social goals with the power of the state and private sector in what has been considered a unique though perhaps contradictory partnership. Lizabeth Cohen has aptly captured the central contradiction of the UDC "between its social mandate to build for low- and moderate-income tenants and its fiscal mandate to do so at no cost to taxpayers." The state's Moreland Act Commission investigation of the UDC's collapse and resulting public debt was concerned with the UDC's possible corruption, its lavish spending, and the very financing and expediting model that sped the completion of projects. Notwithstanding the UDC's loss of credit, the political context was also problematic. Rockefeller's resignation in late 1973 eliminated the governor's promotion and protection. Governor Carey was not so willing in his support and failed to convince the legislature of the need for additional appropriations for the agency that had few loyal friends among upstate political officials.[63]

The UDC's pursuit of a regional and balanced approach—by which low- and middle-income housing would be distributed across metropolitan communities—never came to fruition. The agency's market ethos and public-private partnerships, however, have been incorporated in subsequent state efforts to build affordable housing and pursue statewide development initiatives. By the mid-1970s, a host of state entities were created, all using elements of the New York model that featured independent authority, public-private partnerships, and regional planning.[64] Faded from these efforts is the progressive vision that motivated the UDC's commitment. Scholars, planners, and affordable housing advocates still look to the UDC for a "usable past" that can inform contemporary struggles to create affordable housing.[65] They evaluate the UDC's powers wistfully because the agency had the potential to disregard exclusionary zoning and ultimately reshape metropolitan housing markets, items high on the wish list of today's progressive planners and fair housing advocates.[66]

## NOTES

1. Robert M. Litke, phone conversation with the author, June 14, 2019, and interview with the author, September 22, 2021; Alan Talbot and Steven Lefkowitz, "Origins: How the UDC Began" (opening panel, "Policy and Design for Housing: Lessons of the Urban Development Corporation 1968–1975," Center for Architecture, June 10, 2005), available at http://udchousing.org/images/pdfs/archive/Origins.pdf.

2. "6 State Officials Meet Assaro, Daniels on UR," *Utica Observer-Dispatch*, July 31, 1968.

3. "Annual Report for 1969," New York State Urban Development Corporation Annual Reports, New York State Archives, Albany, 17. Carol DeMare, "New Program Here?" *Yonkers Herald Statesman*, May 15, 1968; Hugh Reynolds, "Ray's Views on the Ghetto Plan," *Kingston Daily Freeman*, May 28, 1968.

4. New York State Urban Development Corporation Directors' Meeting Minutes, January 17, 1973, series B2655, New York State Archives, Albany.

5. Bruce B. Detlefsen, "Rocky: 'Buildingest Governor,'" *Knickerbocker News*, July 1, 1970.

6. Christopher Klemek, *The Transatlantic Collapse of Urban Renewal: Postwar Urbanism from New York to Berlin* (Chicago: University of Chicago Press, 2011).

7. Edward Logue, interview with Ivan Steen, February 4, 1985, 28, transcript, Ivan Steen Papers, 1928–2013, M. E. Grenander Department of Special Collections and Archives, University at Albany, State University of New York.

8. Eleanor L. Brilliant, *The Urban Development Corporation: Private Interests and Public Authority* (Lexington, MA: D. C. Heath, 1977); Louis K. Loewenstein, "The New York

State Urban Development Corporation—A Forgotten Failure or a Precursor of the Future?" *Journal of the American Institute of Planners* 44, no. 3 (1978): 261–273; Lizabeth Cohen, *Saving America's Cities: Ed Logue and the Struggle to Renew America in the Suburban Age* (New York: Farrar Straus and Giroux, 2019).

9. Nicholas Dagen Bloom, *How States Shaped Postwar America: State Government and Urban Power* (Chicago: University of Chicago Press, 2019), 39, 42.

10. During its first year of existence, the UDC was invited to nearly all of the state's sixty-two cities to hash out their development priorities. David K. Shipler, "Across the State, Renewal Hopes Rise," *New York Times*, April 18, 1969.

11. "Annual Report for 1977," New York State Urban Development Corporation Annual Reports, New York State Archives, Albany, 9.

12. Eric David Peterson, "The Urban Development Corporation's 'Imaginative Use of Credit': Creating Capital for Affordable Housing Development," *Journal of Urban History* 45, no. 6 (2019): 1174–1192; Litke, interview.

13. For more on the time lag in rebuilding in New York, see Jon C. Teaford, "Urban Renewal and Its Aftermath," *Housing Policy Debate* 11, no. 2 (2000): 448–450. In New York City, see Gabrielle Bendiner-Viani, *Contested City: Art and Public History as Mediation at New York's Seward Park Urban Renewal Area* (Iowa City: University of Iowa Press, 2018); "Housing on the Edge: A Brief History of Arverne," Architectural League of New York, accessed August 8, 2019, available at https://archleague.org/article/housing-on-the-edge-a-brief-history-of-arverne/.

14. "State in Urban Renewal Picture," *Buffalo Courier-Express*, April 26, 1959; on small cities as recipients of state urban renewal subsidies, see "Urban Renewal to Get 12 Million," *New York Times*, January 2, 1961. When the governor announced UDC to the legislature, he spoke to this legacy: "The State has, since 1959, provided half of the local cost of urban renewal throughout the State. Today there are 151 such projects underway. Yet, many of these projects have not substantially progressed, for a decade or more. The average time, for example, from planning to completion of an urban renewal project is about 10 years." Message related to the creation of an Urban Development Corporation, the Corporation for Urban Research, and Development and the Urban Development Guarantee Fund of New York, February 27, 1968, Public Papers of Nelson A. Rockefeller: Fifty-Third Governor of the State of New York, 1959–1973 (Albany, N.Y., 1968), 193; Charles Grutzner, "State Fund to Aid Nyack's Renewal," *New York Times*, February 12, 1959.

15. Arthur E. Weintraub, "A Report on the Status of the UDC Demonstration Projects in the Mid-Hudson" (presented at the Annual Conference Mid-Hudson Pattern for Progress, Inc., New Paltz, New York, May 28, 1970).

16. New York State Urban Development Corporation Symposium and Exhibition Committee, *Policy and Design for Housing: Lessons of the Urban Development Corporation 1968–1975*, with comments by Stephen Lefkowitz, June 10, 2005, accessed December 23, 2022, http://udchousing.org/document.htm.

17. Urban Development Corporation Task Force, Task Force Report on the Urban Development Corporation, vol. 2, report B.4, 1974, Series A0506-78, New York State Archives, Albany.

18. Moreland Act Commission on the Urban Development Corporation and Other State Financing Agencies, *Restoring Credit and Confidence: A Reform Program for New York State and Its Public Authorities* (Albany, NY: Moreland Act Commission, 1976), 108, 271.

19. "Housing Shortage Held City's Fault," *New York Times*, March 24, 1962; John Sibley, "Need for Housing Dire Here," *New York Times*, January 21, 1961.

20. Charles Grutzner, "Slum Drive Asked in Hudson Counties," *New York Times*, June 18, 1958; David K. Shipler, "The Changing City: Housing Paralysis," *New York Times*, June 5, 1969.

21. "Annual Report for 1969," New York State Urban Development Corporation Annual Reports, New York State Archives, Albany, 9.

22. Though the UDC would create controversy in the Westchester suburbs, by 1975 it had completed five housing projects with three more underway in four Westchester locations. For a concise statement on the ambivalence in Westchester County, see Milton Hoffman, "UDC Was Welcomed, Too," *Yonkers Herald Statesman*, March 7, 1975.

23. Kingston Housing Authority statement, n.d., KURA folder, box 2 of 4, M69-3:6, Joseph Yale Resnick Papers, 1965–1968, M. E. Grenander Department of Special Collections and Archives, University at Albany, State University of New York; Ann Pfau and Stacy Kinlock Sewell, "'Newburgh's Last Chance': The Elusive Promise of Urban Renewal in a Small and Divided City," *Journal of Planning History* 19, no. 3 (2020): 144–163.

24. Philip A. Bean, "The Irish, the Italians, and Machine Politics, A Case Study: Utica, New York, 1870–1960," *Journal of Urban History* 20, no. 2 (February 1994): 205–239; Thomas R. Alexander, *In Gotham's Shadow: Globalization and Community Change in Central New York* (New York: State University of New York Press, 2003), 65–67.

25. Ray Martin, "Utica and Urban Renewal," *Utica Daily Press*, June 17, 1957.

26. Alexander, *In Gotham's Shadow*, 73, 80; John Urbanek, "Utica Now Tops in Redevelopment," *Utica Observer-Dispatch*, August 25, 1957.

27. William Robbins, president of the nonprofit Utica Industrial Development Corporation, quoted in "A Resurgent Utica High on Renewal," *New York Times*, January 21, 1968.

28. Ed Byrne, "Dulan Fires Back at Hot UR Criticism," *Utica Observer-Dispatch*, January 19, 1967; "Urban Renewal in Utica Being Probed by FBI," *Rome Daily Sentinel*, October 11, 1968; "Incorrect, Fass Says of Report," *Utica Observer-Dispatch*, July 24, 1969; David K. Shipler, "Across the State, Renewal Hopes Rise," *New York Times*, April 18, 1969.

29. Ed Byrne, "UR Tax Yield High Says One Aide," *Utica Observer-Dispatch*, August 26, 1969; Rocco Palladino, "Lynch Asks State to Investigate City-UDC Negotiations," *Utica Daily Press*, October 16, 1969.

30. Dominick N. Assaro to Edward J. Logue, August 16, 1968, folder 123, box 244, Edward Joseph Logue Papers (MS 959), Manuscripts and Archives, Yale University Library (hereafter EJL Papers).

31. Palladino, "Lynch Asks State to Investigate"; Social Workers for Social Action issued the "Slumlord of the Year" award to highlight the housing crisis. *Utica Daily Press*, June 10, 1970. In fact, 28.5 percent of Utica's housing was still "substandard" after a decade of much loss of housing. Community Renewal Program, *Final Report* (Utica, NY: Community Renewal Program, 1971).

32. W. D. Clements, "'One Sided', Hanna Says of UDC," *Utica Observer-Dispatch*, February 8, 1974.

33. Lingering criticism for Utica's urban renewal decisions and current state can be viewed on the website Better Utica Downtown, accessed December 23, 2022, available at http://betteruticadowntown.com. In the past decade, Utica's urban renewal agency has sold many remaining parcels. See Steve Howe, "Selling the 'American Dream': Utica Finds Success with Urban Renewal," *Utica Observer-Dispatch*, April 19, 2019.

34. "Program Status Report, NYR-189 East Newburgh Urban Renewal Project," August 1966, box 65-B1b, Newburgh Urban Renewal Agency Files, M. E. Grenander Department of Special Collections and Archives, University at Albany, State University of New York.

35. Pfau and Sewell, "'Newburgh's Last Chance.'" UDC experimented with a variety of formulas of anywhere from 20 to 30 percent low-income residents for many of its projects. Logue wrote that the typical formula was 70 percent moderate income, 20 percent low income, and 10 percent low-income elderly. See Edward Logue to Robert F. Kelley, February 27, 1973, folder 1068, box 40, series 34, Nelson A. Rockefeller Gubernatorial Records, Rockefeller Archive Center; "Annual Report for 1970," New York State Urban Development Corporation Annual Reports, New York State Archives, Albany.; Cohen, *Saving America's Cities*, 290.

36. Because the city of Kingston so botched the relocation process, thus highlighting the city's housing shortage, the UDC became an attractive means by which to solve a local political dispute. On the agreement between Newburgh and UDC for the municipal complex, see "Signatures Pledge Agreement for Newburgh Court Square," *Middletown Times Herald-Record*, July 16, 1971.

37. Harvey Molotch, "The City as a Growth Machine: Toward a Political Economy of Place," *American Journal of Sociology* 82, no. 2 (September 1976): 309–332.

38. "Priority" projects also had "no active opposition from the Mayor." John Stainton to Edward J. Logue, "Potential 1st Phase UDC Projects," July 18, 1968, folder 182, box 245, EJL Papers.

39. "Project Activities," September 6, 1968, folder 200, box 240, EJL Papers.

40. Edward J. Logue to Barry L. Van Lare, September 10, 1969, box 271, EJL Papers.

41. "The UDC: Urban or Suburban?" *Baldwinsville Messenger*, June 21, 1972. A number of legislators said they voted for the UDC believing its application would only be in urban areas. See Milton Hoffman, "Biondo Compromise Bill Would Limit UDC Power," *Tarrytown Daily News*, March 1, 1973; "Excerpts from Address by Rockefeller," *New York Times*, April 19, 1968.

42. "Bulldozing Home Rule," *New York Times*, March 2, 1968.

43. Of the housing planned for the Catskill region, Logue urged more units for elderly residents as this development feature was "locally popular." UDC Directors' Meeting Minutes, October 25, 1972, series B2655, New York State Archives, Albany.

44. "Housing Opportunities: An Analysis of New York City and Its Northern and Eastern Suburbs for the New York State Urban Development Corporation," *Regional Plan News*, September 1969, available at https://s3.us-east-1.amazonaws.com/rpa-org/pdfs/91_RegionalPlanNews.pdf; Peter Kihss, "Housing Here Called Inadequate," *New York Times*, July 22, 1969.

45. Linda Greenhouse, "Black Groups Vie for Greenburgh Renewal Site," *New York Times*, October 24, 1970; David K. Shipler, "Lawsuit to Challenge Suburban Zoning as Discriminatory Against the Poor," *New York Times*, June 29, 1969.

46. Edward J. Logue to Nelson A. Rockefeller, November 25, 1969, box 297, EJL Papers; William J. Lewis, "Suburbs Must Help Blacks: Logue," *Boston Globe*, May 27, 1968; Logue supported a study by the Regional Plan Association that found that more sparsely settled land within thirty miles of New York City would ease congestion in the urban slum. Glenn Fowler, "Land Costs Deter Shift from Slum to Suburb," *New York Times*, August 17, 1969.

47. Edward J. Logue memo, "Roving UDC Ambassador," February 14, 1969, box 271, EJL Papers.

48. Gail Kaplan Guttman, "Division and Diversity: Community Transition in Post-war America, 1945–1970 New Rochelle, New York, A Case Study" (Ph.D. thesis, Columbia University, 2001), 465–472; Housing Council, Urban League of Westchester County, "Urban Renewal in Westchester County: Its Effect on the General Housing Supply and on the Housing Occupied by Negroes," November 16, 1967, box 2, Urban Renewal Collection, White Plains Public Library.

49. Brilliant, *The Urban Development Corporation*, 91; "Annual Report for 1972," New York State Urban Development Corporation Annual Reports, New York State Archives, Albany, 3.

50. Stuart Polly to Edward J. Logue, February 4, 1970, box 297, EJL Papers; Milton Hoffman, "County Housing Program Disclosed, Michaelian Indicates," *White Plains Reporter Dispatch*, February 3, 1970.

51. Nancy Moran, "A Gingerly Step into Westchester Taken by Logue," *New York Times*, February 22, 1970.

52. On UDC's strategy in Westchester, see S. J. Schulman to EJY, June 4, 1970, box 271, EJL Papers; on donations, see Edward Logue to DeWitt Wallace, May 1, 1970, and Nelson Rockefeller to T. J. Watson, Jr., March 9, 1970, box 271, EJL Papers.

53. Linda Greenhouse, "Westchester to Sell 25 Campus Acres," *New York Times*, November 23, 1971; Cohen, *Saving America's Cities*, 312; Brilliant, *The Urban Development Corporation*, 141.

54. "Housing Opposed in Westchester," *New York Times*, July 23, 1972.

55. UDC Board of Directors' Meeting Minutes, November 29, 1972, series B2655, New York State Archives, Albany.

56. In fact, the UDC was besieged by protesters who picketed UDC offices demanding that it use its power to override local zoning ordinances more. See David K. Shipler, "Pickets Ask State Urban Agency to Override L.I. Zoning Laws," *New York Times*, May 7, 1970. The UDC did use its power to override local laws outside of Rochester and Ossining (in Westchester County); these communities mounted unsuccessful lawsuits that challenged the UDC's right to override local building and zoning laws. In about 10 percent of cases, the UDC did in fact override local zoning, building multifamily units in some spots, using prefabricated building methods in others. For the local resistance, see UDC Board of Directors' Meeting Minutes, September 8, 1971, and September 15, 1971, series B2655, New York State Archives, Albany.

57. UDC Board of Directors' Meeting Minutes, November 29, 1972, series B2655, New York State Archives, Albany.

58. "Annual Report for 1972," New York State Urban Development Corporation Annual Reports, New York State Archives, Albany., 17. On the over four decades between relocation and replacement housing in Lower Manhattan, see Bendiner-Viani, *Contested City*. For White Plains' rejection of housing see Donna Greene, "How Much Housing? White Plains Looks for an Answer," *Westchester Commerce and Industry*, January 1, 1973.

59. "Urban Development Curbs Are Voted," *New York Times*, April 13, 1972; Edward J. Logue, "Memorandum for the Governor," re: Status of UDC Ripper Bills, April 23, 1973, folder 1068, box 40, series 34, Nelson A. Rockefeller Gubernatorial Records, Rockefeller Archive Center; Stephen Lefkowitz to Edward J. Logue, "For My Part, There Is More To Do in the Cities, Where We Are Wanted," December 15, 1971, box 271, EJL Papers.

60. The 1949 Housing Act resulted in the creation of numerous middle-income housing projects built away from the urban core. See, for example, Bloom, *How States Shaped Postwar America*, 134, 177.

61. Hoffman, "UDC Was Welcomed, Too"; Cathleen Brooke Holden, "Public Housing in Yonkers, New York: The Impact of Panners on Site Selection in a Segregated Community" (master's thesis, University of Rhode Island, 1987), 41, Open Access Master's Theses, paper 513, available at https://digitalcommons.uri.edu/theses/513.

62. Whereas "local officials have frankly admitted that they refused to talk with UDC before," now they "are reassured and want to cooperate." Hoffman, "UDC Was Welcomed, Too"; "Annual Report for 1974," New York State Urban Development Corporation Annual Reports, New York State Archives, Albany., 58; Brilliant, *The Urban Development Corporation*, 152; Peterson, "The Urban Development Corporation's 'Imaginative Use of Credit,'" 8.

63. Cohen, *Saving America's Cities*, 339; Brilliant, *The Urban Development Corporation*, 173; Moreland Act Commission, *Restoring Credit and Confidence*.

64. Bloom, *How States Shaped Postwar America*, 48–52.

65. Yonah Freemark, "The Entrepreneurial State: New York's Urban Development Corporation, an Experiment to Take Charge of Affordable Housing Production, 1968–1975" (master's thesis, Massachusetts Institute of Technology, 2013), 318.

66. Sarah Mervosh, "Minneapolis, Tackling Housing Crisis and Inequity, Votes to End Single-Family Zoning," *New York Times*, December 13, 2018; Editorial Board, "California Has a Housing Crisis: The Answer Is More Housing," *New York Times*, April 27, 2019; C. J. Gabbe, "Changing Residential Land Use Regulations to Address High Housing Prices: Evidence from Los Angeles," *Journal of the American Planning Association* 85, no. 2 (2019): 152–168.

# 7

# The Dispossessed

*Urban Renewal and Relocation*
*in St. Louis County*

COLIN GORDON

sther Brooks was born in 1897 and lived at 10008 Roberts Avenue in Elmwood Park, an unincorporated African American enclave of about one hundred families a few miles west of the St. Louis city line. She had been commuting (since 1944) to a job as a domestic making thirty-two dollars per week in the tony central county suburb of Ladue. Her modest Elmwood Park home included a living room, a dining room, a kitchenette, a bath, and two bedrooms. To help make ends meet, she took on a boarder, who paid twenty dollars per month for the second bedroom.[1] In 1957, as Brooks approached her sixtieth birthday, St. Louis County officials began discussing the prospect of "renewing" Elmwood Park. As plans progressed, Brooks and others dug in against the county and its efforts to relocate the residents. The county floated a variety of relocation plans but privately—and in their communications with Elmwood Park residents—pressed public housing in St. Louis as the best option. For Brooks, who had owned her own home in Elmwood Park for over thirty years, the option of taking an apartment in the city's notorious Pruitt-Igoe complex (far-removed from family, friends, and her place of employment) was "entirely obnoxious to her."[2]

For displaced residents, urban renewal meant the construction of "dwellings beyond their means, and . . . commercial and industrial improvements completely irrelevant to their well-being." Relocation proceeded with little respect for the deep, multigenerational roots of many residents. "People don't want to be displaced because there is something familiar about where they live, despite the fact that it's a deteriorated area," relocation officials conceded.

"But they feel that it belongs to them and they belong to it, so they are comfortable there."[3] As in so many other settings, the impact was starkly racial: "It's not a land clearance," as on observer put it, "it's a race clearance," adding that renewal projects in St. Louis and St. Louis County "affected ninety-nine percent Negroes."[4] For her part, Brooks received a letter from relocation officials in early 1962 but no further contact as the redevelopment plans progressed.[5]

As residents—some of whom had deep, multigenerational roots in Elmwood Park—saw their homes and their community being confiscated, they turned to the courts. In March 1967, Brooks and her neighbors asked the Missouri Supreme Court for a declaratory judgment—arguing that the state's highest court should intervene because grave constitutional questions were at stake. The court held that the interpretation of Missouri's urban renewal laws might be at stake but not their constitutionality and passed the case on to the Missouri Court of Appeals. By the time the lower court issued its opinion, Elmwood Park had been blighted for over a decade, the land had been cleared, and rebuilding was well underway. These facts alone were enough to guide the opinion. Since the redevelopment authority was "now in possession and the owner of the lands in Elmwood Park previously owned by the plaintiffs," the court reasoned, "it is obvious the latter have no legally protectable interest at stake."[6]

The experience of Esther Brooks neatly captures the logic, the limits, and the often-savage inequity of federal and local urban renewal policies. While federal legislation was animated by the hope of upgrading the nation's housing stock and revitalizing the nation's cities, local administration often frustrated those goals—or turned them on their head. In many settings, "blight" meant not just substandard housing or infrastructure but the "nuisance" of black occupancy itself. Local administration sought not just redevelopment but a "higher use" of land—an imperative that often meant trading residential neighborhoods for commercial or industrial use. And, in project after project, the fate of residents cut loose by redevelopment was at best an afterthought. While federal policy, from 1949 on, specifically guaranteed "decent, safe and sanitary" housing to displaced families, "the bleakness of the relocation landscape," as one observer noted in 1968, "contrasts strikingly with the rosy picture painted by the urban renewal legislation."[7] The sorry history of this era underscores the threat to citizenship—and to democratic voice—embedded in postwar urban renewal.[8]

Greater St. Louis offered a stark case study of the logic and limits of relocation policies. There is no clean count of relocations, as local redevelopment authorities routinely underestimated displacements and overestimated the capacity of public and private housing markets to absorb them.[9] The downtown Mill Creek Valley project (1958) alone displaced 4,200 families (about 15,000 persons); the nearby Kosciusko project (1959) displaced 1,800 families. The city's housing authority estimated 6,700 family displacements due to slum clearance through 1963—a number that more than doubles if displacements due to other government action are taken into account. Once the federal urban renewal program ended, these numbers tailed off: just under 3,000 families were displaced by government action from 1972 to 1977, about 600 of these due to urban renewal.[10] If we assume that the rate of displacement was constant through the 1960s, the number of families displaced by urban renewal runs close to 20,000 families or 75,000 persons—fully 10 percent of the city's 1960 population.

Relocation services were haphazard and half-hearted. A scathing HUD audit (1964) found that more than half of the Mill Creek families never appeared on the local authority's relocation workload. And, when HUD officials spot-checked relocation units, they found that twenty-one of thirty-five units randomly selected from the Mill Creek caseload and thirty of the thirty-one units randomly selected from the Kosciusko caseload were substandard ("no running water, no heating facilities, doors falling off hinges, infestations with vermin, and leaks in roofs and walls"). Most of those displaced, in other words, got no relocation assistance, and most of those who got assistance saw no improvement in their housing. This reflected both the Land Clearance for Redevelopment Authority (LCRA)'s approach to relocation ("federal regulations specifying this obligation were to be considered advisory," as LCRA officials conceded, "to be followed or discarded as necessary") and the fact that many of the displaced wanted nothing to do with the assistance offered by the "Local City Rip-off Artists" who had taken their homes.[11]

St. Louis City officials justified renewal projects in the hope that they would stem residential flight to the suburbs but also relied on that flight to open up units for those displaced. They leaned heavily on the big downtown public housing projects to meet federal thresholds for relocation housing while conceding (by the late 1960s) that "the condition and repute of many public housing projects in St. Louis mitigate against their use as even temporary relocation sites." And they reluctantly admitted that the persistently high ratio of substandard units citywide meant that urban renewal was pushing people around at great public expense and little public benefit—and could even yield "a net decrease in the housing quality city-wide." Indeed, the exodus from "cleared" tracts—some into local public housing, but most into neighborhoods to the west and north—had the effect of both deepening segregation and creating new demand for renewal in neighborhoods overrun by those displaced.[12]

Although its urban renewal program was more modest, these motivations and machinations were even more pronounced in St. Louis County. Like its counterpart in the city, the county LCRA looked to displace pockets of "blighted" black occupancy and convert the land to a "higher use." But residential segregation was much starker west of the city border (even LCRA officials conceded that "St. Louis County has been very closed to the Negro people"), making it harder to make the case for the availability of relocation housing. And county redevelopment plans invariably proceeded from the assumption that blacks displaced from county tracts would and should be accommodated by public or private housing in the city. There was "some concern in Washington for some of the programs in these suburban communities," as the NAACP (National Association for the Advancement of Colored People) noted in 1962, "which in planning seem to indicate a pattern of displacing Negro families back into the city of St. Louis, whether they like it or not."[13]

In Elmwood Park, both early planning and project administration made it clear that the LCRA was less interested in upgrading the local housing stock than in displacing the residents permanently. While federal law envisioned relocation as a step in the renewal process (affording former residents the opportunity to move back to the renewed neighborhoods), redevelopment planning in St. Louis County rested largely on the conviction that these "little ghettos" were out of place: tarpaper shacks and outhouses did not belong amidst the cul-de-sacs of the modern suburban fringe, and their residents did not belong west of the city's border. The municipality of Olivette echoed this reasoning in its planning for the small slice of Elmwood Park that fell within its corporate borders. Olivette targeted forty structures and parcels, including a couple of small businesses and housing for about thirty African American families—at the time the only African Americans living in Olivette.[14] The central goal of Olivette's redevelopment plan was to displace all the area's residents and rezone for industrial development: "the highest and best use . . . [that] will substantially increase the tax base of the community."[15] The goal was to take an area "predominantly populated by Negro citizens," as local officials argued, and transform it into an "economic asset to Olivette." As a local NAACP officer observed, "From all indications the intention of the undertaking of this redevelopment is to move Negroes out of the city of Olivette."[16] Olivette officials worried that their plans would "appear as a conspiracy to rid the community of its Negro population" but made little effort to disguise the fact that this was exactly what they had in mind.[17]

The county's determination to relocate its scattered African American residents to the city was underscored by its resistance to public housing as even a partial relocation strategy. The county's starting assumption was that public housing in the city of St. Louis was appropriate and sufficient as a relocation option. Olivette and county officials saw established housing projects (especially Pruitt-Igoe) as the best destination for those unable to afford market housing in the county. It was this conviction that sank the prospect, floated half-heartedly in the late 1950s, of retrofitting the recently decommissioned Jefferson Barracks in southern St. Louis County as public housing. Local officials, especially in Olivette, rebuffed federal programs and put off even creating local housing authorities for as long as possible. As late as 1970, Olivette lacked a housing authority and the county boasted fewer than 150 units of public housing (there were over 8,000 in the city), all of them in Kinloch, another northern St. Louis County African American enclave.[18]

The county only grudgingly built just enough public housing units to ensure that the federal funds kept flowing. Under HHFA pressure to accommodate displaced low-income families, county planners gave a little. Unable to avoid public housing altogether, they worked to contain it on a few sites, so that Kinloch—and later Elmwood Park—might serve the relocation needs of the entire county.[19] In late 1963, Bishop Primm of the African Methodist Episcopal Church took the lead in sponsoring an application for Section 221(d) assistance (a federal program offering mortgage insurance to nonprofits building or rehabilitating multifamily units). A separate relocation demonstration grant set aside 20 of the planned 210 units (47 townhomes and 160 one-to-three-bedroom apartments) for rent subsidies.[20] At its completion in 1972, Primm Gardens was one of only three apartment complexes in all of St. Louis County to offer a three-bedroom apartment for under $150 a month. By 1973, there were over six hundred families on a waiting list for the subsidized units.[21]

For many Elmwood Park residents (including Esther Brooks), the very idea of public housing, of trading multigenerational homeownership for a subsidized rental apartment, was repugnant. In turn, private housing across St. Louis County was deeply segregated, and redevelopment officials studiously ignored the starkly racial structure of local real estate markets.[22] It was not easy, as the Olivette LCRA admitted in 1963, to come up with a relocation plan that "will meet Federal requirements while simultaneously considering local conditions."[23] Those working with displaced families underscored the problem. As staff of the American Friends Service Committee concluded in 1967,

> Even our experience in the frustrations of community relations work did not fully prepare AFSC staff workers for the webs of obfuscation that have been encountered by them and by homeseekers with whom they have worked in attempts to secure housing. . . . Prospective buyers have found salesmen who are not authorized to sell, unsold homes that are not for sale, prices that suddenly rise, GI certificates and sales contracts that get lost, routine business transactions that spin into months of delay, credit companies that find unpaid bills that were never incurred, and questionable expressions of concern by builders and sales agents that their clients not move into a neighborhood where they "wouldn't be happy."[24]

Local relocation was also hamstrung by financial constraints. For the county, the ramshackle homesteads of Elmwood Park were of little value. But the residents, of course, saw things differently. For those with deep generational ties to Elmwood Park, their homes were worth much more than their assessed value. And the meager options for African Americans elsewhere in the county dramatically inflated the replacement value. In this light, the LCRA's condemnation offers were insulting. Clara Burden, a resident of Elmwood Park for over fifty years, was offered $2,200 for a house she had inherited from her parents. Mary Bryant, who had lived at 9941 Chicago for twenty-four years, got an early offer of $7,000 but no follow-up. Ida Scott and her husband, whose holdings included a salvage yard on eleven lots adjoining 9917 Meeks, were offered $14,000 for everything.[25] The average LCRA settlement (for the subset of properties recording sales or condemnations) was $3,400, while the average price paid by displaced families for new housing outside of Elmwood Park was about $10,000.[26]

These losses were magnified by uneven title documentation. Those who did not own their homes outright often held informal or contract mortgages. Many purchase offers (and later condemnations) by the LCRA ended up in court, with much of the housing value disappearing in contractual disputes and legal fees.[27] Not surprisingly, given these conditions, many rebuffed the LCRA entirely. In the end, almost 80 percent of the properties in Elmwood Park were transferred to county control though condemnation proceedings, which began in December of 1961. Because the project took so long to complete, many displaced owners remained in their homes as tenants of the LCRA, their home equity whittled away in rent on houses they used to own.[28] Those who received early payment for condemned properties were caught: "there was no property available to absorb this payment . . . and by receiving this very payment they became ineligible for [other forms of public assistance]."[29]

Many residents sought options closer to home and pressed for on-site relocation. Federal officials, tiring of the county's recalcitrance, agreed and directed local officials that "unless the Elmwood residents prefer relocating outside of the Elmwood Park area . . . they be relocated in temporary relocation quarters until new homes are available." The county LCRA responded defensively but also grudgingly conceded the point: "Federal representatives from the Washington level have requested that the authority discontinues this method, stating that many letters have been received by the Senators and Congressmen from this district claiming that the minority group in St. Louis County are being pushed out of St. Louis County."[30]

At this point, Elmwood Park residents, the LCRA, and the HHFA struck a deal: For the county's share of the project, the LCRA would make a commitment to staged redevelopment so that the first phase of completed houses could be used to relocate residents from the later phases. No properties west of Dielman Avenue, by this agreement, would be acquired or condemned until those east of Dielman had been rebuilt. Given the extent of vacancies throughout Elmwood Park, the HHFA also hoped that those east of Dielman could temporarily relocate to empty houses on the west side—essentially shuffling families back and forth across Dielman in such a way that none would have to leave the area. The regional director of the HHFA made sure that local officials understood: he "pointed his finger at Mr. Reichert [LCRA]," as one observer recalled, "and he says 'This is what I want done and I want this carried out . . . I have given my word on this.'" A week later, the terms of the deal were outlined in a public meeting in Elmwood Park and adopted by the county council.[31]

The commitment to staged redevelopment was followed in short order by a formal relocation plan, adopted by the LCRA in November of 1962. The plan called for a survey of site residents, dissemination of information about project progress and relocation options and resources, aid and counsel, standards for relocation housing (and provisions for inspection), assistance for those eligible for public housing, and assistance in obtaining mortgages or home improvement loans. And it elaborated a new commitment to multifamily, low-income housing on at least a portion of the project.[32] The plan was more ambitious on paper than in practice. Much of it relied on boilerplate provisions, some of which were irrelevant and some of which were woefully optimistic given the area's deeply racialized housing market. On closer look, the plan outlined relocation efforts that "aside from keeping statistics and the preparation of reports, involve nothing more to be done for the inhabitants than they could do for themselves by merely perusing the 'For Rent' and 'For Sale' columns in the newspapers." And staffing the relocation effort itself was a challenge, given the deep distrust of the LCRA's motives. The county hired Ida Scott, a resident who had deep roots in the community but—by her own admission—no relevant experience or training.[33]

The relocation agreement did not last long. In early 1963, the LCRA began acquiring properties west of Dielman, long ahead of any schedule that would allow residents to relocate. Redevelopment contracts specified that "displaced residents in the Elmwood Park area shall be given priority in the renting or purchasing of apartments or new homes or lots in the area," but—in the absence of staged redevelopment—no such new homes existed. In October of 1963, the Federated Civic Association again pulled together officials from HHFA and the county LCRA, but the latter were uncooperative and clearly resentful of the federal standards. A little over a year later, the LCRA director made it clear that "her understanding of Urban renewal is that it is for the general benefit of the entire community" and that "nowhere in the contract, nor in the urban renewal plan, was it stated that this project is for the specific purpose of the residents of Elmwood Park, nor that these residents were not to be relocated anywhere else. *At no time has the Authority been charged with the responsibility of providing housing for any person*, and specifically low-income housing. This is the responsibility of the County or private citizens."[34] The admission was at once candid and jarring: the "entire community" was clearly something other than Elmwood Park, and the displaced residents were clearly not its citizens.

In its initial planning, the county did what it could to placate federal officials with the promise of staged redevelopment while sticking to its original assumption that most of the Elmwood Park families would never return. But, even on this score, its efforts were patently insincere. The LCRA argued publicly that displaced families had many options but admitted privately that such options were limited. Assessing the relocation prospects for African American families in 1958, realtor Roy Wenzlick counted 155 rental units and 240 sale properties "available to non-whites" in the city and only 6 sale properties and no rental units in the county. Urban renewal officials in Olivette assumed that displaced families would relocate "across the track in Elmwood Park" but were at a loss when Elmwood Park itself was slated for redevelopment: this "poses quite a relocation problem for St. Louis County," a 1958 HUD memo noted, "since housing available to Negroes is very limited."[35]

In violation of federal standards and its own relocation plan, the LCRA routinely offered displaced families substandard housing—sometimes in other African American enclaves in the county, sometimes in north St. Louis, and sometimes on site. The irony of the latter was bitter. Residents were told to leave because their "blighted" homes were substandard threats to the public welfare. The solution, more often than not, was to shuffle them into other blighted homes in order to clear the way for redevelopment. When Lillie Lemmons was forced out of her home, she was offered a short-term rental at 9824 Rebie, a house with no running water and broken windows—and which was itself scheduled for condemnation in a few months. When Fannie White was displaced, she was offered a temporary rental west of Dielman that "wouldn't even fit for an animal to live in, much less a human being."[36] In a 1967 assessment of the Elmwood Park project, the American Friends Service Committee found that redevelopment had magnified local discrimination, violated residents' rights, and—in response to the inevitable complaints—offered "clumsy and grossly inadequate remedial tools."[37]

While some residents were shuffled in and out of substandard dwellings, others were discouraged by the "runaround" they faced in their efforts to actually participate in the redevelopment. The LCRA was reluctant to inform residents of the option to purchase and rebuild on their own lots because they feared that piecemeal rebuilding would discourage developers from bidding on larger chunks of the project. Willis Corbett (who lived at 9823 Chicago and owned the lots at 9623 and 9617 Roberts) was offered $12,000 for the lots on Roberts. When he approached the LCRA about rebuilding, he was given the same contract drafted for large developers and was told that he would either have to bid on the contract to redevelop multiple properties or strike a deal with a developer that won such a contract. For a time, he worked with the Reasor Corporation (the lead developer of the residential properties), but he pulled out of the deal in frustration in 1966.[38]

The glacial pace of redevelopment also frustrated the efforts of those who wanted to stay or return. Initial letters—outlining the plans and residents' options—went out in 1960 and 1961. Within a year, 55 of 146 families and 13 of 39 householders had left Elmwood Park, most with minimal contact with (or assistance from) the LCRA. By the end of 1963, fully three years after the buyouts and condemnations had begun, only one house had been built, and development of the multifamily project (Primm Gardens) was still being hashed out. As of June 1965, the developer had completed and sold a grand total of eleven houses.[39] On the Olivette share of the project, planning commenced in 1961, funding was not assembled until 1967, and the first contract for new development was not tendered until 1972.[40] This pace alone (especially given the demographics of those displaced) made resettlement in a redeveloped Elmwood Park a distant prospect.

Finally, for those who left, relocation assistance was meager (although the half-heartedness of the effort also means that the records on who got what and when are scattered and incomplete). The City of Olivette provided relocation assistance to a total of 12 families and 9 individuals (about two-thirds of the households displaced), but almost all of this came after new federal relocation guidelines were introduced in 1970.[41] On the county side, many refused all assistance. Of the 102 relocations recorded as of 1962, more than three-quarters (63 families and 16 individuals) were listed as "self-relocated"—many with the annotation that they had "refused help," had "no desire to return," or "wants nothing to do with [the LCRA]."[42] This, of course, was especially burdensome for a population that was largely poor and elderly. The average annual income of those facing displacement (63 owners and tenants) in 1963–1964 was $2,667, less than half the median household income for 1963 ($6,249) and barely three-quarters of the median black household income ($3,645).[43]

By the early 1960s, the politics and practice of redevelopment had begun to unravel the social fabric of Elmwood Park. Some residents clung to the original promise of the redevelopment plan, which—despite its many problems—would modernize basic public services (sewer, water, roads) and (once the Primm Gardens project was complete) expand housing options. But others felt that the burden and uncertainty born by displaced residents was too much. "The Elmwood Park owners," as the emerging legal challenge put it, ". . . naturally resented the taking of their homes for public use"—a sentiment exaggerated by the ham-handedness of local authorities. Relocation options were poorly thought out, and relocation assistance was meager. And the prospect of return—especially given local demographics, the pace and staging of redevelopment, and the options presented to residents—seemed both impractical and unaffordable.[44]

In early 1963, residents began complaining that any equity they had realized from sale or condemnation was disappearing in rent to the LCRA, and they asked that rental payments (often on homes they had once owned) be at least partially set aside for down payments on new homes in Elmwood Park. But the LCRA would not budge. By that fall, the LCRA had—by its own estimate—lost all constructive contact with residents. They worked with Ida Scott and others to revamp a local citizen's committee. But rather than assuage resident's anxieties, these efforts widened the gap between local supporters and opponents. Many viewed those who were working with the county as Elmwood Park's "most favored" residents—with the implication that they were getting a better deal. Three of the five members of the community liaison committee (Ida Scott, Wallace West, and Grace Howard) were employed by the county, and opponents accused West of being the "the fair-haired boy for the Land Clearance Authority."[45]

By early 1964, there were now competing local committees—the official Elmwood Park Citizens' Committee and the dissident Elmwood Park Improvement Association. Ida Scott advised the LCRA to not even bother printing a newsletter updating residents on the redevelopment, arguing that it would do little to change the minds of residents who fell into three factions: "those who don't care," "those who care," and the trouble-making "Willis Corbett group."[46]

The dissidents succeeded in getting their case before a grand jury in early 1965. The grand jury's report, in June 1965, offered a scathing indictment of the project—dubbing it an "evasion of responsibility and intent" that had destroyed a stable and long-standing community in one of the few pockets "where there was never any question of the right of Negroes to buy, own and rent property." The jury argued that a project promising "to raise standards and improve the living conditions of the residents of this area" had instead resulting in unrelenting "hardship and inequity." The "apathy and indifference of the entire County Community," it concluded, had allowed the project to proceed without "an honest commitment to the original intent of the Urban Renewal Plan" or the "firm and realistic intention of using the project, first and foremost, for the area residents' benefit."[47]

The extent of the grand jury's recommendation was that such a mistake not be repeated. But the core of its argument was carried forward in the lawsuit launched by Elmwood Park residents seeking a declaratory judgment and a restraining order prohibiting the LCRA from proceeding with the urban renewal plan. The circuit court dismissed the claim in 1966, and the Missouri

Supreme Court, finding no constitutional questions at stake, referred it the court of appeals, where it was tried in 1967–1968.[48] The case, *Esther Brooks et al. v. Land Clearance Authority of St. Louis County*, painstakingly documented the patterns of redevelopment and relocation outlined previously. And its unhappy resolution was the cruel finding that—with the redevelopment and its accompanying displacement now complete—former residents lacked the standing to sue.[49]

Redevelopment drove the residents of Elmwood Park from their homes. The initial hope and presumption of local redevelopment officials that erasing blight meant erasing black occupancy was haphazardly and begrudgingly succeeded by a relocation program that offered little assistance and meager options. The resulting diaspora was shaped by the pace and character of the redevelopment, the demographics of the displaced population, and deep and persistent segregation in the metropolitan labor market. Owners were compensated for their homes but not for the high cost of a split housing market. "I can't get land for that," complained one resident, "at least where they got it for colored people." As the plaintiffs in *Brooks v. LCRA* argued, "Because of the lack of a feasible relocation plan, the greater number of Elmwood park residents has been dispersed indiscriminately throughout widely separated slum areas in the City and County of St. Louis in complete frustration of the avowed purpose and intent of the redevelopment project."[50]

This dispersal, in turn, eroded the local and family ties that might have facilitated return. "It's no longer a community," observed Brooks's lawyer, "but it is individuals as far away as the City of St. Louis, near the river, public housing. Some of them in Wentzville, some of them in Kirkwood, some of them in Kinloch. It's about as wide a dispersal of a formerly cohesive community as anybody could think of."[51] The prospect of resettlement was further eroded by the age of many of those displaced. Many moved out the area, as Ida Scott recalled, and "many of the elderly had passed on or moved on to live with relatives out of the area."[52] The average age of those facing displacement (sixty-three owners and tenants) in 1964 was fifty-six years old. Many of those appearing on the early relocation ledgers had died before the project was complete, and many others, in their sixties or younger before 1970, were unlikely or reluctant to make another move.[53]

If the LCRA neglected the task of relocation, it at least tracked some of the choices made by former residents. Of one hundred relocations recorded though 1964, five had moved out of state and six to other counties in Missouri. The remaining eight-nine relocated across the metro area—the vast majority moving to largely African American tracts on the city's north side, public housing downtown, transitional neighborhoods in the inner suburb of Wellston, or other pockets of African American settlement in the county such as Kinloch and Webster Groves. This reflected both the options available and the persistent recommendation of relocation officials that displaced residents look to public housing in the city or "predominantly negro ghettoes" elsewhere in the county.[54] The longer-term record was only a little bit better. "When this came along, when their properties were sold," Ida Scott recalled, "some of them moved out altogether . . . some of them didn't do any better and then some just bought homes right here. They thought they couldn't afford it but they did."[55] But the reconstitution of Elmwood Park fell far short of the assurance—from the St. Louis County Housing Authority—that, as of 1970s, "the vast majority who had lived there before are back living in Elmwood Park."[56] As of 1974, fifteen families who had lived in Elmwood Park before redevelopment (according to the 1940 census and the LCRA record) had returned and bought homes. At least five others returned to rental housing in the new Primm Gardens complex. In other words, no more than one in six of the pre-redevelopment homeowners returned to the site as homeowners, and no more than one in four pre-redevelopment residents returned at all.[57]

Redevelopment cost the residents of Elmwood Park and Meacham Park their homes and their communities. They were, from the outset, the targets and not the beneficiaries of "renewal." If a "public purpose" was served, they were never considered members of that public. The exercise of eminent domain threatened the sanctity of their homes—a property right, Margaret Radin has argued, that forms "the moral nexus between liberty, privacy, and freedom of association." Involuntary relocation threatened another foundation of local citizenship: the right to move or stay—a right already attenuated, for the county's most marginal residents, by the poor resale value of unevenly serviced homes and the paucity of alternatives in deeply segregated local housing markets.[58] Little wonder that African Americans viewed urban renewal, like policing, as a public policy that conceived of them as targets rather than beneficiaries.

## NOTES

Acknowledgment: This paper is adapted, with permission, from Colin Gordon, *Citizen Brown: Race, Democracy, and Inequality in the St. Louis Suburbs* (Chicago: University of Chicago Press, 2019), 2–3, 80–119.

1. Testimony of Esther Brooks, Transcript on Appeal, vol. 1, 139, *Brooks v. Land Clearance for Redevelopment*, Supreme Court of Missouri (September 1966), No. 52147, *Brooks v. LCRA* Case File, RG 600, Missouri State Archives, Jefferson City (hereafter *Brooks v. LCRA* Case File).

2. Appellant's Brief, *Brooks v. LCRA* Case File.

3. Testimony of Alma Grigsby, Transcript on Appeal, vol. 2, 675, and Appellant's Brief, both *Brooks v. LCRA* Case File.

4. Final Report of the Grand Jury of St. Louis County, January 1965; Appellant's Brief; Transcript on Appeal, Vol. 1, p156, all *Brooks v. LCRA* Case File.

5. Testimony of Esther Brooks, Transcript on Appeal, vol. 1, 137, *Brooks v. LCRA* Case File.

6. Brooks v. LCRA, S.W.2d 545 (1967); Brooks v. LCRA425 S.W.2d 481 (1968).

7. "Judicial Review of Displacee Relocation in Urban Renewal," *Yale Law Journal* 77, no. 5 (1968): 968.

8. Henry W. McGee Jr., "Urban Renewal in the Crucible of Judicial Review," *Virginia Law Review* 56, no. 5 (1970): 826–894.

9. St. Louis City Plan Commission, *Technical Report on a Relocation Analysis for St. Louis, Missouri*, St. Louis: City Plan Commission, February 1972, 2.

10. "Land Clearance for Redevelopment Authority Projects," January 1961, box 2:17, Raymond Tucker Papers, Special Collections, Washington University in St. Louis; Comptroller General of the United States, *Inadequate Relocation Assistance to Families Displaced from Certain Urban Renewal Districts in Kansas and Missouri* (Washington, D.C.: U.S. Government Printing Office, 1964), 8–9; "Mill Creek Valley Urban Renewal Report," n.d., box 12:542, Freedom of Residence Records, Western Historical Manuscript Collections (hereafter WHMC); St. Louis testimony of Charles Farris, St. Louis Housing Authority, Senate Subcommittee on Banking and Currency, *Urban Renewal in Selected Cities*, Washington D.C.: Government Printing Office, 1957, 142; St. Louis City Plan Commission, *Technical Report on a Relocation Analysis*, 2, 15, 20.

11. Comptroller General of the United States, *Inadequate Relocation Assistance*, 8–9; St. Louis City Plan Commission, *Technical Report on a Relocation Analysis*; see also Mark Gelfand, *A Nation of Cities: The Federal Government and Urban America, 1933–1965* (New York: Oxford University Press, 1975), 211–214; quote from "Mill Creek Valley Urban Renewal Report," (n.d.), Box 12:542, FOR Records, WHMC.

12. St. Louis Development Program, *Technical Program: History of Renewal* (St. Louis: City Planning Commission, 1971), 14.

13. Quote from "Minutes of a Regular Meeting of the Land Clearance for Redevelopment Authority of St. Louis County," March 11, 1964, Records of the St. Louis County Land Clearance for Redevelopment Authority, St. Louis County Economic Council, Clayton, Missouri (hereafter County LCRA Records); United States Commission on Civil Rights (USCCR), *Hearings: St. Louis* (January 1970), 260, 299; USCCR staff report, Exhibit 21, USCRR, *Hearings: St. Louis*, 577; Jack Wood (NAACP) to Margaret Rush Wilson (SL NAACP), January 25, 1962, reel 8:212, Papers of the NAACP. [microform] Part 5 (supp.), The Campaign against Residential Segregation, 1914–1955; Gary Orfield, "School Segregation and Housing Policy: The Role of Local and Federal Governments in Neighborhood Segregation," *Equity & Excellence in Education* 17, no. 3 (1979): 51–52.

14. H. Black (St. Louis County NAACP) to Jack Woods, November 19, 1960, reel 1:561, Papers of the NAACP; Statement of the Olivette LCRA, Exhibit 46, USCCR, *Hearings: St. Louis*, 689–693, 699.

15. USCCR, *Hearings: St. Louis*, 408.

16. "Olivette Public Hearing," June 29, 1965, box 19, folder 214, St. Louis County Municipalities Collection, 1930–1976 (SL 74), WHMC; Quarterly Report: City of Olivette (Spring 1963), box 19, folder 212, St. Louis County Municipalities Collection; Illene Dubrow, "Municipal Antagonism or Benign Neglect: Racial Motivations in Municipal Annexations in St. Louis County Missouri," *Journal of Urban Law* 53, no. 245 (1975–1976), 258–259, 260; Minutes of the Citizens Committee in Support of the LCRA, October 1960, reel 1:563, and H. Black (St. Louis County NAACP) to Jack Woods, November 19, 1960, reel 1:561, both Papers of the NAACP.

17. USCCR, *Hearings: St. Louis*, 390, 414–415, 564–565; "Olivette Public Hearing," WHMC; "Olivette Seeks Solution to Elmwood Park Dilemma," *Globe-Democrat*, July 23, 1970, clipping in folder 64, Kay Drey Papers, WHMC.

18. Testimony of Olivette officials, USCCR, *Hearings: St. Louis*, 396–397; USCCR staff report, Exhibit 21, USCCR, *Hearings: St. Louis*, 261, 564; Dubrow, "Municipal Antagonism or Benign Neglect," 260–262; "Olivette Seeks Solution to Elmwood Park Dilemma," Kay Drey Papers; East-West Gateway Coordinating Council, *An Inventory of Housing Conditions, Programs, and Codes in St. Louis County* (St. Louis: East-West Gateway, 1970), 152–154; "Minutes of a Regular Meeting of the LCRA of St. Louis County," January 11, 1958, County LCRA Records.

19. "Minutes of a Special Meeting of the LCRA of St. Louis County," August 20, 1963, County LCRA Records; Transcript on Appeal, vol. 2, 641, and Urban Renewal Plan: Elmwood Park, Project MO R-10, Relocation Plan, n.d., both in *Brooks v. LCRA* Case File; East-West Gateway Coordinating Council, *Inventory of Housing Conditions*, 11; "Minutes of a Special Meeting of the LCRA of St. Louis County," October 9, 1963, County LCRA Records.

20. "Minutes of a Regular Meeting of the LCRA of St. Louis County," November 16, 1963, County LCRA Records; Testimony of Ida Scott, Transcript on Appeal, vol. 2, 608–609, *Brooks v. LCRA* Case File; "Low-Cost Apartments" [*Globe* clipping], October 23, 1968, box 1, folder 17, St. Louis County Municipalities Collection; East-West Gateway Coordinating Council, *Inventory of Housing Conditions*, 158, 165; Testimony of Ruby Koelling, Transcript on Appeal, vol. 2, 691–692, *Brooks v. LCRA* Case File.

21. Handwritten notes on Olivette, n.d., folder 64; "New Neighbors" newsletter, 1972, folder 10; "New Neighbors" Board Minutes, February 1973, folder 14, all Kay Drey Papers.

22. Testimony of Daniel Witt, Transcript on Appeal, vol. 1, 164, *Brooks v. LCRA* Case File; Gary Orfield, "The Housing Issues in the St. Louis Case," report to Judge William Hungate, U.S. District Court (St. Louis, MO), *Liddell v. Board of Education* 693 F. 2d 771 Court of Appeals, 8th Circuit (April 1981), 72.

23. Quarterly Report: City of Olivette, St. Louis County Municipalities Collection; Proposal for Redevelopment of Elmwood Park, MO R-10, First Phase, April 1963, *Brooks v. LCRA* Case File; "Minutes of a Special Meeting of the LCRA of St. Louis County," November 23, 1959, County LCRA Records.

24. "AFSC Experience and Recommendations re: Executive Order 11063 on Equal Opportunity in Housing," May 1967, folder 2, Kay Drey Papers.

25. Testimony of Clara Burden, Transcript on Appeal, vol. 1, 309–310; Testimony of Mary Bryant, Transcript on Appeal, vol. 1, 140–141; Testimony of Ida Scott, Transcript on Appeal, vol. 2, 57, all *Brooks v. LCRA* Case File.

26. Relocation Ledger (Plaintiff's Exhibit 1), *Brooks v. LCRA* Case File. Of 102 relocatees reported in 1962, 46 had purchased new homes. The relocation ledger records the purchase price of 40 of these, from which the average is calculated.

27. Testimony of Elizabeth Harris, Transcript on Appeal, vol. 1, 340–344, *Brooks v. LCRA* Case File.

28. "Minutes of a Regular Meeting of the LCRA of St. Louis County," June 19, 1963; "Minutes of a Special Meeting of the LCRA of St. Louis County," December 19, 1961; "Minutes of a Regular Meeting of the LCRA of St. Louis County," August 14, 1962, all County LCRA Records.

29. Final Report of the Grand Jury of St. Louis County, January Term, 1965, in *Brooks v. LCRA* Case File.

30. "Minutes of a Regular Meeting of the LCRA of St. Louis County," September 25, 1962, County LCRA Records.

31. Testimony of Daniel Witt, Transcript on Appeal, vol. 1, 204–205, and Appellant's Brief, both *Brooks v. LCRA* Case File.

32. "Relocation Plan," Elmwood Park MO R-10, October 1962; Urban Renewal Plan: Elmwood Park; Testimony of Daniel Witt, Transcript on Appeal, vol. 1, 201–204; "Explanatory Memorandum . . . for Change in Plan," Elmwood Park MO R-10, October 1962, all *Brooks v. LCRA* Case File.

33. Appellant's Brief and Testimony of Ida Scott, both in Transcript on Appeal, vol. 2, 582–584, *Brooks v. LCRA* Case File.

34. Testimony of Daniel Witt, Transcript on Appeal, vol. 1, 208, *Brooks v. LCRA* Case File; "Contract for Disposition of Land for Private Redevelopment," September 1963, Recorder Book 5196, 399, St. Louis County Recorder, Clayton, Missouri; "Minutes of a Regular Meeting of the LCRA of St. Louis County," May 12, 1965, County LCRA Records.

35. USCCR staff report, Exhibit 21, USCCR, *Hearings: St. Louis*, 540–542; "Market Analysis and Reuse Appraisal of Meacham Park Urban Renewal Area," 1959, folder 74, box 3, Roy Wenzlick Papers, WHMC; HUD memo cited in USCCR Staff Report, "Housing in St. Louis," 1970, box 3:127, FOR Records, WHMC.

36. Testimony of Willis Corbett, Transcript on Appeal, vol. 1, 86–87; Testimony of Lillie Lemmons, Transcript on Appeal, vol. 1, 254–255; Testimony of Maria Fannie White, Transcript on Appeal, vol. 1, 271–272, all *Brooks v. LCRA* Case File.

37. "AFSC Experience and Recommendations re: Executive Order 11063," Kay Drey Papers.

38. Handwritten notes on Olivette, Kay Drey Papers; "Minutes of a Regular Meeting of the LCRA of St. Louis County," July 16, 1963, County LCRA Records; Testimony of Willis Corbett, Transcript on Appeal, vol. 1, 63–64, 84–86, *Brooks v. LCRA* Case File; "Minutes of a Special Meeting of the LCRA of St. Louis County," October 9, 1963, County LCRA Records.

39. Urban Renewal Plan: Elmwood Park, *Brooks v. LCRA* Case File; "Minutes of a Special Meeting of the LCRA of St. Louis County," September 20, 1961, County LCRA Records; Ida Scott, *The History of Elmwood Park* (self-pub., 2004), 8–9; "Minutes of a Special Meeting of the LCRA of St. Louis County," August 20, 1963, County LCRA Records; Plaintiff's Exhibit 30 and Testimony L. C. Chase (Reasor), Transcript on Appeal, vol. 1, 172–175, both *Brooks v. LCRA* Case File; Dubrow, "Municipal Antagonism or Benign Neglect," 262.

40. USCCR, *Hearings: St. Louis*, 406–408, 441; Olivette LCRA to Residents of Olivette Elmwood Park Mo. R-35, folder 64, Kay Drey Papers; Dubrow, "Municipal Antagonism or Benign Neglect," 263.

41. Quarterly Report: City of Olivette (October, November, December 1969), box 19, folder 212; Quarterly Report: City of Olivette (October, November, December, 1971), box 19, folder 213; Quarterly Report: City of Olivette (January, February, March, 1973), box 19, folder 213, all St. Louis County Municipalities Collection.

42. Relocation Ledger, *Brooks v. LCRA* Case File.

43. United States Census Bureau, *Income of Family and Persons in the United States: 1963*, P-60, no. 43 (Washington, D.C.: U.S. Government Printing Office, 1964); Appellant's Brief, *Brooks v. LCRA* Case File.

44. Appellant's Brief, *Brooks v. LCRA* Case File.

45. "Minutes of a Regular Meeting of the LCRA of St. Louis County," April 9, 1963; "Minutes of a Regular Meeting of the LCRA of St. Louis County," May 14, 1963; "Minutes of a Special Meeting of the LCRA of St. Louis County," October 9, 1963, all County LCRA Records; Appellant's Brief and Testimony of Daniel Witt, Transcript on Appeal, vol. 1, 235, both *Brooks v. LCRA* Case File.

46. Testimony of Daniel Witt, Transcript on Appeal, vol. 1, 151, *Brooks v. LCRA* Case File; "Minutes of a Special Meeting of the LCRA of St. Louis County," January 23, 1964, County LCRA Records.

47. Final Report of the Grand Jury of St. Louis County, January Term, 1965, *Brooks v. LCRA* Case File.

48. Brooks v. LCRA of St. Louis County, 414 S.W.2d 545 (1967).

49. Lead plaintiffs Esther Brooks and Carl Bell, 10008 Roberts; joined by Sallie Bell, Carl Bell, and Annie May Bass (10004 Roberts); Elizabeth and Leo Wallace (1501 Lamson Place); Fred Johnson (9733 Roberts); Elizabeth Johnson (9726 Meeks); Grace Robinson (10161 Roberts); Lena Hendrick (9803 Meeks); Earnest Hannah (10033 Chicago); Roy and Julia Broyles (lots 28 to 34 of block 13); William Broyles and Vivian Broyles (lots 5 to 12 of block 15); Charles Bryant and Mary Bryant (lots 1, 2, 37, and 38 of block 15); Randall Howard and Clara Howard (lots 32–34 of block 5); Charles Phenix and Elizabeth Phenix (10000 Chicago Avenue, lots 16–19 of block 24); and Daisy Nickels (9731 Chicago, lots 37 of block 17), see Transcript on Appeal, vol. 1, 2–3, 10–11, *Brooks v. LCRA* Case File.

50. Appellant's Brief, *Brooks v. LCRA* Case File; Testimony of Herman Davis, USCCR, *Hearings: St. Louis*, 385–386; Statement of the Olivette LCRA, USCCR, *Hearings: St. Louis*, 699; Testimony of Olivette officials, USCCR, *Hearings: St. Louis*, 390–392.

51. Transcript on Appeal, vol. 2, 614, *Brooks v. LCRA* Case File.

52. Scott, *History of Elmwood Park*, 13.

53. Appellant's Brief, *Brooks v. LCRA* Case File.

54. Relocation Ledger; Transcript on Appeal, Vol. 1, 86, 412, 641–643; Elmwood Park Project Area: Relocation Plan (1962), all *Brooks v. LCRA* Case File.

55. Ida Scott Oral History (interviewed by Doris Wesley, November 1996), Box 4, Folder 78, Lift Every Voice and Sing Oral History Project, WHMC.

56. USCCR, *Hearings: St. Louis*, 360.

57. Scott, *History of Elmwood Park*, 13; undated relocation chart and Appellant's Brief, *Brooks v. LCRA* Case File. Post-redevelopment residency based on cross-check with St. Louis County Directory, vol. 1 (telephone listings by name) and vol. 2 (head-of-household by street address), Special Collections, St. Louis County Public Library.

58. Margaret Jane Radin, "Property and Personhood," *Stanford Law Review* 34, no. 5 (1982): 957–1015, quote at 991; Michelle Wilde Anderson, "Cities Inside Out: Poverty and Exclusion at the Urban Fringe," *UCLA Law Review* 55 (2007–2008): 1145–1150.

# Healthy Housing and the Health of the State

Leif Fredrickson

Urban renewal policy was public health policy—in both rhetoric and reality. Advocates justified and framed urban renewal policy in part through the goals of safe, healthy housing and sanitary urban conditions. But the success of urban renewal's public health goals was deeply bound up in the other motives for urban renewal and in the ways local governments implemented urban renewal policies and articulated them with existing public health programs.

Historians have rarely focused on the connection between public health and urban renewal, but this relationship is important for several reasons. First, poor housing has long been a public health problem, and it certainly was in the decades after World War II. The extent to which urban renewal, a major national initiative, did or did not mitigate this problem is important to assess.[1]

Second, foregrounding public health shows us how urban renewal programs and projects integrated with other ongoing programs and objectives of cities. When reading the history of urban renewal, which often focuses on case studies of individual projects, it is easy to get the sense that urban renewal projects were programmatically discrete. In fact, cities administered individual urban renewal projects as part of broader programs that included housing, redevelopment, transportation—and public health.

In this chapter, I zoom out to examine the development of healthy housing policies and urban renewal projects across time and space in Baltimore.

Doing so affords a view of how urban renewal projects were grafted onto existing housing, development, and public health programs. And it allows us to see how the city, and the institutions it worked with, tried successively to modify urban renewal projects in order to better meet their objectives. Focusing on Baltimore, we can see how these programs "worked" in terms benefiting public health. And we can also see how they "worked" in the sense of how the constituencies, administration, control, and goals of the programs changed over time.

Finally, the overlapping histories of urban renewal and public health afford us a view of something more abstract: how the goals and functions of the local state were shaped over time by different contexts (war, urban decline) and different interests (the state itself, real estate capitalists, landlords, public health experts, housing reformers, and residents). In the case of Baltimore, the context of World War II allowed for the emergence of an aggressive local program aimed at healthy housing. But as war faded and the crisis of downtown real estate emerged as a result of mass suburbanization, real estate interests gained a stronger hand, using federal urban renewal as a vehicle for their interests. Urban renewal programs subsumed and eventually marginalized the preexisting public health campaign to improve housing through housing code enforcement.

## Before Urban Renewal

Federal urban renewal began with the Housing Act of 1949, although the term "urban renewal" actually accompanied the revisions in the 1954 Housing Act. Cities embraced the programs and funding these acts created, but local programs did not emerge ex nihilo. Cities grafted urban renewal programs onto existing housing code and redevelopment policies. In the case of Baltimore, those preexisting programs were at the forefront of a modern approach to housing codes and their enforcement.

Housing codes were rooted in the legal authority of "police power"—the power to regulate property for the public good. Baltimore passed its first housing code in 1750, updating it periodically. By 1927, the health commissioner could declare as public nuisances anything "dangerous or detrimental to life or health," at which point the commissioner could order removals, abatements, alterations, and so on. This gave considerable power to the city, but in practice codes were weakly enforced.[2]

"Slums" had existed in Baltimore since the nineteenth century. But the Great Depression exacerbated slum conditions, especially for poor black neighborhoods. Black Baltimoreans had long faced housing discrimination, which packed them into circumscribed parts of the city, and job discrimination, which gave them fewer resources to afford good housing. The Depression made the job situation much worse. And the federal government's New Deal housing programs nationalized discriminatory housing practices.

Worsening slums brought fear of a resurgence of disease epidemics, like tuberculosis, or new types of epidemics, like the discovery in Baltimore of widespread lead poisoning in poor black housing in the 1930s. Health and social service professionals sought to understand slums to mitigate their problems, but what they did in practice was shaped by institutional constraints and other interests.

In the 1930s, the Baltimore City Health Department (BCHD) saw slums and "blighted areas" as being the result of a complex interplay of health, housing, and economics. Slums put people at risk for tuberculosis, according to the BCHD, but people often lived in slums "as a result of having been pushed forcibly down the economic ladder on account of their tuberculosis, unemployment and inability to conquer the disease." Notably absent from this description was housing segregation. Nevertheless, the BCHD did recognize that "the problem of improving housing conditions is one which is intricately involved with the general economic structure of the community, with its real estate and mortgage inheritances and many other determining factors that lie beyond the scope of the Health Department activity."[3] In other words, the health department recognized its own limit to solve problems of healthy housing through nuisance regulation alone without more penetrating changes in labor and housing markets.

Such limits soon became apparent. In the mid-1930s, the social worker Frances Morton carried out a detailed study of slums and disease in the city.[4] In 1939, catalyzed by Morton's study, the city health commissioner, Huntington Williams, recommended the demolition of St. John's Court, an east Baltimore slum, because it was unsanitary and unfit for human habitation. This was the first time the health department had condemned a dwelling.[5] Notably, while rooted in a concern for health, condemnation through nuisance law did not provide any power (let alone funding) to help those individuals most affected by slum conditions: the residents.

By the end of the 1930s, the city gained another tool to clear slums. In 1937, Congress passed the federal Housing Act. The act provided federal funding for public housing, with the dual goals of reducing unemployment and providing safe, sanitary housing that would replace unhealthy slums. To be eligible for funding, local governments had to create laws and agencies that allowed them to condemn and clear property. Maryland passed an enabling act in 1937, and Baltimore subsequently created a housing authority.

In Baltimore's first public housing project, Edgar Allan Poe Homes, the government cleared 385 dwellings, about 90 percent of them black households. Poe Homes had about 100 fewer dwelling units, however, resulting in a net loss. Latrobe Homes, the city's second project, was built at St. John's Court.

It yielded a net gain in dwelling units. But Latrobe was for whites only, and 66 percent of the households displaced from the Latrobe site were black.[6] Both these patterns were common for public housing in Baltimore and elsewhere. Public housing failed to keep pace with housing units destroyed by the state, housing was segregated, and black homes were destroyed to make room for all-white public housing.

With the United States' entry into World War II, public housing construction shifted toward the goal of providing housing for people flocking to cities for the war industry. This construction, however, was far from enough to stave off a major housing crunch. The demand for housing resulted in large-scale conversion of single-family dwellings into multiple-family homes. Building inspectors turned a blind eye, and the resulting housing was often unhealthy and even outright hazardous. Meanwhile, the extremely tight rental market allowed landlords to gouge tenants.

These issues concerned politicians at all levels of government. Slums, unhealthy housing, and short housing supply were not sustainable conditions in the long run for cities. And in the short run, they threatened the stability of the labor force that was churning out industrial products for the war. A healthy workforce was an exigency of war, and therefore so was healthy housing.[7] Thus governments pursued much stronger regulation of the housing market.

Baltimore was a leader. In 1941, the city council passed the first "modern" housing code in the nation: the Ordinance on the Hygiene of Housing (Ordinance No. 384).[8] The key change was that it gave the BCHD broad authority to develop its own regulations. The following year, the department promulgated a series of regulations aimed at healthy housing, including occupancy limits.[9]

Several interests shaped the ordinance and implementation. Low-income housing advocates, including Morton, had pushed for it.[10] But the real estate industry successfully lobbied to shift some aspects of liability to occupants, rather than owners.[11] Still, the law remained relatively powerful. As a result, owners and landlords challenged it in court numerous times. They lost.[12] It was a win for public health regulation. But an effective program would require much more, including the ability to collect information on violations and notify, charge, prosecute, and enforce penalties against tens of thousands of owners and tenants. Finally, if the state was not able to force owners to abate housing issues, it had to have the capacity to abate problems itself, including razing unsalvageable housing.

In the first four years after the passage of the ordinance, the BCHD significantly expanded its organizational capacity. It hired more housing inspectors and promoted an ambitious inspector, G. Yates Cook, to lead the charge. In 1943, the BCHD created a separate housing division in the bureau of sanitation. The BCHD forced some owners to abate nuisances and in some cases required dwellings to be vacated and demolished.[13]

Despite some headway in housing issues, the situation was still dire in 1944. The BCHD had only a handful of inspectors for the more than two hundred thousand buildings in the city.[14] Compliance was low, enforcement was weak, and enforcement that did happen could result in evictions and loss of desperately needed dwelling units.[15]

Because of these problems, the mayor convened a committee in 1944 to study housing problems. It determined that the city would never improve the fifty thousand or so dwellings that were in violation of the healthy housing regulations if the BCHD continued to work on a complaint basis—that is, discovering housing violations only after tenants complained. The committee also suggested the need for cross-departmental coordination.[16]

Another organization, the Citizens Planning and Housing Association (CPHA), also played a critical role in conceptualizing and implementing a modernized approach to housing codes. The CPHA had been formed in 1941 from two organizations: the Citizens Housing Council, a group of social workers led by Morton who were concerned about low-income housing, and the Citizens Planning and Redevelopment Association, a group of professional architects and real estate investors concerned about blight and declining property values.[17] The resulting CPHA thus combined goals of providing decent living conditions for the poor (via public housing, code enforcement, slum clearance, rent control, and education) with goals of preserving property values (via zoning, land use planning, code enforcement, slum clearance, and redevelopment). The goals of the two parent organizations especially overlapped regarding code enforcement and slum clearance.[18]

The CPHA suggested that Baltimore pick one part of the city to test if a coordinated, concentrated, proactive approach to code enforcement could reverse housing deterioration.[19] It also pushed for coordinating the government's response with entities who could assist in revitalizing places targeted for housing conservation and rehabilitation.

In 1945, the city put these recommendations together under the guidance of a new city institution, the Housing Code Enforcement Committee. The BCHD led the committee, which included many other city agencies. It focused on one block—"Block One"—with the idea of enforcing housing regulations to the letter of the law for every structure, forcing owners to either rehabilitate or vacate their homes. It also sought to enlist the residents in the task of cleaning up the block. This block-by-block, proactive approach of code enforcement became known as the "Baltimore Plan" of slum rehabilitation.[20] It was successful in some ways. But the pace was dishearteningly slow. It took four municipal departments and two bureaus coordinating for a year and half to raise *one* block to the *minimum* housing standard. Moreover, by 1947, Block One was already deteriorating again.[21]

By the end of the 1940s, three key problems emerged from the block-by-block program. First, while agencies could order abatements to code violations, landlords often did not take enforcement seriously. Courts were backed up, and penalties were light. To mitigate these problems, the Housing Code Enforcement Committee and the CPHA pushed for the creation of a separate court. In 1947, the state of Maryland gave Baltimore the first housing court in the nation.[22] The second problem was one of scale. Proponents of slum rehabilitation came to believe that because slums surrounded individual blocks, these blocks easily slipped back into slum status.

Finally, Commissioner Williams noted that the plan was not intended to solve housing problems and was not a substitute for redevelopment and public housing. It was a stopgap measure, designed, according to the mayor, Thomas D'Alesandro, to maintain minimum standards until the "slums can be torn down and satisfactory housing built." The plan was like "first aid administered in the temporary absence of a doctor." Enforcement, D'Alesandro noted, did not add one dwelling to the supply of low-rent housing and in fact ended up reducing the supply through condemnation. Thus, strict enforcement would actually increase overcrowding in the remaining slums.[23]

Despite the mixed results of the program, it is significant that, in the 1940s, the problem of housing and slums in Baltimore had been spearheaded by the BCHD, which had been empowered with much greater regulatory authority, expanded capacity, and considerably leeway to experiment with new approaches to code enforcement. The BCHD's efforts had also spurred the creation of the housing court. The war thus catalyzed and sustained an aggressive, public health approach to housing that persevered for almost a decade until 1950. In that year, the city budget contained $200,000 for the Baltimore Plan.[24] By that point, however, the 1949 Housing Act had passed and was setting in motion redevelopment projects that would dwarf investments in housing code enforcement.

## Title I Redevelopment

The Housing Act of 1949 included provisions that extended federally backed mortgages and public housing, along with programs for research and rural housing. Its most radical provision, however, was Title I, a program to fund slum clearance for private redevelopment. The act, and especially Title I, was controversial—rife with tensions among the interests of housing reformers, local governments, and the construction and real estate industries.

One objective that tended to unite its constituencies, however, was the elimination of unsanitary and disease-ridden slums. The act declared the need to secure the "health and living standards" of the American people. And Title I of the act made federal funding for slum clearance dependent on local efforts to maintain and improve healthy and sanitary housing conditions.[25] President Harry Truman praised the slum clearance provisions for their promise of redeveloping areas in a "sound and healthy manner."[26] The surgeon general, Leonard Scheele, hailed the act as the answer to the urgent problem of slums that bred tuberculosis and other diseases. The act, he said, "should greatly strengthen the hand of health officials" in dealing with this problem.[27]

Title I of the 1949 Housing Act provided federal funding for slum clearance and redevelopment. The authority to redevelop lay at the local level in the concept of eminent domain—the power to expropriate property for the public good. Eminent domain allowed municipalities to condemn property to build roads, bridges, parks, and so on. Baltimore's early eminent domain projects (before the 1930s) also occasionally entailed clearing "slums," and in some cases this was done not just to use the space but to remove unwanted people who were seen as a threat to property values, morality, health, and white control of city space.[28]

In contrast to earlier uses of eminent domain, redevelopment under Title I had a much broader vision of urban problems and solutions. Along with that came a broader understanding of how eminent domain could be used, including in the condemnation of private property for redevelopment by other private interests. The use of eminent domain for private redevelopment was not new, but the earlier uses had primarily been for creation of transportation infrastructure used by a huge swath of the public. Title I redevelopment was more loosely connected to the public interest by the argument that slum clearance would reduce disease and increase property values.[29]

As with the 1937 Housing Act, the 1949 Housing Act required that local governments pass enabling legislation related to slum clearance and redevelopment. Many states had already identified slum clearance as a public good and thus passed such enabling legislation. In 1943, legislators introduced a bill that authorized the creation of a Baltimore Land Development Commission with the power of eminent domain. But Baltimore's Mayor McKeldin did not create the commission, in part because he and the city solicitor, Simon Sobeloff, believed the Housing Authority of Baltimore City (HABC) should oversee dealing with blight and slums. Sobeloff argued that even though public redevelopment would reduce the tax base, it would guarantee the city would get what it wanted: low-income housing development and the replacement of housing destroyed in slum clearance. Private developers, he argued, were not likely to build housing for the very poor because it would not be profitable. McKeldin also argued that the initial legislation was vulnerable to charges of unconstitutionality. To fix the latter problem, the legislators proposed an amendment to the state constitution allowing for such a commission in 1944. The mayor, under great pressure from the real estate industry, created the Baltimore Redevelopment Commission (BRC) in 1945.[30]

The purpose of the BRC was to identify, obtain, and clear slums and blighted areas for resale for private development. In addition to leveraging eminent domain, the program subsidized private investment in urban land by using state funds to carry out the research, physical clearance, and legal procedures necessary to procure and sell land. Although some of the initial proposed legislation to create a redevelopment commission emphasized the creation of "low rent housing and collateral facilities" via private investment, the final amendment said nothing about low-rent housing.[31] The stated goal of the commission was to eliminate slums and blight and facilitate "redevelopment."[32]

Also in 1945, the Commission on the City Plan (CCP) released a report on blight and housing problems in the city. It noted that people living in blighted areas could not afford to pay rents that provided "decent living conditions." This produced an inherent tension because even if BRC's "sole interest," as the report put it, was "doing away with the slums, not the provision of low-rent housing," the BRC still had to contend with whether simply displacing poor people would re-create slums elsewhere in the city. Ultimately, while the CCP found the BRC to be a "radical" idea, it believed that when used alongside subsidized low-income housing, it was a worthwhile experiment.[33]

Redevelopment, it turned out, was a disaster for low-income residents, especially African Americans. Redevelopment plans began with the creation of the BRC, but the passage of Title I kicked things into high gear. The BRC completed its first plan—Project 1-A—in May of 1950. The council and mayor quickly approved it.[34] In less than a year, the federal government approved the plan, kicking in two-thirds of the $1.5 million budget for the project.[35]

The BRC described Project 1-A, located in South Waverly, as a "bad slum." But neither photos nor statistics of the area support that. Of the five blighted areas the CCP studied, South Waverly had the newest houses, the lowest need for repairs, and the highest ownership rate. And it had a *lower* rate of tuberculosis and meningitis than the city average.[36] Instead of focusing on the worst housing or health conditions—as the purpose of the 1949 Housing Act might dictate—the BRC chose Waverly because the "better residential sections of Waverly north of this area were constantly in danger from the close proximity of this isolated slum section."[37] And Waverly was probably also chosen because although the area had a significant mix of both white and black residents, it had become increasingly black over the 1940s.[38]

Between 1951 and 1953, Baltimore demolished every one of the 162 residential dwellings in South Waverly, along with 31 commercial buildings. Then it sold the twenty-three acres of land to an ambitious developer, James Rouse. Rouse built a shopping center and 321 "garden apartments," the latter with the help of federal mortgage insurance. When completed in 1957, Waverly became the second Title I project to be completed in the nation and the first with an FHA-insured rental housing project.[39]

For the city, the project was a net gain in housing quality and quantity. But not for most of Waverly's former residents and their health. Rouse's apartments were for whites only, but of the 192 households from South Waverly, 62.5 percent were black. People displaced by Title I projects were given priority for public housing, but demand overwhelmed supply. Only 16 Waverly households got public housing. For the others, the city offered relocation counseling but no reimbursement for moving expenses. Most families simply ended up in other "blighted" sections of town. Homeowners who moved paid more for their new housing than the government paid them for their demolished housing—a result, according to those displaced, of the government's hardball negotiating. Black homeowners were paid about $3,700 for their homes but paid an average of $7,800 for their new homes. These higher prices may have indicated the purchase of better housing. But they also likely reflected the premium black Baltimoreans had to pay for the same housing that whites had—a direct result of racially exclusionary housing. High housing costs forced many black Baltimore families to double up in houses or defer maintenance. Both practices led to housing deterioration.[40]

Thus, from the beginning Title I redevelopments were dubious in terms of their public health goals. The Waverly neighborhood was hardly a priority in terms of public health in Baltimore. And these Title I redevelopments made little effort to ensure that displaced residents ended up in better—healthier—housing. Most did not.

Subsequent Title I projects in Baltimore similarly demolished housing without providing good options for displaced residents. A detailed 1961 study found that most displaced families moved into surrounding neighborhoods, remaining in the "rundown sections of the city."[41] Displaced people also paid more for housing. Renters paid an average of ten dollars more per month in rent (about ninety dollars in 2021 dollars). Homeowners, meanwhile, could barely afford their new homes. As a result, people crowded into housing to relieve costs. Unsurprisingly, therefore, the city found no improvement in crowding before and after displacement.[42] And, again, homeowners stretched thin with housing costs probably deferred maintenance. Deferred maintenance and crowded housing further "blighted" neighborhoods and yielded unhealthy housing conditions, such as lead paint exposure.

## The Pilot Program and Mount Royal

As the BRC drafted more urban redevelopment plans and fired up the bulldozers, ambitious housing code enforcement programs also proceeded. In

1951, the city launched its "Pilot Program" in east Baltimore. This "Pilot Area" targeted by the program included fourteen blocks. The area was 80 percent black, and most residents were workers with steady jobs. The neighborhood had a reputation for stability. Unlike the earlier test blocks, the Pilot Area included substantial homeownership (about 40 percent). Also, unlike the test blocks, the Pilot Area was predominantly "blighted" rather than a "rock bottom slum." Conditions were still quite bad, however, with 40 percent of homes "seriously deteriorated." Many lacked central heat or refrigeration. Rats, trash, and sewage were problems.[43]

With this project, the BCHD further elevated its housing wing, creating a housing bureau headed by Cook. It was Cook's job to coordinate city agencies with code enforcement powers, including the bureau of building inspection and the fire department. Cook was also charged with ginning up voluntary support to help clean up neighborhoods.[44]

The hope was that the Pilot Program would be a blueprint for reclaiming all the slums in Baltimore, as well as an inspiration to other cities. It certainly succeeded in this latter goal, eventually gaining national notoriety as the Baltimore Plan. But in practice, it was a mixed bag. As before, landlords openly resisted the program. It was cheaper to pay fines, which averaged twenty-two dollars an incident, than make repairs. With a good lawyer, landlords could easily delay for months. In the meantime, they might make the repairs or sell the property.[45] If they made repairs, they often raised rents. In one study, landlords spent from $800 to $8,000 (in 2021 dollars) on repairs and raised rents 11 percent, making them unaffordable for some tenants. For this reason, as well as fear of retaliation for reporting violations, tenants were often deeply distrustful of the code enforcement program.[46]

As for the homeowners, many lacked the capital to even make improvements required by code. As a result, code enforcement could make their situations more precarious. The crackdown on overcrowded houses, for example, meant an end to boarders, who supplemented homeowners' incomes.[47] Moreover, many owned their houses on "contract." Contract selling was basically a lease-to-own system. But it was poorly regulated and open to tremendous exploitation. Lessors, for example, could repossess a house after just one missed payment. Faced with strict code enforcement, landlords often forced their tenants to buy their residences on contract or be evicted. By leasing, the landlords could avoid both rent control caps and liability for fixing housing code violations.[48]

To deal with the problem of poor homeowners, a private group started the Fight Blight Fund in 1951 to provide a revolving fund of loans for needy homeowners.[49] In addition, the BCHD created a hearing board to hear hardship cases and work out extra time and accommodations for homeowners who were struggling to come into compliance. These institutions helped code enforcement work, in terms of both getting compliance and not producing outright revolt against it. And the program did bring results. For the first time, for example, mothers found they did not have to fear that rats would bite their babies. In 1954, the program even expanded its borders at the request of adjacent residents.[50]

But success was qualified and fleeting. The program never got compliance from landlords. Homeowner compliance was for bare minimum standards, which did not even include a toilet in each house. Crowding never improved because slum clearance projects elsewhere pushed more people into the area. Gains made were unsustainable. When the program ended in 1954, the BCHD discovered (once again) that it could not maintain compliance without enforcement. The rats returned. Within a few years, the program's effect on the area was not discernible.[51]

Those involved with the Baltimore Plan identified several problems with it, though they did not agree on all the solutions. One issue was that some enthusiastic businesspeople took the plan to be an unmitigated success, implicitly or explicitly making the case that public housing was not needed. As a result, the Baltimore housing authority became unenthusiastic about the plan, which it saw as a legitimate threat to its budget. Another issue, again echoing what Commissioner Williams had said about the earlier test bock program, was that the plan included no eminent domain authority. For example, areas could not be cleared to create a park for kids to play.

Finally, there was the issue of administration. The BCHD took the lead in coordinating the program with other departments. But some agencies, particularly the Bureau of Building Inspection (BBI), did not want to be coordinated and refused to assign inspectors full time to the project because it said it needed inspectors for new construction. Other agencies were also indifferent. Cook and the head of the citizens' advisory council to the housing bureau, James Rouse, reported to the mayor that having the BCHD's housing bureau coordinate these programs was hopeless. The council suggested that a new agency be invested with all the city's legal and organizational powers to fight slums on its own. This idea, however, was vigorously opposed by Williams, who argued that the responsibility to protect the health of the people should remain with the health department. The mayor backed Williams, resulting in the resignations of both Cook and Rouse.[52]

Rouse, however, took his approach to the level of state and national government to help get legislation passed that could instantiate his vision for dealing with slums. In the meantime, at the local level, housing code enforcement shifted to the Mount Royal neighborhood of Baltimore.

The Mount Royal project continued several trends in Baltimore's code enforcement program. The program had started with Block One, a small, mostly black, and very poor area. The Pilot Program was a bigger area that was still poor and black, but it had more homeowners and more whites. Having ultimately failed in these slums and blighted areas, the city now focused on an even larger area—which supposedly made it less susceptible to the "spread" of blight—with higher home-ownership rates, more wealth, and residents who were mostly white. The hope was that code enforcement might be more successful in an even bigger area and in an area that was in an even earlier stage of threat from "blight." Similarly, the experience with poor homeowners resulted in the hope that wealthier homeowners would have more resources to comply with codes.[53]

Previous code enforcement programs had been initiated by the city, rather than by residents, who had little voice in initiating or approving programs. But that changed with Mount Royal. Before World War II, Mount Royal had been a middle- to upper-class white neighborhood. After the war, it largely retained that profile, but new groups began moving in, too: rural whites and blacks from the South and black Baltimoreans from other parts of the city. There was tremendous prejudice against all these groups from established Mount Royal residents. These residents were also concerned about physical changes to the neighborhood, such as noise, trash, overcrowded and deteriorating housing, and the conversion of single-family homes to multifamily residences. As a result, in 1953, several prominent residents of Mount Royal pushed city hall for a code enforcement and rehabilitation program aimed at their neighborhood.[54]

The health department led and coordinated the code enforcement program in Mount Royal. While there were many fewer substandard houses in this neighborhood compared to the Pilot Area (only 20 percent in the 1950 census), most of them had some sort of violation of the city code. In addition, the BCHD had just issued additional and more stringent healthy housing regulations. Thus, Mount Royal was held to a higher standard than the Pilot Area. Despite attempts by the BCHD to streamline its code enforcement process, and despite working in an area with better housing and wealthier residents, progress was still slow. Middle-class residents balked at the idea that they, too, had to bring their homes into compliance, not just the overcrowded multifamily homes inhabited by rural white southerners and African Americans. These latter homes were, as usual, operated by landlords who again resisted compliance. The residents of these homes also tended to be more transient than the homeowners of the Pilot Area and hence less interested in investing in housing rehabilitation.[55]

After a year, Mount Royal residents became increasingly disillusioned with code enforcement. At the heart of this was the question of who and what code enforcement was for. At its most benign, the call from Mount Royal's white, middle-class residents for code enforcement was a call to keep or restore the aesthetics of their neighborhood. To put an end to trash, overcrowded housing, and noise. But there was strong evidence that for many the goal was more pernicious. The long-standing neighborhood group in the area was the Mount Royal Protective Association, which included among its prerogatives keeping black people out of the neighborhood. (The association eventually brokered a deal with the Urban League to allow a percentage of black residents in the neighborhood.) There was likewise open hostility to the "hillbillies" from the South. What some of these white, middle-class residents wanted was the removal of these groups from their neighborhood.[56]

The BCHD, however, pursued its program of bringing housing up to the minimum health standards. That meant that most of the multifamily dwelling stayed crowded within the limit of the law. Similarly, housing code violations often pertained to the insides of houses, which meant there was little outward evidence of the program. In addition, the program did not do much to remove or stop the influx of groups that some of the white, middle-class residents objected to. Thus, whatever goal drove residents to seek the power of the state, the BCHD's strict housing code enforcement program was not doing the job. Middle-class residents soon requested a more robust program to address their concerns—a program coming out of the recent 1954 Housing Act known as urban renewal.[57]

## The 1954 Housing Act and Urban Renewal

The 1954 Housing Act was the first major update of the 1949 Housing Act. Like the 1949 act, the 1954 act was justified in part through public health.[58] What was new in the 1954 act was an approach called urban renewal. At the time, "urban renewal" referred to a planned approach that integrated conservation (upkeep of homes, mostly through code enforcement), rehabilitation (improvement of deteriorated homes with code enforcement and financing), and clearance and redevelopment. Although public housing remained part of the 1954 Housing Act, it was relegated to acting as a place for displaced families or a holding pen for the very poor, rather than a broader project to providing decent, suitable housing for people who could not get it in the housing market. On the other hand, the act provided funding for conservation and rehabilitation projects and required cities to modernize their housing codes, as Baltimore had done over a decade before. Thus, in many cities, and especially Baltimore, federal urban renewal programs increasingly merged with housing code enforcement programs in the 1950s and 1960s.[59]

The 1954 Housing Act had a strong connection to Baltimore. In the late 1940s and early 1950s, real estate and building interests latched on to the Baltimore Plan as an alternative to public housing, which they opposed. As noted, the original proponents of the Baltimore Plan, including Frances Morton, Commissioner Williams, and Mayor D'Alesandro, consistently argued that concentrated code enforcement had to go along with a major investment in public housing. But the real estate and construction industries distorted the Baltimore Plan—a plan with an (at best) equivocal track record—into a program that could, by itself, cure blight.[60] In 1949, the National Association of Home Builders (NAHB) produced a filmstrip based on the Baltimore Plan, presenting the story as one in which the actions of code enforcement and private industry *ended* slum conditions. That same year, a member of Congress argued for something like the Baltimore Plan as a preferable alternative to public housing.[61] Media portrayal of the plan reached a peak around 1953, with frequent glossing over of the problem of slumlord recalcitrance, resident approval, and any evidence of a long-term effect.

It was also at this time that consensus around how to deal with code enforcement began to break down. Rouse and Cook abandoned further involvement with Baltimore's code enforcement programs. Cook went to work for the NAHB. Rouse, along with other bankers and developers, ended up in an advisory position helping draft the new 1954 Housing Act. The 1954 Housing Act bore a strong stamp of influence of the Baltimore Plan, as filtered through the worldview of real estate developers. To them, the Baltimore Plan showed that much could be done with code enforcement, voluntarist action, and better access to financing. And if these could be used with slum clearance and redevelopment tools, slums and blight could be effectively battled with little or no public housing.[62]

Dissatisfied with concentrated code enforcement, the white, middle-class residents of Mount Royal clamored for an urban renewal program in their neighborhood. The city initially rebuffed them. But after they organized a protest at city hall, the mayor promised them urban renewal. Meanwhile, Rouse and other downtown business leaders formed the Greater Baltimore Committee to get private businesses involved in renewal and redevelopment plans. Rouse urged Mayor D'Alesandro to convene a study board. The mayor did so, and in 1956 the Urban Renewal Study Board handed its report to the mayor.[63]

Among its myriad points, the report made one overarching suggestion: that clearance, redevelopment, and code enforcement powers should be vested in one agency with the ability to use them in large, planned urban renewal areas. The next year, the city created the Baltimore Urban Renewal and Housing Authority (BURHA) to do just that. The housing bureau from the BCHD was relocated to BURHA, which took up the primary responsibility for code enforcement.[64]

BURHA facilitated the creation of the two large urban renewal projects in the 1950s: Mount Royal and Harlem Park. Primarily, what the new urban renewal project added to ongoing efforts in Mount Royal was more slum clearance on the south end of the neighborhood—the part that was poorer and more black. Ultimately, in the 1960s, the project displaced over three thousand people, the majority of whom were black. As in the past, only some of this cleared housing was replaced. And those displaced were "unable to capitalize on their move to improved housing in a better neighborhood so as to raise their overall standard of living," according to one study. The study also noted that pushing people into other neighborhoods could cause "rapid deterioration" of those places.[65] The northern—wealthier and whiter—part of the project did meet with some success in staving off "blight." It was one of the few places in inner-city Baltimore that experienced immigration from affluent white people in the 1960s.

In addition to Mount Royal, Baltimore launched the Harlem Park urban renewal project. Like Mount Royal, it consisted of a combination of clearance, redevelopment, and housing code enforcement. Harlem Park—which had much more deteriorated housing and more rentals than Mount Royal—emphasized rehabilitation: the restoration of deteriorated houses. In addition, the project developed aesthetic standards for housing. This was to get FHA rehabilitation loans (part of the 1954 Housing Act), which were not available for strictly making houses healthier. The houses had to be marketable too. As experience had shown, poor homeowners could not afford code compliance, and landlords refused compliance. The government hoped FHA loans would provide resources for the former and incentives for the latter. But it was only partially successful because the increased financing came with requirements for more housing improvements.[66]

BURHA's reign over housing code enforcement was short lived. Although the agency did code enforcement, enforcement was marginalized by other projects (clearance and redevelopment) or subsumed under broader goals (rehabilitation). Williams charged that the housing bureau had become less active under BURHA than under the health department.[67]

Dissatisfaction with BURHA and code enforcement in general—the 1960 census showed continuing, serious housing problems in the city—as well as confusion over jurisdiction of health code enforcements in places outside urban renewals areas (such as the suburbs) prompted the mayor to form a task force to study code enforcement. The report argued that code enforcement—both building and health codes for all parts of the city—should be located in one agency. Despite many department heads and local housing experts warning against it, the mayor chose to lodge that authority with the BBI in 1961. The BBI was widely regarded as lacking the capacity and expertise to carry out this job and being too politically close to the property owners it would have to regulate. Dissatisfaction thus continued, and the BBI faced continuous criticism resulting in further reorganizations in 1969.[68] By then, federal urban renewal programs themselves had come under intense criticism. In 1974, the federal government ended the urban renewal program.

Meanwhile, Baltimore hemorrhaged people to the suburbs, and huge tracts of inner-city housing went vacant. Interstate building further compounded the deterioration of inner-city housing and facilitated decentralization. Attempts to fix blight and ensure healthy housing continued. But the expansive and aspirational approaches to housing, including healthy housing, that characterized the post–World War II period, at both the local and federal level, were gone.

Federal urban redevelopment and renewal programs had been, from the beginning, justified in part through their public health effects. But they never delivered on that goal. Unhealthy slum housing was destroyed. Some families may have ended up in better housing. But many did not. Moreover, urban renewal programs often exacerbated unhealthy conditions for families and neighborhoods. The story of urban renewal in Baltimore reveals a program that was unable to counteract the forces that pushed and kept people in unhealthy housing. There were two reasons for that.

First, even in the hands of administrators dedicated to public health, the urban renewal tool kit was inadequate while racial discrimination in housing prevailed and public housing production was meager. Many of Baltimore's residents lived in deeply squalid slum housing. Many others lived in housing that, while solid in some ways, contained serious health threats, such as lead paint. Code enforcement and, in some cases, clearance were necessary tools to deal with unhealthy housing. But on their own, they had the effect of simply moving the people most affected to similar housing in a different part of the city. And they were employed in deeply unfair and discriminatory ways. Without open housing and, perhaps most important, strong public investment in new affordable housing, these tools were doomed—just as public health advocates had argued from the beginning.

Second, the administration of urban renewal was vulnerable to influence or capture by urban developers and landlords. Those interest groups deprioritized or suppressed urban renewal's public health goals. The strong position of the BCHD in the 1940s and 1950s stemmed from the war and the overlap between public health and wartime exigency. As the war receded, national objectives aimed at economic growth and development came to dominate housing policy. Affordable housing and public health advocates initially backed the Housing Act of 1949. But urban renewal became highly influenced, and in some cases even administered, by urban real estate developers. Eventually, the seemingly intractable problem of code enforcement was passed off to the BBI, with its close ties to builders and landlords. Thus, not only did urban renewal programs in Baltimore initiate little in the way of public health protections, but they sapped energy, and ultimately an entire housing bureau, from a city health department that had begun the 1940s as a national leader in healthy housing.

## NOTES

1. The few historical takes include Russ Lopez, "Public Health, the APHA, and Urban Renewal," *American Journal of Public Health* 99, no. 9 (September 2009), 1603–1611; Mindy Fullilove, *Root Shock: How Tearing Up City Neighborhoods Hurts America, and What We Can Do About It* (New York: Random House, 2009).

2. Virginia Ermer, "Street-Level Bureaucrats in Baltimore: The Case of Housing Code Enforcement" (Ph.D. diss., Johns Hopkins University, 1972); City of Baltimore, *Ordinances and Resolutions of the Mayor and City Council of Baltimore* (Baltimore: King Bros., 1927), 915–917.

3. "The Baltimore City Health Department and the So-Called Blighted Areas," *Baltimore Health News*, June 1936, 31–32, Maryland Room, Enoch Pratt Library.

4. Frances Morton, "A Social Study of Wards 5 and 10 in Baltimore, Maryland," Baltimore Council of Social Agencies, April 1, 1937, folder 2, box 2, series I, Health and Welfare Council (HWC) Records, Langsdale Library Special Collections (LLSC).

5. Baltimore City Health Department, *Annual 1939*, 9–10, 48, 250, Baltimore City Health Department Archives.

6. Housing Authority of Baltimore, *Public Housing in Baltimore 1941–1942*, 2–56, folder 56, box 20, series X, Greater Baltimore Committee (GBC) Records LLSC; Baltimore Urban Renewal and Housing Authority, "Data Sheets: Urban Renewal and Public Housing Projects," May 1961, folder 21, box 4, series X, BURHA Records; Urban Renewal and Public Housing Fact Sheets, various years, folder 43, box 1, series VI, Citizens Planning and Housing Association (CPHA) Records, all LLSC.

7. U.S. Congress, *National Defense Migration: Hearings Before the United States House Select Committee Investigating National Defense Migration, Seventy-Seventh Congress, First Session, on July 1, 2, 1941, Part 15, Baltimore Hearings* (Washington, D.C.: U.S. Government Printing Office, 1941); "Warns of Slums in Housing Rush," *Sun*, March 14, 1941. For the nexus of the state, war, and disease, see Mark Harrison, *Disease and the Modern World: 1500 to the Present Day* (New York: John Wiley and Sons, 2013).

8. National Commission on Urban Problems, *Building the American City* (Washington, D.C.: U.S. Government Printing Office, 1968), 274. City of Baltimore, *Ordinances and Resolutions of the Mayor and City Council of Baltimore* (Baltimore: King Bros., 1942), last updated October 17, 2012, available at http://archive.org/details/ordinances42balt.

9. Baltimore City Health Department, "New City Housing Regulations," *Baltimore Health News*, April 1942, 25–31.

10. Interview with Frances Morton Froelicher, November 22, 1977, folder 17, box 2, series I, CPHA Records, LLSC.

11. "Council Studying New Housing Code," *Sun*, January 28, 1941, 9; Franklyn Baumgart, "Under the Dome of the City Hall," *Sun*, February 9, 1941, 16.

12. Baltimore City Health Department, "Court Upholds New Housing Ordinance, and Regulations," *Baltimore Health News*, December 1942. *Petrushansky v. State*, 182 *Md.* 164, 32 A.2d 696 (1943).

13. Baltimore City Health Department, *Annual 1943*, 236–246, Baltimore City Health Department Archives.

14. Cynthia Neverdon-Morton, "Black Housing Patterns in Baltimore City, 1885–1953," *Maryland Historian* 16 (1985): 41–56.

15. Baltimore City Health Department, *Annuals*, various years, Baltimore City Health Department Archives.

16. "Round-Table Discussion on Housing Scheduled," *Sun*, April 6, 1945, 9; Ermer, "Street-Level Bureaucrats in Baltimore."

17. "Let's Look at Housing in Baltimore: President's Report of the First Year's Activities of the Citizens' Housing Council of Baltimore," (May 1941), 1, folder 2, box 1, series I, Citizens Housing Council of Baltimore (CHCB) Records, LLSC; "Need for Stiffer Zoning Stressed," *Sun*, July 1, 1941, 5; "Plans to Survey Blighted Areas," *Sun*, June 21, 1941, 5.

18. Gaudreau to Morton, August 1, 1941, and Morton to CHC Members, August 11, 1941, both in folder 7, box 1, series I, CHCB Records, LLSC.

19. "Information Requested of Citizens Planning and Housing Association by the Baltimore Council of Social Agencies," July 1947, folder 3, box 2, series I, CPHA Records, LLSC.

20. Martin Millspaugh and Vivian Breckenfeld, *The Human Side of Urban Renewal: A Study of the Attitude Changes Produced by Neighborhood Rehabilitation* (New York: Ives Washburn, 1960).

21. "Court Action as a Warning to Slum Profiteers," *Sun*, April 30, 1947, 10.

22. Millspaugh and Breckenfeld, *The Human Side*.

23. Huntington Williams, "Law Enforcement and the 'Baltimore Plan,'" in *Housing and Health* (New York: Milbank Memorial Fund, 1951), 19–30.

24. Millspaugh and Breckenfeld, *The Human Side*.

25. Housing Act of 1949, Pub. L. 81–171, 63 Stat. 413 (1949).

26. Harry Truman, *Public Papers of Harry S. Truman, 1949* (Washington, D.C.: U.S. Government Printing Office, 1999), 299.

27. "City Slums Breed Higher Disease Rates, Parley Told," *Boston Globe*, November 14, 1949.

28. "Aimed at Plague Spots," *Sun*, August 9, 1917.

29. Jon C. Teaford, "Urban Renewal and Its Aftermath," *Housing Policy Debate* 11, no. 2 (2000): 443–465.

30. "Sobeloff Makes Report on Slums," *Sun*, October 22, 1940, 24; "Mr. McKeldin and the Belated Land-Development Commission," *Sun*, December 11, 1944, 10.

31. Chapter 664 (House Bill 761), "Land Development Commission," May 4, 1943, in *Laws of the State of Maryland* (Baltimore: King Bros., 1943), 871.

32. Chapter 649 (House Bill 731), Article XI-B, "Baltimore Redevelopment Commission," May 5, 1943, in *Laws of the State of Maryland* (Baltimore: King Bros., 1943), 849.

33. Commission on the City Plan, *Redevelopment of Blighted Residential Areas in Baltimore: Conditions of Blight, Some Remedies and Their Relative Costs* (Baltimore, 1945), 1, 57–59.

34. Baltimore Redevelopment Commission, *Redevelopment Project No. 1-A* (Baltimore, May 1950), available at https://jscholarship.library.jhu.edu/bitstream/handle/1774 .2/36886/Baltimore%20Redevelopment%201-A.pdf; "2 Blighted Area Plans Approved," *Sun*, July 12, 1950, 34.

35. Baltimore Urban Renewal and Housing Authority, "Data Sheets: Urban Renewal and Public Housing Projects," December 1962, folder 28, box 13, series XII, Baltimore City Department of Planning (BCDP) Records, LLSC.

36. Commission on the City Plan, *Redevelopment of Blighted Residential Areas*, 16, 22; Baltimore Redevelopment Commission, "Redevelopment Project No. 1-A," 6.

37. Baltimore Redevelopment Commission, "Redevelopment Project No. 1-A," 4.

38. Commission on the City Plan, *Redevelopment of Blighted Residential Areas*, 20.

39. Baltimore Urban Renewal and Housing Authority, "Data Sheets: Urban Renewal and Public Housing Projects," December 1962, LLSC; "Waverly Cleanup," *Sun*, February

7, 1953, 24; "Baltimore's Pioneer Project in Private Slum Redevelopment," *Sun*, November 30, 1952, 16.

40. "Displaced Persons, Baltimore Style," *Sun*, July 2, 1950, 10; "The Waverly DP's," *Sun*, July 12, 1952, 8; Baltimore Urban Renewal and Housing Authority, *Ten Years of Relocation Experience in Baltimore, Maryland* (Research Division, Baltimore Urban Renewal and Housing Authority), 1961.

41. Baltimore Urban Renewal and Housing Authority, *Ten Years of Relocation Experience*. The exception was Waverly, where black residents had to move far away due to racial exclusion.

42. "Baltimore's Displaced Persons: Some Improved Housing in Move from Area 3C," *Sun*, January 2, 1961, 22. Even the Greater Baltimore Committee, traditionally opposed to public housing, admitted that Baltimore's urban renewal program was unfeasible "unless subsidies are made available to substitute low-cost housing that is being demolished with new housing at rental levels within reach of the people being displaced." Memo, "Review of the Urban Renewal Program in Baltimore," GBC Committee Staff to GBC Urban Renewal Subcommittee, ca. 1964, box 25, series XIII, GBC Records, LLSC.

43. Millspaugh and Breckenfeld, *The Human Side*.

44. Millspaugh and Breckenfeld.

45. Millspaugh and Breckenfeld.

46. "Slum Work Bears Fruit," *Sun*, August 4, 1948, 7.

47. Millspaugh and Breckenfeld, *The Human Side*.

48. Millspaugh and Breckenfeld. Eventually, courts determined that it was the lessor's responsibility to do repairs. Lessors then simply added the new expenses into the principle of the contract.

49. Fight Blight Council, "Private Enterprise Fights Blight," ca. 1956, box 5, series XIII, GBC Records, LLSC.

50. Millspaugh and Breckenfeld, *The Human Side*.

51. Millspaugh and Breckenfeld; Ermer, "Street-Level Bureaucrats in Baltimore."

52. Millspaugh and Breckenfeld, *The Human Side*.

53. Urban Renewal Study Board, *Report of the Urban Renewal Study Board to Mayor Thomas D'Alesandro, Jr.*, 1956, folder 35A, box 2, series III, American Civil Liberties Union Collection, LLSC.

54. Millspaugh and Breckenfeld, *The Human Side*.

55. Millspaugh and Breckenfeld.

56. Millspaugh and Breckenfeld; Ward to Rouse, March 31, 1964, folder 2, box 37, GBC Records, LLSC.

57. Millspaugh and Breckenfeld, *The Human Side*.

58. Housing Act of 1954, P.L. 560; President Eisenhower connected national housing policy to "good health" when he helped pass the 1954 Housing Act. Dwight Eisenhower, *Public Papers of Dwight Eisenhower, 1954* (Washington, D.C.: Government Printing Office, 1960), 193.

59. Nicholas Bloom, *Merchants of Illusion: James Rouse, America's Salesman of the Businessman's Utopia* (Columbus: Ohio State University Press, 2004), 56–75; Charles Rhyne, "The Workable Program—A Challenge for Community Improvement," *Law and Contemporary Problems* 25, no. 4 (October 1, 1960): 685–704.

60. Thomas Winship, "Remedy of Home Builders Is Mere Palliative, Says Senator Sparkman," *Washington Post*, April 31, 1949, B1; Housing Act of 1949, H.R. 4009, 81st Cong. (June 23, 1949), app. A4128; Frances Morton Froelicher, "The History of Neighborhoods

in Baltimore from 1936–1969," typewritten draft, n.d., folder 11, box 2, series I, CPHA Records, LLSC; Williams, "Law Enforcement."

61. Bloom, *Merchants of Illusion.*

62. Bloom.

63. Memo, "Review of the Urban Renewal Program in Baltimore," folder 16, box 32, GBC records, LLSC.

64. Baltimore Urban Renewal Study Board, *Report of the Urban Renewal Study Board to Mayor Thomas D'Alesandro,* (Baltimore, September 1956), folder 14, box 20, GBC Records, LLSC.

65. Health and Welfare Council, "Background Material for Use by the Relocation Project Evaluation Committee," June 1965, folder 18, box 24, series I, HWC Records, LLSC.

66. Baltimore Urban Renewal and Housing Agency, *A Demonstration of Rehabilitation: Harlem Park, Baltimore, MD* (Baltimore City, June 1965); M. Carter McFarland, *Residential Rehabilitation in the Harlem Park Area, Baltimore, Maryland* (Washington, D.C.: Federal Housing Administration, June 1962).

67. Confidential interview with Huntington Williams, April 26, 1960, folder 2, box 37, GBC records, LLSC.

68. Urban Renewal Subcommittee of GBC, ca. 1962, folder 15, box 32, GBC records, LLSC; Citizens Planning and Housing Association, "Statement by Citizens Planning and Housing Association Position on Housing Law Enforcement," November 13, 1963, folder 16, box 32, GBC records, LLSC.

# Urban Renewal through Rehabilitation and Restoration

FRANCESCA RUSSELLO AMMON

W hen Congress passed Title I of the Housing Act of 1949, it provided essential government support to enable the clearance of blighted areas of U.S. cities and the stimulation of primarily private efforts to rebuild them. That act of clearance—of creating deceptively blank slates for new, modern development—was foundational to the program as it was the only type of renewal activity for which federal funds would be granted. As a result, politicians, planners, and many members of the public celebrated demolition itself as progress in forums ranging from public demolition ceremonies to children's books about demolition and construction. Nationwide, the Housing Act of 1949 spurred demolition on a scale that was previously unseen in the United States. During the 1960s—the peak decade for urban renewal demolition—an average of one out of every sixteen or seventeen dwelling units fell across the country. In cities that were most actively implementing this policy, like New Haven, Connecticut, that number was closer to one out of every six dwelling units.[1]

But it soon became clear that demolition and new construction alone could not adequately or economically cure all the physical ills of cities. Thus, with the Housing Act of 1954, rehabilitation and conservation joined demolition as federally funded means for renewal. This oft-overlooked alternative method held the potential to reduce the scale of both building demolition and resident displacement. While rehabilitation and historic preservation are often seen as the antithesis of urban renewal, this chapter examines how they were deployed as corollary tools within the larger postwar revitalization effort.[2] Using a national urban renewal data set and the cases of individual projects from around the country, it considers the motivations behind this more conservationist approach; the practical constraints to its wider adoption; and its prevalence, character, and impact on the ground—particularly in contrast to the clearance approach that preceded and continued alongside it.

## Why Rehabilitation?

There are multiple reasons why rehabilitation appealed to postwar policy makers and practitioners over clearance alone—at least as a complement, if not as a replacement—but cost and speed were primary among them. Large-scale demolition proved to be both expensive and slow. It produced massive amounts of rubble, the disposal of which was difficult and costly. To rid themselves of such refuse, some developers unscrupulously buried materials on site; not until the subsequent sinking of rebuilt properties did the truth become clear. Other pieces of debris littered cleared lots for years as it often took much longer to rebuild than it did to tear down. This was particularly the case as developers were initially slow to sign on for new construction, thereby imposing a different kind of blight on renewal neighborhoods. Further, although whole blocks were envisioned to come down en masse, difficult relocations and legal opposition by some residents often meant structures came down in a more patchwork pattern instead. This slowed down demolition and dramatically increased the price of the work as contractors had to switch to smaller, less efficient equipment. It even bankrupted some companies in the process while also costing the city much needed tax revenue while new construction was delayed. For all too long, many cities saw parking lots as the replacements for the former sites of dense urban neighborhoods.[3]

By contrast, rehabilitation could potentially be much swifter, cheaper, and culturally sensitive. A basic rehabilitation job could be completed for roughly the cost of demolishing a building—never mind the additional expense of building a new structure on that site afterward.[4] Plus, much rehabilitation work could be funded by property owners, rather than the government. For historic preservationists, rehabilitation also appealed for its conservation of historical fabric. But making preservation synonymous with modernization required a cultural leap of faith for some. As the HHFA wrote in late 1960, "architectural character in individual buildings, blocks of buildings, or whole neighborhoods can be achieved or retained, if false conceptions of 'modernization' are not followed."[5] That is, an acceptance of rehabilitation as renewal required that "modernization" not be strictly synonymous with new construction. Instead, updated buildings from the past could also satisfy contemporary needs.

In November 1963, nearly a decade after passage of the Housing Act of 1954, William Slayton, commissioner of the Urban Renewal Administration, testified to Congress about the impact of the rehabilitation-based legislation thus far. There was an understandable lag between legislation and action. By that point, he reported, there were 225 projects that included a significant amount of rehabilitation—about three-fifths of which were already in execution. This represented roughly 17 percent of the more than 1,300 urban renewal projects that had been initiated nationwide to date. But rehabilitation encompassed variable portions of each of these projects, and building counts provide perhaps a better estimate of the extent of rehabilitation versus demolition. By mid-1963, urban renewal had demolished approximately 129,000 structures and rehabilitated over 17,000 structures. Thus, cities had applied rehabilitation to about 12 percent of the buildings on which urban renewal was then complete. They tore the other structures down. Although demolition had gotten a head start, the future looked bright for rehabilitation. As Slayton concluded, "Especially gratifying is the fact that the number of dwelling units on which rehabilitation had been completed rose nearly 37 percent during the last fiscal year."[6]

## Challenges to Rehabilitation

Despite this promising beginning, several factors limited the pace and scale of rehabilitation progress. Foremost among these were the individualized attention required with rehabilitation, relative to clearance, and the challenge of financing for owners and developers of smaller-scale properties. Whereas large developers would typically take the lead in remaking sites with a clearance-based approach—often utilizing superblock designs with towers in a park—rehabilitation often required the efforts of many more individual investors. With most properties needing tailored solutions, this kind of support was also difficult to scale. Given limited local staff resources, rehabilitation could only proceed as quickly as owners negotiated individually with contractors, lenders, and other involved actors.

Recognizing this strain, the federal government offered additional supports over time. An amendment to Title I provided grants to test new rehabilitation approaches. The Housing Act of 1961 "would enable local public agencies to carry out rehabilitation demonstrations in urban renewal projects."[7] But financing was perhaps the larger challenge. The Housing Act of 1954 anticipated this by introducing Section 220, which provided a new FHA mortgage insurance program "for use in rehabilitating dwellings and constructing new dwellings in urban renewal areas."[8] By basing its assessment of mortgage risk on the future development of the area, rather than a property's current condition, the FHA would be able to insure mortgages in areas where it had been unable to do so before. As the HHFA concluded, "Section 220 makes possible larger loans and smaller equity investment by private capital than would normally be possible under conventional lending practices."[9]

Slayton reported to Congress about one exemplar case of the new mortgage policy in practice. In New Haven, 220 financing not only enabled rehabilitation work for a multifamily house but even decreased the net monthly mortgage premiums—by half—due to the lower interest rate and longer repayment term (even with the additional rehabilitation loan).[10] While this was an extreme example, Slayton expressed his hope that "through the 220 refinancing device we are going to make it possible for property owners to refinance the property and not have to pay more in monthly charges. . . . I call this the magic of the 220 refinancing, and it is the real key to making rehabilitation work."[11]

But the policy did not always work like magic in practice. Officials in Philadelphia, for example, reported on several challenges property owners faced as they applied for 220 mortgages in a low-income area undergoing rehabilitation-based renewal. In this project, 490 properties were to be rehabilitated, yet by 1964, the city could identify "only one example . . . of any affirmative FHA action in [that] area over the past five years"—and it was for a property located on a boundary street. Instead, they reported numerous instances of owners who were turned down for FHA 220 insurance due to, for example, "evidence of rapid deterioration and obsolescence" in the surrounding area, which would "limit long-term marketability and economic life which precludes favorable consideration." Further, when mortgages were offered, they often did not match the amounts owners required.[12] While this type of housing was precisely what the program was intended to address, banks' hesitancy to lend could partly be explained by the fact that, relatively speaking, "the highest volume of defaults occur[red] in projects located in urban renewal areas and insured under Section 220."[13]

## Rehabilitation and Displacement

Not long after the clearance approach to urban renewal was put into action, the program became the subject of criticism and protest—most memorably in a few critical texts. Sociologist Herbert Gans relocated to Boston's West End to uncover a lively community of "urban villagers" in a neighborhood that planners had labeled as blighted and marked for removal. In *The Death and Life of Great American Cities*, urbanist Jane Jacobs profiled the mixed-use buildings and sidewalk ballet of street life in New York's Greenwich Village to argue for the conservation of both. From an entirely different perspective, Martin Anderson's *Federal Bulldozer* analyzed the economic impacts of urban renewal to show that the program was not benefiting city coffers either.[14]

On top of all these critiques, the destruction of community was one of the program's most egregious transgressions. Across the country, urban renewal displaced nearly a million families and over a hundred thousand businesses by 1980.[15] These burdens were unevenly distributed. Non-whites experienced almost two-thirds of the displacement, earning the urban renewal program the nickname "Negro removal."[16] Sociologists studied those who had been displaced and discovered the damaging psychosocial impacts of this sudden rupture of community.[17] Social psychiatrist Mindi Fullilove has termed this emotional trauma "root shock."[18] Rehabilitation, however, offered the possibility of reducing displacement. As Slayton told Congress in 1963, "The emphasis is on maintaining the same occupancy. Rehabilitation is to bring the area up, to improve the area for the residents who are there, so that there is not the exodus, the movement of people, the relocation of families. Rehabilitation makes it possible for people to stay in their neighborhood."[19]

In the case of clearance and new construction, a best-case scenario was that existing residents would receive temporary relocation housing while their homes were demolished and would then be able to move into the redeveloped units years later, once new construction was complete. Oftentimes, however, the new housing constructed was too expensive for previous residents to afford. Such was the case in Southwest Washington, D.C., where developers initially agreed to make one-third of newly constructed units affordable to prior area residents only to plead economic hardship while successfully petitioning for the removal of that provision after development began.[20] Slayton argued, however, that rehabilitation could be different. Existing property owners could have the option of staying or going. But even if such a choice were offered, it was not always possible for existing owners to accept. Staying in one's home required committing to implement often costly rehabilitation standards—requiring funds that some owners did not have. For the "impecunious family," as Slayton described them, "who may own his home outright and cannot afford any mortgage on that home," even a mortgage with good terms was impractical.[21]

Levels of urban renewal displacement can be measured, in part, through the Urban Renewal Administration's quarterly *Urban Renewal Project Characteristics* report. This report includes best estimates of the level of projected displacement by project across the country (including U.S. territories). Although the report does not distinguish the extent of demolition versus rehabilitation in each project, if rehabilitation were truly effective in reducing displacement, one would expect a reduction in the rate of displacement per affected building following the Housing Act of 1954. That does appear to be the case. In 1955, the *Characteristics* report projected that one family would be displaced for every 1.24 dwelling units affected by urban renewal. In 1960, when rehabilitation was likely only to have had a small impact on average project progress, the report projected the displacement of one family for every 1.38 affected dwelling units. Finally, by 1966, when the impact of the Housing Act of 1954 was more fully being felt (and the last year when these statistics were collected nationally), the report projected the displacement of one family for every 1.5 affected dwelling units.[22]

Displacement levels in some of the earliest rehabilitation projects further support this trajectory. Cleveland's Garden Valley project claimed to be the "first in the U.S. to combine clearance and conservation under the Housing Act of 1954."[23] This project incorporated many different actions, including redevelopment, rehabilitation, public housing, private housing, and institutional and public facilities. On average, across 364 dwelling units, one family was displaced for every dwelling unit. On a 370-acre project in Mercedes, Texas, which was "predominantly conservation with some clearance areas," the levels of displacement were similar, with one family displaced for every 1.06 dwelling units (over a total of 426 dwelling units).[24]

## Rehabilitation and Conservation Projects in Practice

Looking beyond displacement levels alone in some early projects adds texture to these raw numbers, making clear that while rehabilitation and conservation saved many buildings from destruction, they did not significantly stop the federal bulldozer in its tracks. Rehabilitation could essentially take the form of a facelift with some internal updates, with the mayor of Little Rock, Arkansas, describing the typical job as "a rundown house, that you can put a new roof on it, change the lines, and put a carport in front of it, paint it up, and put new screens on."[25] But a more extensive rehabilitation, particularly when oriented toward historic restoration, involved additional investment and work. This approach was typically described as "conservation" (a term also synonymous with "preservation"—particularly outside the United States). If bringing buildings up to code was sufficient for basic rehabilitation projects, conservation projects often imposed another level of standards.

At least two documents helped formalize the application of historic preservation in urban renewal. Providence, Rhode Island, pioneered this type of work in its College Hill project, itself the product of a government demonstration grant. The project's 1959 report advised on how to utilize zoning and planning to preserve the distinctive built environment while also modernizing the overall area. The project combined demolition, infill, and restoration at a neighborhood scale.[26] Less than four years later, the Urban Renewal Administration itself sought to further stimulate such projects by publishing *Historic Preservation through Urban Renewal*, which used the example of fourteen projects in progress—Providence among them—to demonstrate the applications of Title I to conservation.[27] While fourteen exemplars may seem like a relatively long list, the limited extent of historic preservation within these examples suggests that there was still a long way to go in making conservation an integral—rather than token—outcome of urban renewal.

Several of the featured projects focused on applying demolition to help select buildings of historic importance stand out within the context of what were effectively historic districts.[28] In York, Pennsylvania—at four-tenths of an acre, the smallest urban renewal project to date—just two buildings were being saved. These were Gates House, which served as a headquarters during the American Revolution and a banquet site for the Marquis de Lafayette, and Plough Tavern, a half-timber "architectural gem." Both structures demonstrated the limited temporal scope of what was considered "historic" (i.e., that dating back to before the Revolutionary War era). As the publication noted, seemingly in triumph, "When the project was decided on, rundown buildings covered the area. Now only the two historic buildings will remain."[29] In some ways, demolition was as much—if not more—of a goal as preservation at this site.

The report also highlighted several other projects in which cities identified a few select buildings for conservation. The Marcy-Washington Streets project in Portsmouth, New Hampshire, proposed to save "at least 12 buildings in this 9½-acre area," while "some 60 structures" would be removed. Bethlehem, Pennsylvania, proposed to save twenty buildings across nine acres in its Monocacy Creek project. The East Church Street project in Mobile, Alabama, proposed to save ten buildings across six blocks while clearing two-thirds of the area for public use. All these projects took a more curatorial approach to preservation, endorsing demolition to help illuminate restoration-worthy gems. Some also proposed to relocate historic buildings from elsewhere in the city to these new districts for safekeeping. The result would be an "outdoor history museum" of sorts.[30]

Notably, these projects were all located in predominantly white neighborhoods, even as roughly two-thirds of those displaced by urban renewal were non-white. This meant that most of the benefits in the minimization of lost buildings and residents would be experienced by white residents, rather than those communities that were most negatively impacted by the urban renewal program. The demographically uneven location of preservation-based urban renewal projects suggests that preservation was deemed most appropriate in communities of a certain racial character. Yet the report highlighted at least one exception to this trend. In the 560-acre Southwest project in Washington, D.C., African Americans represented 70 percent of existing residents. This project incorporated historic preservation as well, integrating six historic buildings into a new townhouse development (rather than cordoning them off as museum exhibits). But urban renewal destroyed roughly 99 percent of the buildings that previously occupied the neighborhood, making these six structures noteworthy but, again, largely token in their significance.[31]

The greater outliers in the report—in terms of the prevalence of preservation, rather than the demographics of preexisting residents—were the Society Hill project in Philadelphia and the Wooster Square project in New Haven. In each, restoration represented a more substantial portion of the approach. It also operated at the scale of the neighborhood, rather than that of just individual buildings. The result was the integration of conserved buildings into everyday life throughout the area, rather than their segregation as museum pieces. In New Haven, although an interstate highway would decimate much of the neighborhood, planners sought to retain much of what survived to the west of the new roadway. They aimed to restore 400 of 450 buildings across 235 acres, plus supplement those with new construction. Philadelphia's Society Hill neighborhood shared certain similarities with Wooster Square. Another interstate highway would cut alongside that area, and ethnic whites also represented the majority of prerenewal residents (in Wooster Square, these were Italians; in Society Hill, they were largely Eastern Europeans). While the building retention goals were more modest there—75 percent of all residential structures or roughly 50 percent of total structures—Society Hill still vastly surpassed the retention of existing fabric achieved on the typical urban renewal project.[32]

Both Wooster Square and Society Hill stood out nationally for their large-scale preservation-based approaches to urban renewal. This is likely why William Slayton highlighted both projects in his comments to Congress. Upon viewing the before and after photographs that Slayton presented, one congressman noted, "The transformation of those houses is so dramatic that I would think that either the rent or the cost would be so . . . substantial that I would wonder if the same families could live in those." Slayton confirmed his suspicion.[33] Thus, large-scale conservation practices, when applied, may have saved significant numbers of buildings but did not necessarily save their inhabitants as well.

## The Urban Renewal of Society Hill

Taking Society Hill as a closer case study helps us move beyond project-level statistics to consider the impacts of rehabilitation-based renewal approaches on individual properties and residents. Society Hill took its name from the Free Society of Traders, a business entity that settled along the Delaware River during the eighteenth century in what is now the eastern side of Center City, Philadelphia. The name fell out of use around the time of the Revolution but was resurrected by architect and architectural historian Charles Peterson as a way to rechristen the revitalizing neighborhood. While official postwar planning documents designate the area as Washington Square East, Society Hill is the name that has endured since urban renewal.

During the era when the Free Society of Traders was active in Society Hill, mansions were located along its main streets and mixed with the housing and businesses of area tradesmen, with more modest structures lining secondary roadways; over time, the neighborhood evolved physically and socially. At the turn of the twentieth century, working-class residents of Jewish, largely Eastern European origin occupied much of the neighborhood. An African American population concentrated in the southwest corner of the neighborhood, extending into the Seventh Ward of W.E.B. DuBois's famous social survey.[34] By the start of renewal, African Americans represented 20 percent of the neighborhood population. Starting in the late nineteenth century, owners subdivided larger row houses into multifamily units to accommodate the changing population. Commercial, industrial, and residential development mixed throughout the area.[35]

By the mid-twentieth century, the neighborhood had grown increasingly physically dilapidated, as indicated by the ratings of D and E (on a scale of A to E) on a 1930s appraisal map.[36] This assessment was further reinforced by a 1940 public health survey of Society Hill and the Old City area to its immediate north. The survey concluded that "the excessive mixture of land uses indicates that this Area is not a desirable place in which to live." Further, the survey found the "deterioration index" of the area to be high, with 39 percent of dwelling units exhibiting "extreme deterioration." Inadequate toilet and bath facilities were just one contributing factor. On Society Hill's eastern side, in particular, roughly half of the dwelling units lacked indoor private toilets; baths were even more scarce.[37] Planners identified the need for revitalization of the area, and they turned to urban renewal as the solution.

Between 1958 and 1960, the city introduced plans for the area in two main geographic parts: Unit 1 (to the north and east) included large swaths of clearance and new construction, along with elements of restoration, while Unit 2 (to the south and west) more significantly foregrounded the restoration approach.[38] The combined five-by-four-block area was generally bounded by Walnut Street to the north, Lombard Street to the south, S. Front Street to the east, and S. Seventh Street to the west. (A later and much smaller Unit 3 stretched the boundaries one block further west and included both demolition and restoration.) In Unit 1, the city replaced a wholesale food market with three thirty-one-story high-rise towers, accompanied by new row house developments, designed by architect I. M. Pei. This was classic, clearance-based urban renewal as practiced in cities across the country. But in Unit 2, the city applied what came to be known as the "Philadelphia Cure"—that is, "clearing cities with penicillin, not surgery" in a way that joined rehabilitation with new construction.[39] Philadelphia implemented such an approach earlier and at a larger scale than most other cities, and it gained national prominence for its leadership in publications from *Architectural Forum* to *Time* magazine.[40]

The plans yielded four major categories of outcomes for existing residential properties. First, and least disruptively to the existing community, property owners could undertake rehabilitation and remain in place after renewal. In 1960, the city reported that over 70 percent of owners of the roughly three hundred rehabilitation-designated buildings in Society Hill expressed interest in completing that work, suggesting a strong potential for these residents to avoid displacement.[41] Second, urban renewal could displace existing residents so that new owners could complete the rehabilitation work. This could occur, for example, when residents lacked the will or resources to complete that work on their own—although new owners were often held to a higher and more expensive restoration standard. Third, urban renewal could displace existing residents and businesses to complete a more substantial building facelift that shifted usage from mixed use to residential. Finally, and most dramatically, an existing residence could be demolished to create an entirely new building for an entirely new owner.

The most straightforward outcome was the restoration of an existing building for continued residential use. In Unit 1, the city marked all properties for acquisition and then offered existing residents the chance to buy back their building if they agreed to restore the exterior to architectural standards prescribed by the Philadelphia Redevelopment Authority. Such standards often included cleaning brickwork, installing operable shutters, replacing windows, repointing chimneys, replacing roofs, building marble steps, and completing other publicly visible alterations that would help transform a building's street-facing facade to more closely resemble its historical form from the late eighteenth or early nineteenth century.[42]

The ten row houses on the north side of the 300 block of Spruce Street offer an illustrative case study of how such rehabilitation worked. As shown in Figure 9.1, a 1942 land use map identifies each of these properties as a three-story multifamily building (although, in fact, they were largely three and one-half stories, given the dormered attic on the fourth floor).[43] The properties were 20 feet wide and 100 to 109 feet deep—both dimensions of which were spacious for Center City, Philadelphia. The city acquired these sites for redevelopment through a court condemnation in mid-1959.[44] Shortly after, the prior owners of five of the ten repurchased their properties from the redevelopment authority for the same prices they had received as compensation for the condemnation. Before renewal, in 1942, all five repurchased properties had been strictly residential, whereas four out of the remaining five prop-

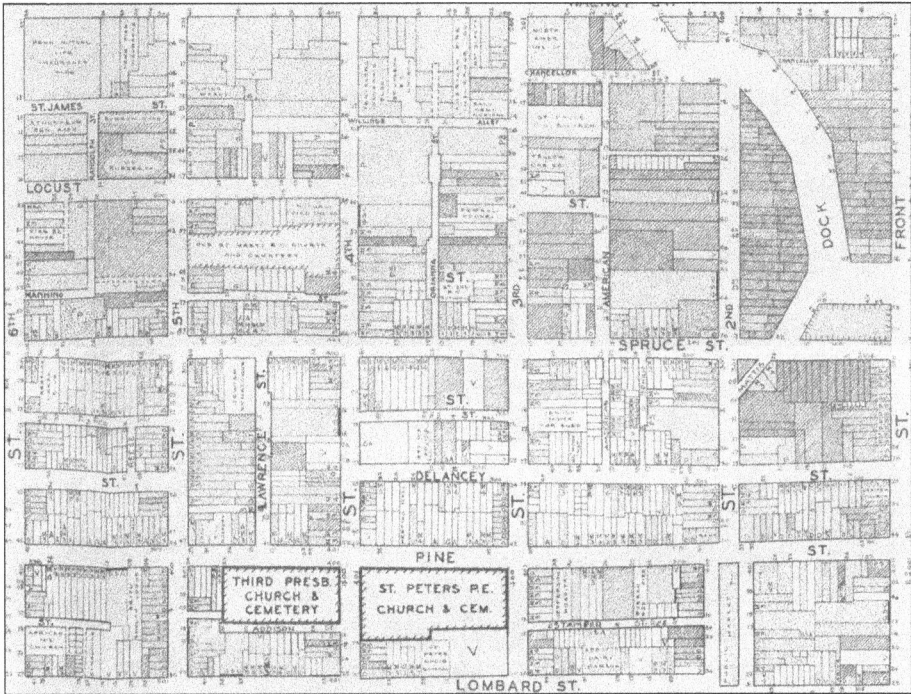

**Figure 9.1** Land use map from 1942 showing a central portion of the Society Hill neighborhood prior to urban renewal. Lots denoted with dots were commercial, with diagonal lines were industrial, and without any coloration were residential; some properties were multiuse. *M* indicates multifamily dwellings, while *D* (or no letter on a residential lot) indicates a single- or two-family dwelling. *V* indicates a vacant lot. *G* indicates a garage. *S* indicates gasoline service. *A* indicates accessory use. Numbers on lots indicate the number of stories, while numbers in streets indicate address numbers. In Philadelphia, address numbers follow street numbers; that is, all properties between Second and Third Streets have a number in the 200s, between Third and Fourth Streets have a number in the 300s, and so on. The examples that follow discuss several sites that are located on this map.
(Source: Works Progress Administration, *Philadelphia Land Use Map*, 1942, Map Collection, Free Library of Philadelphia, accessed via Greater Philadelphia GeoHistory Network.)

erties that permanently changed hands during renewal had housed commercial space on the ground floor and residential above.[45] The fact that any property owners remained in possession of their buildings after renewal was a stark contrast to what typically happened in the case of clearance. Prior existence of mixed use, however, proved to be a strong indicator of displacement.

One of those five repurchased properties, 311 Spruce Street demonstrates the nondisplacement story. Figure 9.2 depicts the facades of this building and its neighbors before and after urban renewal. In 1935, sometime after they

**Figure 9.2** 313 and 311 Spruce Street in 1949 (*left*) and 1999 (*right*). Prior to renewal, a luncheonette operated on the ground floor of 313 Spruce Street, with apartments above. After renewal, the new owners restored the property to purely residential use, while the Matkowski family funded the restoration of their own residential property at 311 Spruce Street.

(Source: Atheniasis T. Mallis, "Fronts of 311 and 313 Spruce Street" [*left*] and "311 Spruce Street" [*right*]. Photos courtesy of PhillyHistory.org, a project of the Philadelphia Department of Records.)

had emigrated from Poland and started a family, property owners Andrew and Catherine Matkowski purchased this Greek Revival brick row house that had been built in 1815.[46] The 1940 census shows husband and wife residing in the property, along with their seven children, then ages ten to twenty-six. Andrew Matkowski worked in a shoe factory, while Catherine was a home-maker; two of their older children worked, respectively, as a laborer at a con-tracting company and a soda jerk in a department store. Both the class and ethnic character of the Matkowskis were typical of the neighborhood prior to urban renewal. What was relatively unusual, however, was the fact that they owned and occupied the entirety of such a large-size building on their own, in contrast with the division of many neighboring properties into multifam-ily rental properties. For example, their neighbor at 313 Spruce Street at that time included two families—both renters—sharing the same building. Fur-ther down the block, at 315 Spruce Street, two different families plus three lodgers resided in a single building. Again, they were all renters.[47] The Mat-kowski house would remain in the family until it was sold in 2013.[48]

Two properties located five and six doors down from the Matkowski residence, at 319 and 321 Spruce Street, respectively, experienced a different fate: the demolition of the first and the arrival of a new owner to complete the rehabilitation of the second. 319 Spruce Street had been the site of the Al-Moe Bar, purportedly so named because of the two bartenders who worked there: Al during the day and Moe at night.[49] The condition of the building was such that it was the only one of the ten properties on that side of the block that the Philadelphia Redevelopment Authority marked for demolition. After urban renewal, the site became a side garden for the house to its immediate west, 321 Spruce Street, which in 1940 housed an extended family and one lodger. In 1957, the death of the then current owner of 321 Spruce Street led the executors of his will to put the house on the market; with urban renewal in the offing, it appears that absentee landlords acquired the property. Although they repurchased the building from the Philadelphia Redevelopment Authority, they eventually decided to sell it in what was effectively a delayed urban renewal transfer. The new owner, Philip Price Jr., purchased the building from them in 1965 for $15,000.[50] Price described the state of the building at that time:

> Just before it became vacant, it was carved up as a rooming house. I remember going in for the first time and seeing false partitions dividing rooms in the house, with numbers on the doors. It was probably a rooming house in which maybe fifteen people lived on three floors. . . . Well, it was absolutely appalling, poor condition. In fact, there had been a fire on the third floor. The whole roof was gone. . . . It required a total rehabilitation.

Price worked with an architect to turn the building back into a single-family property, recalling that he spent $80,000–$90,000 completing a year and a half of extensive restoration work.[51] He continued to reside there for a decade before renting out the full house to others and eventually selling it in 2005.[52] Figure 9.3 depicts Price's properties both before and after urban renewal. Not many existing owners would have the capacity or will to take on this scale of rehabilitation work. Thus, some properties changed hands because of renewal, even as the buildings themselves endured.

Across the street from these houses, the Philadelphia Redevelopment Authority denied another owner's petition to rehabilitate his own property since he wished to continue mixed use on the site. Harry and Anna Altman purchased the three-story row house at the southeast corner of S. Fourth and Spruce Streets in 1947. There, continuing a business Harry's father had started in the neighborhood two decades prior, Harry operated the Royal Hand Laundry on the ground floor. The site served only as a drop-off and pick-up

**Figure 9.3** 319–321 Spruce Street in 1957 (*left*) and 1999 (*right*). Urban renewal led to the demolition of the building housing the Al-Moe Bar and the purchase and restoration of the residences to its immediate west.

(Source: Cuneo, "321–327 Spruce Street" [*left*] and "321 Spruce Street" [*right*]. Photos courtesy of PhillyHistory.org, a project of the Philadelphia Department of Records.)

site for laundry, and all cleaning occurred off premises. Harry and Anna lived on the floors above. As planners sought to use urban renewal to eliminate mixed use from the neighborhood, the city told Altman—along with roughly sixty other businesses in Unit 2—that they would have to relocate elsewhere. Altman petitioned the Philadelphia Redevelopment Authority to make an exception, even hiring an architect to draw up plans to alter the facade to fit with the restorations occurring in the area. He was willing to pay to complete this rehabilitation work, and twenty-six near neighbors signed a petition endorsing his request.[53] As one resident stated, "He not only cleans my clothes beautifully, but he cashes checks for me . . . or I run out of bread and he loans me a loaf of bread, anything, anything. Harry Altman is a magnificent neighbor, and I'm very proud to have him as a next-door neighbor."[54] But the Philadelphia Redevelopment Authority denied his request, refusing to make exceptions that would permit commercial use in a residential area, even when neighbors wanted him to stay. The Philadelphia Redevelopment Authority acquired the property in a court condemnation on the day after Christmas in 1962. In 1968, new owners purchased the property for $9,400 and subsequently rehabilitated it in a way that eliminated the commercial storefront to reflect the building's conversion to purely residential use.[55] Figure 9.4 shows the building before and after that rehabilitation work.

**Figure 9.4** The building at the southeast corner of Spruce and S. Fourth Streets transformed from mixed use (1957, *on the left*) to residential (1969, *on the right*). In the 1950s, Harry Altman's Royal Hand Laundry operated on the ground floor. During urban renewal, new owners purchased the building and eliminated its commercial frontage in its conversion to residential use.

(Source: "S. E. cor. 4th & Spruce Street" [*left*] and "340 Spruce Street, Southeast Corner, 4th & Spruce" [*right*]. Photos courtesy of PhillyHistory.org, a project of the Philadelphia Department of Records.)

Urban renewal also brought more direct displacement to those areas of the neighborhood where planners targeted new construction. Even when those buildings were owner occupied and used strictly as residences, and those same owners agreed to complete rehabilitation work, that could not save them from clearance if the existing properties conflicted with the renewal plan. Such was the case for six attached houses on the 400 block of Addison Street, located just two blocks south of Royal Hand Laundry. Constructed by individual builders starting around 1830, these houses were of a more modest scale than those on Spruce Street.[56] Old Pine Presbyterian Church and Cemetery abutted Addison Street, and the church worked out a plan with the Philadelphia Redevelopment Authority to use urban renewal to expand their property holdings. Specifically, on the expanded grounds, they hoped to build a neighborhood community center and a historical society for the entire U.S. Presbyterian Church.[57] All that stood in their way were the buildings and residents still occupying that land.

Unlike the Al-Moe Bar, which the Philadelphia Redevelopment Authority also slated for demolition, the properties on Addison Street were not in poor physical condition. In 1940, most of the houses were occupied by single families of Russian or Polish decent. (See Figure 9.5.) Residents worked as dishwashers, chauffeurs, cooks, butchers, ironworkers, firemen, and other

**Figure 9.5** 400 block of Addison Street, 1960, showing six row houses that the city eventually demolished during urban renewal to make way for the Presbyterian Historical Society and Old Pine Community Center.

(Source: "Addison Street." Photo courtesy of PhillyHistory.org, a project of the Philadelphia Department of Records.)

working-class occupations.[58] At least two Addison Street residents addressed city council members at the same public hearing at which Harry Altman also spoke. Tillie Wilinski, almost seventy years old and living at 410 Addison Street, testified in Polish, breaking down in tears at the prospect of having to relocate from the block where she had raised her family for many decades. Her neighbor Margaret Sobel, of 412 Addison Street, spoke proudly of having finally paid off the mortgage on her house—in which she was raising four daughters and one son—just six months prior to the hearing. Yet she told the council members that she would be happy to go back to work, if necessary, to pay for the rehabilitation costs that would be required of redevelopment—if only her home could be saved from demolition.[59] While their testimony appeared to move some of the council members, the church's plan ultimately prevailed. They completed construction of the Presbyterian Historical Society in 1966 and the Old Pine Community Center in 1977. Although the new historical society building, in particular, had a neocolonial style that fit with much of the neighborhood, the construction of this historically styled and oriented building was enabled only by the destruction of houses and communities that had histories of their own on that same site.

Although these individual examples from Society Hill only touch the surface of the experience of rehabilitation- and restoration-based urban renewal, they suggest the range of possible outcomes. And, across the entire project area, they added up to a major demographic change that continues to define the neighborhood today. While many buildings remained after renewal, the population residing in them was quite different. Between 1950 and 1980, Society Hill's population declined from roughly 7,000 to 5,200 residents. The portion of nonwhite residents dropped from twenty percent to just five percent of the total population. Median income increased from one-half the city average before renewal to two and a half times the city average after renewal, education levels skyrocketed, owner occupancy more than doubled, and the costs of the housing units increased from three-fourths of the city average to seven times the city average.[60] Undoubtedly, owing to an approach that incorporated rehabilitation instead of just wholesale clearance, many more families were able to stay in Society Hill after renewal. But, on average, the neighborhood's social and economic character transformed along with its building facades.

## Conclusion

The Housing Act of 1954 ushered in a new rehabilitation-based approach to urban renewal that broke significantly with the demolition-oriented tradition of the Housing Act of 1949. It offered federal funding to improve upon existing buildings, rather than seeing clearance as the necessary first step to urban modernization. Through tailored, relatively smaller-scale interventions, it empowered individual property owners to better their built environment instead of relying only upon large-scale, developer-funded efforts. It introduced financing mechanisms and local administrative support to help make the aspirations of those individual property owners materially possible. And it held out the potential to reduce the impact of renewal-based displacement.

But this next federal iteration on urban revitalization also shared much in common with its prior policy. Demolition remained a major part—typically a dominant element—of renewal projects going forward. The experiences of early adopter cities suggest that demolition maintained a particularly strong presence in minority neighborhoods, whereas white communities benefited more often from rehabilitation. The promised financing was initially difficult to obtain in communities where the postrenewal residents would have more modest incomes. When historic preservation was incorporated, it was often curatorial in its orientation rather than integrated into the everyday life of the broader community. And business and residential displacement continued in substantial numbers, despite the theoretical prospect of many more residents opting to stay. Examining urban renewal rehabilitation at scales ranging from the individual project to the individual property suggests that, while the practice diverged from the previous clearance approach quite noticeably from a policy perspective, its implementation actually proved to have much in common with it.

## NOTES

1. Francesca Russello Ammon, *Bulldozer: Demolition and Clearance of the Postwar Landscape* (New Haven, CT: Yale University Press, 2016).

2. Abundant scholarship focuses on the demolition side of urban renewal; see, for example, Ammon, *Bulldozer*; Samuel Zipp, *Manhattan Projects: The Rise and Fall of Urban Renewal in Cold War New York* (New York: Oxford University Press, 2010); Jon C. Teaford, *The Rough Road to Renaissance: Urban Revitalization in America, 1940–1985* (Baltimore: Johns Hopkins University Press, 1990); Christopher Klemek, *The Transatlantic Collapse of Urban Renewal: Postwar Urbanism from New York to Berlin* (Chicago: Chicago University Press, 2011). Other scholars have also begun to explore the rehabilitation dimensions of the program; see, for example, Stephanie R. Ryberg, "Historic Preservation's Urban Renewal Roots: Preservation and Planning in Midcentury Philadelphia," *Journal of Urban History* 39, no. 2 (2012): 192–213; George Walter Born, "Urban Preservation and Renewal: Designating the Historic Beacon Hill District in 1950s Boston," *Journal of Planning History* 16, no. 4 (November 2017): 285–304.

3. Ammon, *Bulldozer*, chap. 3.

4. In Mercedes, Texas, for example, the average rehabilitation cost was $2,000 per structure, with over 360 structures completed to date; Housing and Home Finance Agency, Urban Renewal Administration, "Urban Renewal Is for Small Communities Too," in *Urban Renewal Notes* (January–February 1961). In South Dalworth, Texas, renewers spent

an average of roughly $1,500 per property in rehabilitating 148 properties to date; United States, Urban Renewal Administration, *Report on Urban Renewal: Statement of William L. Slayton, Commissioner, Urban Renewal Administration, Housing and Home Finance Agency, before the Subcommittee on Housing, Committee on Banking and Currency, United States House of Representatives, November 21, 1963* (Washington, D.C.: U.S. Government Printing Office, 1964), 418, Proquest. William Slayton, "Statement of William Slayton, Commissioner, Urban Renewal Administration, Housing and Home Finance Agency," in *Urban Renewal: Hearings Before the Subcomm. on Housing of the Comm. on Banking and Currency*, Part 1, H.R. 88th Cong., 1st sess., at 418 (1963), Proquest. These costs were roughly on par with the cost of demolition of individual buildings in New Haven at this time; Ammon, *Bulldozer*, 151.

5. Housing and Home Finance Agency, Urban Renewal Administration, "Conserving Neighborhood Character," in *Urban Renewal Notes* (November–December 1960).

6. Slayton, "Statement of William Slayton," 404, 409, 415, 416.

7. Comm. on Banking and Currency, *Housing Act of 1961*, H.R. Rep. 87–6028, at 25 (1961), Proquest.

8. Slayton, "Statement of William Slayton," 392–393.

9. Urban Renewal Administration, *Replacing Blight with Good Homes* (Washington, D.C.: Housing and Home Finance Agency, 1956), 3–4, 10.

10. Slayton, "Statement of William Slayton," 418.

11. Slayton, "Statement of William Slayton," 453–454.

12. "The Philadelphia Conservation Program," 1963, box 12, folder: Redev—General, 1963, City Planning Commission Files, City Archives of Philadelphia.

13. Louis W. Hunter, "Statement of Louis W. Hunter, Assistant Director of Civil Accounting and Auditing Division, General Accounting Office; Accompanied by Frank M. Mikus, Supervisory Auditor," in Subcomm. of the Comm. on Banking and Currency, *FHA Mortgage Foreclosures: Hearings Before a Subcomm. of the Comm. on Banking and Currency*, S. 88th Cong., 2nd sess., at 62 (1964), ProQuest.

14. Herbert J. Gans, *The Urban Villagers: Group and Class in the Life of Italian-Americans* (New York: Free Press of Glencoe, 1962); Jane Jacobs, *The Death and Life of Great American Cities* (New York: Random House, 1961); Martin Anderson, *The Federal Bulldozer: A Critical Analysis of Urban Renewal, 1949–1962* (Cambridge: MIT Press, 1964).

15. Ammon, *Bulldozer*, 5.

16. Through 1961, non-whites made up 66 percent of families living in and relocated from areas slated for urban renewal (among those for whom "color" was reported); United States Housing and Home Finance Agency, *Relocation from Urban Renewal Project Areas: Through December, 1961* (Washington, D.C.: U.S. Government Printing Office, 1962), 6. Among those relocated for urban renewal and neighborhood development projects by June 30, 1970, 40 percent of families who reported their race were white; Department of Housing and Urban Development, *1970 HUD Statistical Yearbook* (Washington, D.C.: U.S. Government Printing Office, 1971), 73.

17. Daniel Thursz, *Where Are They Now? A Study of the Impact of Relocation on Former Residents of Southwest Washington, Who Were Served in an HWC Demonstration Project* (Washington, D.C.: Health and Welfare Council of the National Capital Area, 1966); Marc Fried, "Grieving for a Lost Home," in *The Urban Condition: People and Policy in the Metropolis*, ed. Leonard J. Duhl, 151–171 (New York: Basic Books, 1963).

18. Mindy Thompson Fullilove, *Root Shock: How Tearing Up City Neighborhoods Hurts America, and What We Can Do About It* (New York: One World/Ballantine Books, 2004).

19. Slayton, "Statement of William Slayton," 483.

20. Francesca Russello Ammon, "Commemoration amid Criticism: The Mixed Legacy of Urban Renewal in Southwest Washington, D.C.," *Journal of Planning History* 8, no. 3 (July 2009): 188.

21. Slayton, "Statement of William Slayton," 482–483.

22. Based upon analysis of Urban Renewal Administration, *Urban Renewal Project Characteristics* (Washington, D.C.: U.S. Government Printing Office, 1955, 1960, 1966).

23. Garden Valley was noteworthy for being an urban renewal housing specifically aimed at middle-income African Americans. Yet it had its own failings, serving as an example of environmental racism; Todd M. Michney, "White Civic Visions versus Black Suburban Aspirations: Cleveland's Garden Valley Urban Renewal Project," *Journal of Planning History* 10, no. 4 (2011): 282–309.

24. Urban Renewal Administration, *Urban Renewal Project Characteristics*, June 1966; Urban Renewal Administration, "Urban Renewal Is for Small Communities Too."

25. Byron R. Morse, "Statement of Hon. Byron R. Morse, Mayor, Little Rock, Arkansas; Accompanied by Dowell Naylor, Jr., Executive Director, Little Rock Housing Authority," in *Urban Renewal: Hearings Before the Subcomm. on Housing of the Comm. on Banking and Currency*, Part 1, 88th Cong., 1st sess., at 62–63 (1963), ProQuest.

26. Providence City Plan Commission, Providence Preservation Society, and Housing and Home Finance Agency, *College Hill: A Demonstration Study of Historic Area Renewal* (Providence, RI: City Plan Commission, 1959).

27. Slayton, "Statement of William Slayton," 419; Urban Renewal Administration, *Historic Preservation through Urban Renewal* (Washington, D.C.: U.S. Government Printing Office, 1963).

28. On the growth of district thinking in response to urban renewal, see Lauren A. R. Poole and Douglas R. Appler, "Building a Local Preservation Ethic in the Era of Urban Renewal: How Did Neighborhood Associations Shape Historic Preservation Practice in Lexington, Kentucky?" *Journal of Urban History* 46, no. 2 (March 2020): 383–405.

29. Housing and Home Finance Agency, Urban Renewal Administration, "Smallest Urban Renewal Project," in *Urban Renewal Notes* (November–December 1960).

30. Urban Renewal Administration, *Historic Preservation through Urban Renewal*. See also "Historic Preservation via Urban Renewal," *Journal of Housing* 19 (August 1962): 297–315.

31. Ammon, "Commemoration amid Criticism," 175–220.

32. Wright, Andrade and Amenta, Architects, *Washington Square East Urban Renewal Area, Technical Report, May 1959: Prepared for the Redevelopment Authority of the City of Philadelphia* (Philadelphia, 1959), appendix.

33. Slayton, "Statement of William Slayton," 483.

34. W.E.B. DuBois, *The Philadelphia Negro: A Social Study* (Philadelphia: University of Pennsylvania Press, 1899).

35. George W. Dowdall, "Society Hill," in *Encyclopedia of Greater Philadelphia* (2015), accessed January 3, 2023, available at https://philadelphiaencyclopedia.org/essays/society-hill/.

36. J. M. Brewer, *J. M. Brewer's Map of Philadelphia*, 1934, South Section, Free Library of Philadelphia, available at http://www.philageohistory.org/rdic-images/view-image.cfm/JMB1934.Phila.002.SouthSection.

37. Philadelphia City Planning Commission, Philadelphia Redevelopment Authority, and Philadelphia Housing Authority, *Philadelphia Housing Quality Survey: Old City Area*, (Philadelphia: Philadelphia City Planning Commission, November 1949), 2, 4.

38. Philadelphia Redevelopment Authority, *Washington Square Redevelopment Area: Washington Square East Urban Renewal Area, Unit No. 1: Redevelopment Proposal* (Philadelphia: Philadelphia Redevelopment Authority, 1958); Philadelphia Redevelopment Authority, *Washington Square Redevelopment Area: Washington Square East Urban Renewal Area, Unit No. 2: Redevelopment Proposal, Urban Renewal Plan, Relocation Plan* (Philadelphia: Philadelphia Redevelopment Authority, 1960).

39. "The Philadelphia Cure: Clearing Slums with Penicillin, Not Surgery," *Architectural Forum*, April 1952.

40. "Urban Renewal: Remaking the American City," *Time*, November 6, 1964.

41. S. Schraga, "News Release: Office of the City Representative," February 4, 1960, Housing Association of Delaware Valley Records, series 1, box 265, folder 4435, Special Collections Research Center, Temple University Library, Philadelphia.

42. Wright, Andrade and Amenta, Architects, and Philadelphia Redevelopment Authority, *Standards for Rehabilitation of Existing Buildings, Washington Square East, Urban Renewal Area, Unit I and Unit II* (Philadelphia: Philadelphia Redevelopment Authority, 1959).

43. Works Progress Administration and Philadelphia Bureau of Engraving, Surveys and Zoning, *Philadelphia Land Use Map*, 1942, Free Library of Philadelphia, available at http://www.philageohistory.org/rdic-images/view-image.cfm/LUM1942.4B-1.

44. "Condemnation Proceedings in the Court of Common Pleas No. 5, March Term 1959, No. 3585," June 23, 1959, City Archives of Philadelphia.

45. Works Progress Administration and Philadelphia Bureau of Engraving, Surveys and Zoning, *Philadelphia Land Use Map*.

46. Dennis J. Dougherty to Andrew and Catharine Matkowski, Deed, 311 Spruce Street, November 19, 1935, Deed Book JMH 3917, page 355, City Archives of Philadelphia, available at https://www.phila-records.com/historic-records/web/.

47. United States Census Bureau, *U.S. Census of Population, 1940*, enumeration district 51-110, sheet 3-A, available at https://www.ancestrylibrary.com/.

48. Antonia and Charles Dougherty to Konstantinos Macos, Deed, 311 Spruce Street, October 10, 2013, City Archives of Philadelphia, available at https://epay.phila-records.com/phillyepay/web/.

49. Philip Price Jr., oral history interview, November 10, 2009, Project Philadelphia 19106, Special Collections Research Center, Temple University Library, Philadelphia, available at https://preservingsocietyhill.org/oral-histories/philip-price-jr.

50. Morris and Bessie Betty Rothman and Abraham and Anna Orocofsky to Philip Price Jr., Deed, 321 Spruce Street, June 1, 1965, Deed Book JRS 461, page 70, City Archives of Philadelphia, available at https://www.phila-records.com/historic-records/web/.

51. Price, oral history interview.

52. Philip Price Jr. to Michael and Sharon Salzberg, Deed, 319–321 Spruce Street, May 2, 2005, City Archives of Philadelphia, available at https://epay.phila-records.com/phillyepay/web/.

53. Philadelphia Committee on Municipal Development and Zoning, *Public Hearing for the Washington Square Redevelopment Area, Washington Square East Urban Renewal Area, Unit 2*, September 14, 1960, transcript, Athenaeum of Philadelphia.

54. Vault of MIT, *"Big City" (1961)*, January 20, 2016, YouTube video, available at https://www.youtube.com/watch?v=foaQTrm9Z7o.

55. Redevelopment Authority to Martin H. and Libby Baumholtz, Deed, 340 Spruce Street, July 7, 1968, Deed Book JRS 150, page 140, City Archives of Philadelphia, available at https://www.phila-records.com/historic-records/web/.

56. Philadelphia Committee on Municipal Development and Zoning, *Public Hearing for the Washington Square Redevelopment Area.*

57. "Friends of Old Pine Street—Publication No. 125," July 10, 1961, Philadelphia Presbytery Congregations "Old Files," Philadelphia, box 6, folder: Friends of Old Pine—1960–61, Presbyterian Historical Society, Philadelphia.

58. United States Census Bureau, *U.S. Census of Population, 1940*, enumeration district 51-114, sheet 4-B, available at https://www.ancestrylibrary.com/.

59. Vault of MIT, *"Big City" (1961).*

60. Francesca Russello Ammon, "Picturing Preservation and Renewal: Photographs as Planning Knowledge in Society Hill, Philadelphia," *Journal of Planning Education and Research* 42, no. 3 (September 2022), 12; United States Census Bureau, *1950 Census of Population* (Washington, D.C.: U.S. Government Printing Office, 1952); United States Census Bureau, *1950 Census of Housing, General Characteristics, North Carolina-Tennessee* (Washington, D.C.: U.S. Government Printing Office, 1953); United States Census Bureau, *1980 Census of Population and Housing, Census Tracts, Philadelphia, P.A.-N.J.* (Washington, D.C.: U.S. Government Printing Office, 1983).

# Contributors

**Francesca Russello Ammon** is a social and cultural historian of the urban built environment. She is the author of *Bulldozer: Demolition and Clearance of the Postwar Landscape*, winner of the 2017 Lewis Mumford Prize for best book in American planning history. She is Associate Professor of City and Regional Planning and Historic Preservation at the University of Pennsylvania.

**Douglas R. Appler** is Associate Professor and Chair of the Department of Historic Preservation at the University of Kentucky. His teaching addresses city planning history and historic preservation. He is also coeditor of *Urban Archaeology, Municipal Government and Local Planning* with Sherene Baugher and William Moss.

**Brent Cebul** is Assistant Professor of History at the University of Pennsylvania. He is the author of *Illusions of Progress: Business, Poverty, and Liberalism in the American Century* (University of Pennsylvania Press, 2023). With Lily Geismer and Mason B. Williams, he is also coeditor of *Shaped by the State: Toward a New Political History of the Twentieth Century* (University of Chicago Press, 2019).

**Robert B. Fairbanks** is an urban historian and Professor Emeritus at the University of Texas at Arlington. He has written or coedited seven books. Temple University Press published his latest, *The War on Slums in the Southwest* (2005). He has also served as Editor for the Americas for *Planning Perspectives* for thirteen years.

**Leif Fredrickson** is Director of the Public History Program at the University of Montana. He produces the podcast *Death in the West* and is a writing a book about the history of lead poisoning.

**Colin Gordon** is the F. Wendell Miller Professor of History at the University of Iowa. He is the author of four books, most recently *Citizen Brown: Race, Democracy, and Inequality in the St. Louis Suburbs* (2019). His current research is supported by the National Endowment for the Humanities and the Russell Sage Foundation.

**David Hochfelder** is Associate Professor of History at University at Albany, State University of New York. He is working on a National Endowment for the Humanities–funded digital/public history of urban renewal with colleagues Stacy Sewell and Ann Pfau. The project is called Picturing Urban Renewal.

**Benjamin D. Lisle** is Assistant Professor of American Studies at Colby College. His work examines urban geography and cultural history in the United States after World War II. He is the author of *Modern Coliseum: Stadiums and American Culture*, published by the University of Pennsylvania Press in 2017.

**Robert K. Nelson** is Director of the Digital Scholarship Lab at the University of Richmond. He is the editor of *American Panorama: An Atlas of United States History* and the creator of a number of other digital history projects. He teaches courses about topics such as antislavery and slavery in the United States and the digital humanities.

**Stacy Kinlock Sewell** is Professor of History at St. Thomas Aquinas College in Sparkill, New York. Along with David Hochfelder and Ann Pfau, she is a member of the Picturing Urban Renewal team, which is building a multilayered website on the history of urban renewal in New York State.

# Index

www.ingramcontent.com/pod-product-compliance
Lightning Source LLC
Chambersburg PA
CBHW050353270326
41926CB00016B/3723